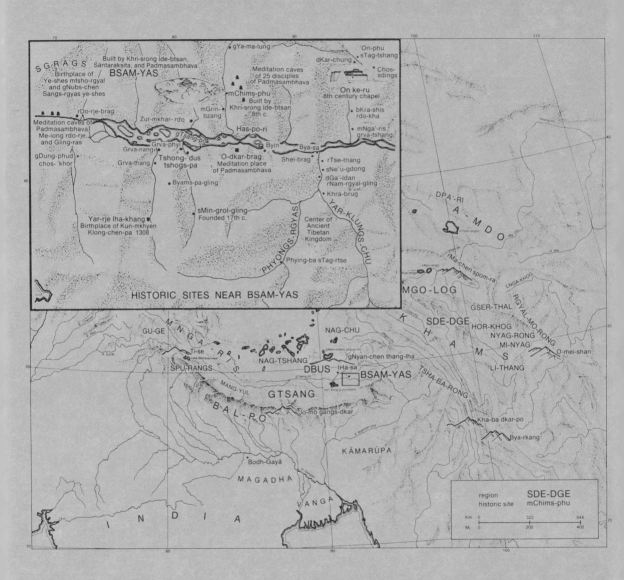

The Land of Tibet: Home of Ye-shes mTsho-rgyal

བོད་ཀྱི་ཇོ་མོ་ཡེ་ཤེས་མཚོ་རྒྱལ་གྱི་མཛད་ཚུལ་

རྣམ་པར་ཐར་པ་གབ་པ་མངོན་བྱུང་

རྒྱུད་མངས་དྲི་ཟའི་གླུ་ཕྲེང་བཞུགས་སོ

Bod-kyi jo-mo ye-shes mtsho-rgyal-gyi mdzad tshul
rnam-par-thar-pa gab-pa mngon byung
rgyud-mangs dri-za'i glu phreng bzhugs-so

Mother of Knowledge:

The Enlightenment of Ye-shes mTsho-rgyal

Plate 1: White Tārā

Mother of Knowledge:

The Enlightenment of Ye-shes mTsho-rgyal

Text by
Nam-mkha'i snying-po

Oral Translation by
Tarthang Tulku

Edited by Jane Wilhelms

Dharma Publishing

TIBETAN TRANSLATION SERIES

Buddha's Lions
Calm and Clear
Elegant Sayings
Golden Zephyr
Kindly Bent to Ease Us
Legend of the Great Stupa
The Life and Liberation of Padmasambhava
The Marvelous Companion
Mind in Buddhist Psychology
The Voice of the Buddha

Library of Congress Cataloging in Publication Data

Nam-mkha'i snying-po, 8th/9th cent.
    Mother of knowledge.

    (Tibetan translation series)
    Translation of: Bod kyi jo mo Ye-śes Mtsho-rgyal gyi
mdzad tshul rnam par thar pa gab pa mṅon byuṅ rgyud
maṅs dri za'i glu phreṅ.
    Includes index.
    1. Ye-śes-mtsho-rgyal, 8th cent. 2. Lamas—China—
Tibet—Biography. 3. Yogis—China—Tibet—Biography.
4. Yoga (Tantric Buddhism) I. Tarthang Tulku.
II. Wilhelms, Jane. III. Title. IV. Series.
BQ998.E757N3513 1983   294.3'923'0924   [B]   83–23208
ISBN 0-913546-90-9
ISBN 0-913546-91-7 (pbk.)

Typeset in Fototronic Garamond with Garamond Open Initials.
Printed and bound in the United States of America by Dharma Press,
Oakland, California.

9 8 7 6 5 4 3 2 1

Dedicated to all Dharma students
inspired by the Vajrayāna teachings

Table of Contents

Publisher's Preface   xvii

Publisher's Introduction   xxi

Prologue   5

Chapter 1   Ye-shes mTsho-rgyal Sees That the   11
               Time Has Come for Her to Teach
               and Appear in the World

Chapter 2   The Arrival and Manifestation of   15
               Ye-shes mTsho-rgyal in the Land of Tibet

Chapter 3   Ye-shes mTsho-rgyal Recognizes the   21
               Impermanence of All Things
               and Relies Upon a Teacher

Chapter 4   Ye-shes mTsho-rgyal Asks Her Teacher   33
               for Instruction in the Dharma

Chapter 5   The Manner in Which   79
               Ye-shes mTsho-rgyal Did Her Practices

Chapter 6   A Summary of the Auspicious Signs Which   111
Occurred as Ye-shes mTsho-rgyal Practiced
and the Siddhis She Manifested
After Achieving Realization

Chapter 7   The Manner in Which Ye-shes mTsho-rgyal   117
Acted to Benefit Sentient Beings

Chapter 8   How Ye-shes mTsho-rgyal Reached Her Goal,   167
Achieved Buddhahood, and Entered
the Expanse of All That Is

Glossary   221

Index   237

List of Sacred Art

Color Plates

Plate 1: White Tārā   vi

Plate 2: Ye-shes mTsho-rgyal   xvi

Plate 3: Guru Padmasambhava and 25 Disciples   2

Line Drawings: 9 Manifestations of Padmasambhava

Padma 'byung-gnas   4

Orgyan rDo-rje 'chang   10

Padmasambhava   14

Blo-ldan mchog-sred   20

Padma rgyal-po   32

Nyi-ma 'od-zer   78

Guru Śākya seng-ge   110

Seng-ge sgra-sgrog   116

rDo-rje gro-lod   166

Plate 2: Ye-shes mTsho-rgyal

Publisher's Preface

When I first came to this country, and before there were so many large and difficult projects to take up so much of my time, I was able to give regular Tibetan and philosophy classes. A few of my students kept up their studies, and I recommended various texts for them to read in Tibetan. Jane Wilhelms, one of these students, began to read the life of Ye-shes mTsho-rgyal. As her interest in the text increased, I encouraged her to translate certain passages, and gave her guidance as she proceeded. Eventually we decided that a translation of the whole work would give Dharma students a valuable resource for understanding the authentic Tibetan Buddhist tradition.

Once we began work on the translation, I read the text aloud to Jane, and provided a word for word translation. This process continued for some time, but in 1978, as work began on the Nyingma Edition of the bKa'-'gyur and bsTan-'gyur, we had to set this project aside, along with many others. When we resumed work on the text this year, I once again reviewed difficult passages in detail. Later, Deborah Black and Leslie Bradburn edited the completed manuscript.

Rendering the life of Ye-shes mTsho-rgyal into English has been a difficult undertaking. The Tibetan is in the old style, and contains a mixture of prose and poetry which is rich in images and examples that have no parallel in Western culture. There are many esoteric terms and descriptions for which there are no meaningful English equivalents. Most important, even the simple narrative contains multilevel meanings, and it is impossible for the translation to present them all.

Faced with these difficulties, we have decided to present the text as clearly and simply as possible. Ye-shes mTsho-rgyal's life story is a revelation of spiritual transformation, and the original Tibetan reveals the depth of her experience, the inner meaning of her initiations, and her visionary understanding. Tibetans have spent hundreds of years finding ways to express the power and richness of such experience within the constraints of language, and, at the time this book was written, possessed a terminology developed for precisely this purpose.

Until the English language develops similar resources, we felt that the inner beauty and wonder of Ye-shes mTsho-rgyal's life story would shine forth most clearly through a direct and straightforward presentation. Pursuing the esoteric implications of the text would only risk confusion. And in any case the conceptual mind would find itself unable to grasp the significance of much of what was being said. Still, it is good to bear in mind that a translation of this work on the esoteric level would look very different.

Even in terms of simply presenting the narrative of the story, I do not feel that we have always been completely successful. Although we have presented a number of the most important technical terms in a glossary, this does not resolve every problem or remove every imperfection. In the future, when Western students of Tibetan and the Dharma have gained more experience with this kind of work, we can hope to do better. Yet there is no reason to delay publication for years by chasing after perfection. Our readers have been waiting many years for this work, and I sincerely believe that its publication can be of benefit.

However, readers of the life of Ye-shes mTsho-rgyal should also bear in mind that the experiences and the practices undertaken by Ye-shes mTsho-rgyal on her path toward realization can only be successfully carried out by those with proper preparation. Even then, the guidance of an established and qualified spiritual teacher, one who is a complete master of the tradition, is essential. The risk for anyone attempting to pursue such practices on their own, or without full preparation, is simply too great.

I would like to dedicate this book to all Dharma students interested in the Vajrayāna path. Studying the life of Ye-shes mTsho-rgyal, they will find an excellent example of the relationship between student and teacher and the importance of devotion.

Publisher's Introduction

In 1958, when I was still in Tibet, I visited an area known as Dar-yongs rdzong. There in a beautiful valley is located the cave used for meditation by gNubs-chen Sangs-rgyas ye-shes, a great practitioner and holder of the Vidyādhara lineage of the Tantrayāna, and a direct disciple of Padmasambhava. Not far from there is Brag-dmar, the palace of the eighth century Dharma King Khri-srong lde'u-btsan, who invited Padmasambhava to Tibet. Close to the palace is a rugged canyon, and at the top of the canyon are many large caves used for centuries by meditators. At the bottom of the canyon is a lovely village. Tall trees grow there, like willows but with distinctive silver leaves; nearby is a small lake. It is here that the great yoginī Ye-shes mTsho-rgyal was born, more than twelve hundred years ago.

Ye-shes mTsho-rgyal was the youngest of three daughters born to a local nobleman. She was a reincarnation of the goddess Sarasvatī, and many miraculous events took place at her birth. One in particular seized the imagination of her family: The small lake that bordered on their village suddenly expanded greatly in size. From this, her father gave his daughter the name mTsho-rgyal, which means 'vast ocean'. The name Ye-shes, which she received later, refers to unending primordial wisdom. In Sanskrit her name would be Jñānasāgarā.

Ye-shes mTsho-rgyal was so unusually beautiful that by the time she was twelve years old, suitors from all the surrounding regions had come to seek her hand in marriage. Her parents feared that a decision in favor of one of the powerful lords would provoke the wrath of the others, and in the end, they decided that they would have to send Ye-shes mTsho-rgyal away.

Until that moment, the young girl had lived an idyllic life, but now her fortune rapidly changed. Sent away from home, her wishes to lead a life devoted to religious practice brushed aside, Ye-shes mTsho-rgyal tried to escape into the mountains, but to no avail. For several years she suffered greatly, until at last she came to the attention of King Khri-srong lde'u-btsan, who took her as one of his queens. Soon after, to show his faith in the Dharma and in Padmasambhava, the king symbolically gave his teacher his entire kingdom, and allowed mTsho-rgyal to go with Padmasambhava as the Guru's disciple. Thus, by the age of sixteen the fortunate girl had become a student of the greatest tantric master of the age.

Once she had become Padmasambhava's student, Ye-shes mTsho-rgyal soon mastered the basic teachings of the Sūtras and the śāstras. After she matured her understanding in the inner, outer, and esoteric teachings, she was given the complete teachings of the inner Tantras, the Mahā, the Anu, and the Āti, and in particular the oral teachings of the Ātiyoga, known in Tibetan as rDzogs-chen. She also received from Padmasambhava the mKha'-'gro snying-thig, the heart of the ḍākinī teachings.

After achieving great realization, Ye-shes mTsho-rgyal devoted her life to instructing others and encouraging them in their practice; although she underwent many hardships herself, she overcame even the greatest obstacles for others. She brought inconceivable benefit to so many people, it is difficult to imagine how much suffering she removed from the world. Her songs of realization brought her listeners immediate understanding, and her very presence radiated joy. She performed many miraculous deeds, only a small number of which are recounted in this volume. She had many other wonderful qualities as well, some beyond human expression. Perhaps in another time and place it will be possible to say more about these.

Her intelligence, perseverance, devotion, and pure motivation all were exceptional, even in the company of the many accomplished masters who were Padmasambhava's disciples. As well as being the most important woman in the rNying-ma lineage, truly Ye-shes mTsho-rgyal was one of Padmasambhava's greatest disciples. She occupies a place of central importance within the Vajrayāna and especially the lineage of Padmasambhava, the great teacher who embodies the enlightened state. For Ye-shes mTsho-rgyal received all of Padmasambhava's teachings, as if the contents of one vessel were poured into another. Traditionally she is compared to a crown, a jewel, a leader, and a guide. Her accomplishments and realizations have seldom been equalled, and the merit of her actions is beyond description.

But Ye-shes mTsho-rgyal is by no means the only important woman in the tradition. As Padmasambhava himself said: "Male or female—there is no great difference. But if she develops the mind bent on enlightenment, to be a woman is better." The female energy is especially respected in Padmasambhava's lineage, having a special place in the enlightened transmission—for it could be said that all of Padmasambhava's teachings came to us through Ye-shes mTsho-rgyal.

She is one of the greatest in the tradition of those who preserved Buddhist texts, especially the esoteric texts of the rDzogs-chen tradition. Teachings of both the oral and treasure tradition passed through her; and after Padmasambhava left Tibet, Ye-shes mTsho-rgyal and gNubs-chen Sangs-rgyas ye-shes worked closely together to transmit the teachings of the heart of realization, which are necessary for the rest of the teachings to bear fruit.

One of the most important contributions Ye-shes mTsho-rgyal made to future generations was in regards to the gter-ma texts. The gter-ma are treasures of many different kinds, including special kinds of teachings, texts, ritual objects, and relics which were concealed for the use of future generations. A great many of the gter-ma, and the most important of the gter-ma texts, were concealed by Padmasambhava and Ye-shes mTsho-rgyal for the purpose of transmitting the esoteric aspect of the three inner tantras.

Under the direction of Padmasambhava, Ye-shes mTsho-rgyal transcribed many of these teachings, and concealed them in the appropriate places, thus making it possible for later masters, themselves reincarnations of disciples of this great master, to rediscover them and make them available to others in the future. The most important gter-ma texts were preserved through Ye-shes mTsho-rgyal's inspiration and activity and are thus in the direct lineage of her teachings and her blessings. In this way, the heritage of Padmasambhava was preserved and protected throughout the centuries, and the direct path of his teachings was kept open.

Thus the gter-ma treasures figure prominently in the rNying-ma teaching tradition. Concealed at the time of Padmasambhava, they are found not only in Tibet, but all over the world; in fact, they can be thought of as existing throughout time and space. Preserved in their original form, protected from the distortions and mistakes that so often arise from centuries of interpretations and recopyings, the gter-ma texts retain their true meaning, remaining pure and fresh, and present a direct path to enlightenment.

The rNying-ma tradition recognizes one hundred and eight great gter-ma masters, the first of whom appeared several centuries after the time of Padmasambhava. There are many additional gter-ma masters, who also found texts tracing directly to Padmasambhava. Some of these texts had been transcribed in their entirety and hidden away; others had been written in ḍākinī language, a kind of code accessible only to the discoverers through meditative awareness. Most of the gter-ma texts fall into this latter category, and the gter-ma masters, in order to make these texts accessible to others, first needed to rewrite them in language understood by a more general audience.

Although the tradition of the gter-ma treasure texts ensured the continued transmission of many of the teachings, a large number of the gter-ma were lost again soon after their revelation. Over a period of a thousand years and more, there appeared innumerable treasure texts which were revealed by hundreds of gter-ma masters—many of whom lived only a short time and had only a few students to carry on their lineages. With the treasure texts appearing in so many different times, places, and circumstances, only the works found by the major gter-ma masters and the works gathered into great collections were certain to survive.

Fortunately, late in the nineteenth and early in the twentieth century, many of the major and minor gter-ma cycles, important supplementary teachings, and information on initiations and instructions for practice, were searched out and preserved for posterity. This was due to the work of three great masters: mChog-gyur bde-chen gling-pa, his major disciple 'Jam-dbyangs mkhyen-brtse'i dbang-po, and mKhyen-brtse's principal disciple Kong-sprul blo-gros mtha'-yas. Although mKhyen-brtse'i dbang-po (1820–1892) and Kong-sprul (1811–1899) were technically members of the bKa'-brgyud-pa school, they were also leaders of the ris-med movement which accepted the teachings of all the schools of Tibetan Buddhism, thus reversing the sectarian tendencies of the previous century. The result of their work in collecting and bringing order to the gter-ma teachings is the Rin-chen gter-mdzod, the 'Great Storehouse of Treasures'.

A massive collection in sixty volumes, the Rin-chen gter-mzdod contains many of the smaller basic texts of the major gter-ma cycles, sādhanas, and other essential teachings. The entire collection was printed in at least two editions in Tibet, both published under the auspices of bKa'-brgyud-pa monasteries. The mTshur-phu Monastery edition, published by the fifteenth Karma-pa mKha'-khyab rdo-rje, contains three extra volumes of information on the life of Kong-sprul as well as on the history and contents of the gter-ma. The dPal-spungs edition of Kong-sprul's "Five Treasures" contains the Rin-chen gter-mdzod in sixty volumes. Recently this treasury has been reprinted in Bhutan, and is now again available.

Large as it is, the Rin-chen gter-mdzod contains only a sample of the rich teachings available through the inspiration and vision of Padmasambhava. It would have been very difficult to include them all, for there are eighteen different types of gter-ma, and the texts alone contain thousands of initiations, sādhanas, and practices. Thus many gter-ma texts are not included in the collection—some, such as the collections of the major texts of the great gter-ma masters, because they were widely available, others because copies could not be found.

Why are there so many gter-ma teachings? The gter-mas were specifically fashioned for a variety of times and circumstances in order to meet the needs of people living in different eras and cultures, and having different types of karma and ways of understanding. These teachings were designed to directly touch the heart, to help the process of awakening realization. When one practices these teachings with total devotion and surrender, it becomes possible to transform body, speech, and mind.

In these troubled times of the Kāli Yuga, when there is so much confusion on both global and individual levels, it is especially important to make such teachings available. These teachings which come to us through Ye-shes mTsho-rgyal are direct and pure representations of the Vidyādhara lineage; they are very powerful, easily healing suffering and removing obscurations, promoting peace and unity.

It is good to remember that it is through a woman that these teachings have come down to us; and that the great Buddhist teachers have always emphasized the importance of the wisdom nature of women. The dākinīs that helped to spread the teachings and helped the practice of Buddhism during the time of Padmasambhava are available to help us today. As Ye-shes mTsho-rgyal herself told her disciples as she was leaving to join Padmasambhava in the Southwest: "I have not died; I have not gone anywhere. Pray to me—even if I do not appear in person, I will give the desired siddhis to those with one-pointed devotion."

Just by opening our hearts to the Buddhist teachings of love and compassion, we can bring their blessings into the world today. A sādhana does not have to be elaborate or difficult to be effective; not all such practices are as difficult as the ones Ye-shes mTsho-rgyal undertook. Nor are Padmasambhava's teachings confined to space and time;

as he himself said: "I am never far from those with faith; or even far from those without it, though they do not see me." Our practice can be as simple as visualizing Padmasambhava and Ye-shes mTsho-rgyal together. With this clear practice we can bring their presence into our lives; we can invite their teachings into our hearts.

Through visualizing the unity of Padmasambhava and Ye-shes mTsho-rgyal, the outer and inner aspects of experience flow together, deepening into a unity of subject and object, male and female, self and world, student and teacher. In this way the sense of isolation imposed by the self struggling to survive in the hostile world of the Kāli Yuga is transcended.

Though this is a very simple sādhana, it can open the heart, enabling us to overcome obstacles to understanding, penetrate all samsaric illusions, and break the karmic chain that binds us to suffering. We can learn to recognize and value our own enlightened nature as we experience an inner awakening. With faith and devotion, we can enter the mandala of teachings established by Padmasambhava and transmitted through Ye-shes mTsho-rgyal, and receive specific knowledge and blessings which have a power that goes beyond words. Through sustained devotional practice we can embrace the whole vidyādhara lineage; we can share in the full blessings of enlightenment and transmit them to others. Then we will be following in the tradition of Ye-shes mTsho-rgyal herself.

Plate 3: Guru Padmasambhava and 25 Disciples

Mother of Knowledge:

The Enlightenment of Ye-shes mTsho-rgyal

Amitābha   Vajrasattva   Samantabhadra   dGa'-rab rdo-rje   Avalokiteśvara

Mandāravā   Ye-shes mTsho-rgyal

Padma 'byung-gnas

rDo-rje drag-po   Seng-ge gdong chen-ma

Śāntarakṣita   Khri-srong lde'u-btsan

Padma 'byung-gnas

Prologue

Herein is contained the hidden life story of Ye-shes mTsho-rgyal, the great lady of Tibet: a story as lovely as the music the gandharvas play upon their lutes.

The life story of Ye-shes mTsho-rgyal is told here in eight chapters.

ན་མོ་གུ་རུ་དེ་ཝ་ཌཱ་ཀི་ནཱི་ཧཱུྃ༔

NĀMO GURU DEVA ḌĀKINĪ BHYĀ!
Homage to all gurus, gods, and ḍākinīs!
Homage to the host of lamas of the lineage,
to the Lord of beings and the Triple Gem,
to the Teacher endowed with the Three Kāyas—
Padmasambhava, manifestation of the compassion
of Avalokiteśvara and Amitābha, Lord Protectors.
Homage as well to the Mother
of all the Buddhas of the three times—
the White Lady of Great Bliss.

I bow low to the ḍākinī of the Dharmakāya realm,
the most joyous Samantabhadrā;
to the ḍākinī of the Sambhogakāya realm,
Vajra Yoginī;
to the ḍākinī of the Nirmāṇakāya realm,

Ye-shes mTsho-rgyal-ma
who delights the Buddhas of the three times
by translating the symbols.

The Great One of Orgyan committed the Teachings to her care—
for the Lady has the power of complete retention.
From her the profound treasures come forth—
the supreme siddhis, the Rainbow Body, the Vajra Body
are her attainments.
The name of this ḍākinī, this Teacher, is Ye-shes mTsho-rgyal.
This is her Life Story.

Her biography and collected teachings,
the heart's blood of the ḍākinī, were committed to writing
for the benefit of sentient beings yet to come.
They were concealed and then guarded by the Protectors,
the Lion-faced Demon Protector and the Flaming Black Demon Lord.

པ་ལཿ རྒྱུརྒྱུ༔ ཁྲི༔ ཟྲཿ ཟྲོཿ བྲོ་བགྲོ༔

E Ma Ho!
Padma Thod-phreng-rtsal is the Mantra Holder,
essence of the Buddhas of the three times.
No mother's womb stained this great siddha—
spontaneously he arose from a lotus.
He displays the charismatic activity
of the Buddhas of the three times,
surpassing even Śākyamuni's great deeds.

He preserved for posterity the imperiled Mantrayāna teachings,
the ones so difficult to convey;
he tamed the wild Tibetan barbarians and the southwestern savages,
the ones so difficult to discipline;
he mastered all demons, heretics, gods, and evil spirits,
the ones so difficult to subdue,
merely by the power of his mind.
In an instant he educated
the ones so difficult to teach

by magic and miraculous changes of form.
He achieved the siddhi of life without death,
the one so difficult to obtain.

In order to spread the Mantrayāna doctrine,
he worked through appropriate and mystic consorts,
more numerous than the sesame seeds it would take
to fill the four walls of a house.
He found his consorts in the highest Akaniṣṭha realm,
and throughout all the lands of gods and men,
among nāgas and gandharvas,
in cemeteries and power centers across the earth.
No less than seventy thousand such fortunate women
lived in this special part of the world
which encompassed India and China, Tibet and its neighbors,
Turkestan, Khotan, Kucha, Mongolia, and other lands.

But never was he separated
from the five manifestations of Vajravārāhī—
her body incarnation was Mandāravā;
her speech incarnation was Ye-shes mTsho-rgyal;
her heart incarnation was Śākya De-ma;
her quality incarnation was Kālasiddhī;
her activity incarnation was bKra-shis spyi-'dren;
and her essence incarnation was the ḍākinī Prabhādharā.
These were the six great manifestations of Vajravārāhī.
The two greatest of these were
Mandāravā of India and Ye-shes mTsho-rgyal of Tibet.
Mandāravā's story is told elsewhere.
These eight chapters relate a little of the life of Ye-shes mTsho-rgyal:

How Ye-shes mTsho-rgyal saw that sentient beings
needed instruction and manifested in this world;

How she entered the world;

How she saw the nature of impermanence
and relied upon a teacher;

How she listened to instructions in the Dharma;

How she engaged in meditative practices;

How signs of realization arose;
How she benefitted sentient beings;

How she vowed to reach her goal
and became a Buddha in the expanse of the Dharmadhātu.

Hūmkara

Nam-mkha'i snying-po

Shel-dkar rDo-rje mtsho

Orgyan rDo-rje 'chang

rGyal-ba'i blo-gros

rNgom-se 'od

Orgyan rDo-rje 'chang

Ye-shes mTsho-rgyal Sees That
the Time Has Come for Her to Teach
and Appear in the World

Ye-shes mTsho-rgyal, the manifestation of the Nirmāṇakāya, is everywhere renowned as the Mother of the Buddhas of the three times. After accumulating merit and removing obscurations for ages too numerous to count, she generated great waves of benefit for all sentient beings.

At the time of Ārya Sadāprarudita, 'Ever-weeping', she appeared as a lady merchant. Together with five hundred other women she approached the Buddha Dharmodgata and vowed never to return to the world except to benefit beings. After passing from that life, mTsho-rgyal wandered for a time in Sambhogakāya realms, and then again appeared in the world of men, this time as the goddess of the river Ganges. She honored the Victorious One, Śākyamuni, and made collections of his Teachings.

Again, she resided in the Sambhogakāya realms and was known as Sarasvatī, Goddess of Euphony, who aided many beings. It was then that the great Dharma King Khri-srong lde'u-btsan reigned in the land of Tibet. A manifestation of Mañjuśrī, the king intended to introduce and stabilize the holy Dharma in Tibet. For this very same reason, the

Buddha Amitābha came to the world of men as the great Teacher Padmasambhava, the one whose body is untouched by birth and death. The king invited the Teacher to the land of Tibet, and Padmasambhava promised to cover the far reaches of the land with innumerable temples of learning such as the magnificent bSam-yas. He vowed to make the teachings of the Dharma rise and shine like the sun.

It was then that the great Teacher reflected: "Now is the time for the goddess Sarasvatī to manifest and help me spread the Mantrayāna teachings." In an instant, in less time than it takes for a star to fall into the sea, he travelled to his home in Orgyan.

Rumor had it that the Tibetan ministers-of-state had banished Padmasambhava to the barbarous hinterland of Turkestan; the Dharma King had heard that he was staying in a meditative retreat in the Lion Fortress of the Three Attainments in Bhutan. The common folk even suspected that he had actually left the country, eloping with one of the queens to India.

In fact, Padmasambhava had been wandering about in hundreds of Nirmāṇakāya realms for seven years as men count them. Then he appeared in the Sambhogakāya realm, gathering about him Vajra Yoginī, the goddess Sarasvatī, and Tārā Bhṛkuṭī, as well as all the ḍākinīs of the power centers of the world, and the ḍākinīs of the four lineages. Together they engaged in the play of joy and the dance of bliss, while he exhorted them thus:

"HRĪ!
Non-attachment resides in the secret space of great attachment.
Non-attached attachment is the diamond scepter of bliss.
By the radiant light of the tainted, the untainted is realized.
The time has come to embrace the play
of the most profound and secret Great Bliss."

Sarasvatī arose from among the assembly of goddesses and replied:
"HO!
Heruka, Hero, Sublime Dancer, God of Bliss!
Already you have danced in nine aspects.

12

Holy Padma, happiest of all who dwell in Great Bliss,
who suffered no pain or unhappiness in the womb,
I will now manifest in Tibet,
that most barbarous of border countries."

The Yab spoke: "SAMAYA HO!"
The Yum spoke: "SAMAYA SATTVAṀ!"
Again the Yab spoke: "SAMAYA HRĪ!"
And the Yum spoke: "SAMAYA TIṢṬHAḤ!"
The Yab spoke: "RAHO! HAM!"
The Yum spoke: "RĀGA YAMI!"

The Vajra of the Yab joined the Lotus of the Yum, and together they entered a state of great equanimity. The five goddesses of the senses bestowed offerings and praise, and the male Herukas destroyed all hindrances. A rain of blessings poured down from the Bodhisattvas, while the Vajra goddesses danced. The mandala door-keepers kept vigil, and the four protectors set a guard around them. The Lord and Lady Dharma Protectors of all the ten directions agreed to protect the Teachings. The Great Bliss of the Yab-Yum penetrated everywhere into all the realms of the world, and great tremors and earthquakes shook the universe.

Light rays burst forth like shooting stars from the union of the Yab and Yum. The red letter A came into view, and from it spiralled a garland of white vowels. The white letter VAṀ appeared and from it spiralled a chain of red consonants. The lights and letters penetrated into the world, striking the ground in sGrags-gi se'u valley in the land of Tibet.

ས་ཨལ་ཡ༔ ཀུ་ཀུ་ཀུ༔ ཧ་མ་ག་ཇ་ཧ༔

This Completes the First Chapter Concerning How
Ye-shes mTsho-rgyal Saw the Need for Beings
to be Taught and Manifested in the World.

Padmasambhava

The Arrival and Manifestation of
Ye-shes mTsho-rgyal in the Land of Tibet

The earliest Tibetan king was gNya'-khri btsan-po; his reign was the first of a dynasty which continued up through King gNam-ri srong-btsan. gNam-ri's first-born son became the great Dharma King Srong-btsan sgam-po, a powerful man who revered the Teachings of the Buddha—he brought all of Tibet under his dominion and did much to advance the country. Tibet had become divided into seven regions during the reigns of his predecessors, and Srong-btsan sgam-po chose seven men to rule these provinces. Each of these men took the name of his region: mKhar-chen-pa and Zur-mkhar-pa, mKhar-chu-pa, Gong-thang-pa and rTse-pa, sGrags-pa, and Rong-pa.

The province of mKhar-chen-pa was the home of many followers of the old Bon religion. The son of the first mKhar-chen-pa was mKhar-chen gZhon-nu-pa; his son was mKhar-chen rDo-rje-mgon; his son was mKhar-chen dPal-gyi dbang-phyug. When dPal-gyi dbang-phyug of mKhar-chen was fifteen years old, he married a girl of the gNub family named dGe-mtsho. Shortly thereafter, his father was struck down and died, leaving dPal-gyi dbang-phyug as ruler of the province. The young leader was especially attracted to the Dharma and encouraged all his subjects, including the nobles, to study and respect the Dharma in accord with the decree of Khri-srong lde'u-btsan, the King of the Realm.

One evening, when dPal-gyi dbang-phyug was twenty-five years old, some amazing visions appeared to both the young lord and his lady as they were lying together. In dGe-mtsho's vision, there came from the west a stream of golden bees, their buzzing more beautiful than the music of a lute. In single file they flew into the crown of her husband's head. In dPal-gyi dbang-phyug's vision, his wife appeared to have three eyes.

Then a small and lovely eight-year-old girl appeared to both of them. She played a lute and sang: "A, Ā, I, Ī, U, Ū, R̥, R̥I, L̥, L̥I, E, AI, O, AU, AM̐, AH̐." After crying out: "HRĪ! HRĪ! HRĪ! HRĪ! HRĪ!" she completely disappeared. At the same time the earth trembled and rays of light criss-crossed the sky; an ear-splitting din rent the air, followed by a great rushing, clashing sound, and a little spring of water near the palace grew into a small lake.

That same night, the lord and his lady both had very strange dreams. dPal-gyi dbang-phyug dreamt he held an eight-petalled lotus in his hands, and from the lotus rays of light emanated in all directions, filling all the three thousand realms of this universe without exception. A coral stūpa grew from the crown of his head, attracting men from all the neighboring regions of China, Turkestan, Tibet, Khams, Mongolia, Nepal, Bhutan, and so on.

Some of these men were saying: "I will gain access to the stūpa!"
Others were saying: "I will have it!"
Still others were saying: "I will steal it!"
And others were saying: "I will take it away by force!"

Then dPal-gyi dbang-phyug took the stūpa in his hands and from it came sounds like a fine lute which were heard in all the three thousand worlds. Countless beings of all kinds crowded around to listen. The music enchanted them all, and no one tired of hearing it. This was dPal-gyi dbang-phyug's dream.

dGe-mtsho dreamt that she held a garland of shells and red coral in her hands; from the shells flowed milk and from the coral, blood.

Unimaginably great crowds of people partook of the blood and milk that ceaselessly poured forth, filling all the worlds in the universe. She dreamt that the red and white nectar would continue to flow until the end of the age. Such was dGe-mtsho's dream.

The next morning, just as the sun was rising, a strange and beautiful maiden appeared at the palace. Like a daughter of the gods, she was dressed all in white, and she sang: "Into the palace of the Father-king comes the Buddha, comes the Dharma, comes the Sangha. O how wonderful!" And then she disappeared without a trace.

Nine months later, strange sounds were heard, including a catena of vowel sounds, the syllables HRĪ and GURU PADMA VAJRA Ā. Tantric mantras spoken in Sanskrit sounded continuously and clearly, though no one knew their source. At dawn of the tenth day of the bird year, in the monkey month, amid many miraculous events, dGe-mtsho gave birth without pain.

The earth trembled and roared like a dragon. Flowers fell from the sky, and the little lake near the palace became much larger. Strange and wonderful flowers appeared on the surface of the lake—flowers of red and white and many colors, shimmering and glowing. A rainbow of five colors arched out of the palace, soaring upwards where all could see it. For a long time, the air was filled with the sound of lutes and other instruments. Lovely goddesses appeared in the sky showing the upper half of their bodies above the clouds and singing songs of good will and joy:

"HRĪ!
The Dharmakāya, the Great Bliss, is Samantabhadrā;
the Sambhogakāya is the ḍākinī Vajra Yoginī;
you are the Nirmāṇakāya, Great Mother of the Buddhas;
rejoice and be happy!

"The Dharmakāya is the Vajraḍākinī,
the expanse of openness;
the Sambhogakāya is Sarasvatī,
Mother of the Buddhas of the three times;
you are the Nirmāṇakāya,

wondrous lady marked with perfection.
May you be victorious!

"The Dharmakāya is the presencing
of the expanse of Pristine Awareness;
the Sambhogakāya is the seven-eyed White Tārā,
mother of the Āryas;
you are the Nirmāṇakāya, the supreme one among men—
we bow low to you!"

As soon as the song was done, a rain of flowers fell, and all the goddesses vanished into the expanse of the sky.

At the moment of her birth, the little incarnation sang in a clear voice: "Hail, Padmasambhava! Great Wise One of Orgyan!" She was able to sit cross-legged and to kneel; she was alert and watched all that went on around her. Unstained by the womb, her complexion was fresh and healthy, white and rosy from the start. Her remarkably white teeth coiled like conch shells, and her hair, of bluish color, hung down to her waist. When her mother gave her yak butter to eat, she sang:

"I am an incarnation, a girl yoginī.
Since consuming the nectar that never deteriorates,
I have forgotten all food that decays.
But so my mother may accumulate merit,
I will eat this food.

"How will I eat this?
The same way I consumed the secret teachings.
How will I swallow this?
The same way I swallowed all samsara.
How will I be satisfied?
The same way I was satisfied
by Pristine Awareness and Pure Wisdom.
A YE!"

And so she ate the butter.

Her father considered: "What an unusual girl! There is something saintly about her. Perhaps she is a great female siddhā of the Buddhist

18

or Bon tradition. Or maybe she will become the queen of a World Ruler. Since our little lake has become much larger since she was born, I will call her mTsho-rgyal, 'the Lake Conquers'."

After only one month, mTsho-rgyal was in all ways like an eight-year-old child. Realizing this could cause gossip, her mother and father kept her hidden for ten years. At the end of that time, mTsho-rgyal had matured into a woman of extraordinary beauty in both face and form. Any who chanced to see her were amazed and delighted. Soon, large numbers of people were coming from the many lands of Tibet, China, Mongolia, Turkestan, Nepal, and more—just to look upon her.

ཨ་ལ་ལ༔ ཧྲཱི༔ ཧ་མ་ཡ་ཙ་རྒྱ་ཀ་མ་ཧ༔

This Concludes the Second Chapter on How
Ye-shes mTsho-rgyal Manifested in Nirmāṇakāya Form
in the Land of Tibet for the Purpose of Training Beings.

Mañjuśrīmitra

Ting-nge-'dzin bzang-po

Ye-shes gzhon-nu

Blo-ldan mchog-sred

dKon-mchog 'byung-gnas

Sog-po lHa-dpal

Blo-ldan mchog-sred

Ye-shes mTsho-rgyal Recognizes the Impermanence of All Things and Relies Upon a Teacher

With the arrival of many suitors, the time had clearly come for mTsho-rgyal's mother and father to discuss their daughter's future with the nobles and ministers-of-state. They agreed that should mTsho-rgyal be promised to any one of the suitors, the others would become very angry. Only the express command of the sovereign king of Tibet could then prevent a great deal of trouble. So mTsho-rgyal's parents did not give her to anyone and sent all the suitors away.

But then dPal-gyi gzhon-nu, powerful lord of the mKhar-chu province, appeared with an offer of three hundred horses and mules fully laden with goods in return for mTsho-rgyal. Soon after, rDo-rje dbang-phyug, ruler of Zur-mkhar province, appeared with an equal offer. Still the problem remained. No matter which of the two was given the girl, the other could be expected to cause trouble. Finally her parents decided that mTsho-rgyal herself should choose.

But mTsho-rgyal pleaded with her mother and father not to force her to make such a choice: "To go with either of these men would be to enter the prison of samsaric suffering, from which it is so very difficult to escape."

Though she urgently begged them, her parents remained adamant. Her father reproached her: "In this whole land, you will find no more powerful men than these our neighbors. For a well-born girl, you are not very agreeable. I would not send you far away, not to China or Mongolia—but I have told these two most eligible men that one of them would have you, and I have given my word. Now you refuse to go with either one. If I give you to one of them, the loser will be upset, and there may be fighting.

"Though you are my daughter, above all I want to prevent trouble. Therefore, I will send you away, and whoever finds you first shall have you. The other must promise not to provoke any conflict. If he breaks his word, I will inform the King of the Realm that his laws against interprovincial war have been broken."

Thus, powerless, mTsho-rgyal was forced to leave home. Dressed in fine silks, she was led away in a caravan of one hundred laden horses and yaks to face whatever disasters lay ahead.

The Lord of mKhar-chu was the quickest of the two rivals to respond. As soon as he heard dPal-gyi dbang-phyug's decree, he sent his officer Śānti-pa to catch and bind mTsho-rgyal. Seeing the officer coming from afar, mTsho-rgyal fled, leaping across great boulders, leaving footprints in them as if they were mud. But Śānti-pa finally caught her as she was climbing in the mountains.

Still, no one could control her. The evil Śānti-pa stripped her and beat her with a thorn whip, trying to make her submit. "Girl, you are a demoness!" he cried. "Your father and mother could not control you. But you will yield to me, or I will kill you!" And then he beat her even more.

mTsho-rgyal answered him:

"After tens of thousands of ages,
I have achieved this body of realization.
Even if I were not to use it
for the purpose of enlightenment,
should I use it to create more suffering in this world?

Lord mKhar-chu may rule the steppes with great power,
but he lacks even one day's inclination to achieve enlightenment.
I would rather die than surrender and be his wife."

The officer Śānti-pa replied:

"Outwardly, girl, you are beautiful,
but inside you are rotten.
Outwardly, your face is fair,
but you make trouble for your country.
Outwardly, you are soft,
but inside you are hard as lentils.
Girl, you must accept Lord mKhar-chu!"

But mTsho-rgyal responded:

"It is difficult to achieve a human body,
one which is a unique occasion and right juncture.
But it is not so hard to get a body like yours—
your body is wicked and hurtful; it is not really human.
What good would come from my marrying mKhar-chu?"

The officer and his men beat her again with thorn whips until the
bristles were red with her blood. Finally, mTsho-rgyal could bear it no
longer and collapsed. Unable to stand, she fell before them like an arrow.
The soldiers were delighted and danced around, singing with joy.

mTsho-rgyal was in great despair. Lying there bloody and in tears,
she could think of no way to escape. So she sang this sad song to the
Buddhas of the ten directions:

"Kye Ma Hud!
O Buddhas of the ten directions,
Bodhisattvas and Protectors of beings,
Masters of great compassion and power,
possessors of the Wisdom Eye and magical abilities,
O great-hearted ones,
the time has come to show your mercy!

"My mind is white, whiter than the white snow mountains;
it will turn dark, darker than rust,

contaminated by the minds of these alien demons.
Please look upon me with a little compassion!

"My mind is good, its quality like gold;
it will turn bad, worse than the worst bronze,
contaminated by the minds of these alien demons.
You who have the Eye of Wisdom,
look to me with understanding!

"My intention is good, like a precious jewel;
it will become bad, worthless as stone,
contaminated by the intentions of these alien demons.
You who have power, please bring it forth now!

"In one lifetime, in one body,
I can realize the highest Dharma.
But these alien demons will envelop me in the mire of samsara.
You who have compassion, return me quickly to the Path!"

While mTsho-rgyal sang this song to herself, the soldiers were celebrating, becoming quite drunk with beer. So they all fell asleep, which gave mTsho-rgyal a chance to escape. Running more swiftly than the wind, she fled through valleys and mountain passes, always heading toward southern Tibet.

In the morning the men awoke to find her gone. Regretful and afraid, they searched far and wide, but could not find her anywhere. They searched her home in mKhar-chen, but she was nowhere to be found. Finally they returned to mKhar-chu.

About this same time, the teacher Padmasambhava unexpectedly appeared at mChims-phu near bSam-yas. When the anti-Buddhist ministers heard of this, they headed there at once, intending to kill him. But as they drew near, they saw a great fire burning all around. Terrified, they returned and complained to the king:

"Kye Ho!
King of the World, Lord of Men, Son of the Gods—listen to us!
That vagabond from some unknown hinterland
did not go to Turkestan as we commanded.

Instead he must have gone to mChims-phu.
Shall we kill him now or try once more to banish him?
What shall we do?"

Inwardly, the Dharma King was more than happy when he heard that Padmasambhava was close by, for Padmasambhava knew certain oral teachings of the Buddha which did not require the emotions to be conquered. The king greatly desired these teachings, so he sent three scholars to Padmasambhava with gifts of golden bowls and an invitation to come to bSam-yas.

As Padmasambhava started down the mountain from mChims-phu, he became aware that the antagonistic ministers planned to ambush him. Heavily armed, they were lying in wait on a precipitous footpath. So he sent the three scholars on ahead and said he would follow later.

He then made the finger-pointing mudrā with his hand and after crying out: "HŪṀ! HŪṀ! HŪṀ!" in a loud voice, he rose up into the air. A mountain of flames reaching to the farthest realms surrounded him, and within the circle of flames, he manifested as Guru Drag-po. All those who saw this manifestation fell unconscious out of sheer terror.

When the Guru arrived at the palace, even the king was utterly terrified and fell senseless before him. Other people also saw him, but in many different guises. He then returned to his peaceful manifestation and seated himself in the mandala of the guru. The king soon recovered his senses and after bowing before his teacher with reverence, circumambulated him countless times and offered him mountains of gifts. Again, the king asked Padmasambhava for his teaching.

The Teacher replied: "This is not the proper time to teach you the secret Mantrayāna. First you must study the other Dharma vehicles and train and purify your mind. Next year at this time I will give you what you are asking for."

While this exchange was taking place, mTsho-rgyal was in the wilderness near 'On-phu Tiger Cave, wearing only cotton garments and living on fruit. The lord of Zur-mkhar, having heard where she had gone, took three hundred men to search for her. Again, she was captured and carried off.

When Lord mKhar-chu-pa heard of this, he sent a letter to the mKhar-chen-pa, mTsho-rgyal's father:

"Most excellent dPal-gyi dbang-phyug:
You gave your daughter to me,
but then she disappeared, and I could not find her.
Now I hear Lord Zur-mkhar has captured her
in a land a long way from here.
Is this true, what I hear?
What can you tell me of these rumors?
If you have had any part in this, I will fight you!
If you know nothing, I will fight Zur-mkhar!"

After sending the letter, mKhar-chu at once began to gather a great army. And then the lord of mKhar-chen sent back this reply:

"rDo-rje, Lord of mKhar-chu:
What do you mean by your letter?
Please do not threaten me with harsh words I do not understand.
My daughter has left my house; I know nothing more.
How can fighting with me give you what you want?"

But he also set about raising a large army. Soon he received a letter from Zur-mkhar as well:

"Excellent King dPal-gyi dbang-phyug:
Your daughter was hiding in a far distant borderland.
I searched her out and found her—she is here with me now.
If I offer you great riches and priceless goods,
will you give your wonderful daughter to me?"

Zur-mkhar received this reply from mTsho-rgyal's father:

"Some time ago, I solemnly promised
that the one who reached mTsho-rgyal first could have her.
If I now accept more riches for my daughter,
there will surely be fighting.
Therefore, whatever will make mTsho-rgyal happy,
even if it is to wander alone in the borderlands,
is all right with me."

But when Zur-mkhar-pa received this letter, he decided not to let mTsho-rgyal go. So he put her in chains and locked her away while he gathered a great army in preparation for war.

When the King of the Realm heard news of this dispute, he sent this letter to dPal-gyi dbang-phyug of mKhar-chen:

"mKhar-chen dPal-gyi dbang-phyug:
Listen to me. Attend carefully to what I say!
If you do not heed the words of your Sovereign King,
I will quickly overthrow you!
You have a wonderful and beautiful daughter—
I wish to make her my wife.
Remember that in accord with my law,
whoever makes war in my domain will be executed."

The letter was delivered by seven ministers-of-state. As soon as mKhar-chen dPal-gyi dbang-phyug received the letter and confirmed that it was genuine, he sent back a reply offering mTsho-rgyal to the king:

"Ho! World King, most powerful of men:
My daughter is truly incomparable!
Why would I not rejoice in your making her your queen?
Until now, I had feared there would be war,
but the vast armies of the Sovereign King
can take care of anything."

The king was very pleased and went with nine hundred horsemen to Zur-mkhar to fetch mTsho-rgyal—intimidating the lord of Zur-mkhar considerably.

dPal-gyi dbang-phyug of mKhar-chen actually had three daughters. He was able to give the eldest, bDe-chen-mtsho, to Lord rDo-rje of mKhar-chu, making him quite happy and content. Lord gZhon-nu of Zur-mkhar was satisfied when given the middle daughter, Nyi-ma-mtsho. The youngest daughter, mTsho-rgyal, was taken by the king himself, and so the others had to relinquish all hopes of possessing her. Thus the threat of war was dispelled and harmony restored.

The king welcomed mTsho-rgyal with rich robes of fine silk and adorned her with many precious jewels. They then journeyed to bSam-yas where the king celebrated her arrival with three months of festivities.

Because mTsho-rgyal had great faith in the Dharma, the king encouraged her to study and appointed learned men to teach her. They taught her only the most fundamental subjects—first the alphabet, reading, and writing, then the five branches of learning, and the cultivation of inner and outer good qualities—but this was enough for her practice.

After some time had passed, the king again invited Padmasambhava to come to the palace. Khri-srong lde'u-btsan prepared a jewelled throne and offered a veritable mountain of earthly goods to his great Teacher. He decorated a mandala of silver with clusters of gold, and a mandala of gold with ornaments of turquoise to give to the Guru. He even offered Padmasambhava the whole of his realm as if it were a symbolic mandala of Mount Meru and the four great continents.

He offered the central provinces of dBus and gTsang as if they were Mount Meru, and he offered the three regions of the East—China, 'Jang, and Khams—as if they were the great eastern continent, islands, and subsidiary regions. He offered the three regions of the South—Byar, Kong, and Mon—as if they were the great southern continent, islands, and subsidiary regions. He offered the three regions of the West—the three lands of mNga'-ris—as if they were the great western continent, islands, and subsidiary regions. He offered the three regions of the North—Hor, Sog, and 'Brog—as if they were the great northern continent, islands, and subsidiary regions. Thus, he offered his whole kingdom, including his wives, and all available worldly pleasures. Having done this, he asked:

"Great Guru Rinpoche! I offer all that is under my power to you. I offer my realm in the form of a mandala, Guru Rinpoche! Because of your great compassion for all beings, including all gods and men, I will follow you devotedly in all ways forever. I seek the secret Mantrayāna teachings that go beyond cause and effect and karmic relations. This is no time for the ordinary Dharma: Please give me the special teachings of the Buddha that give realization in one lifetime, in one body."

Having asked this, the king bowed before the Teacher nine times. The great Guru then answered him in verse:

"E Ma Ho!
Great Dharma King, listen well.
I am the Lotus-born One, Padmasambhava.

"From the vajra light
of the body, speech, and mind of Amitābha,
free from birth and death,
from the realm of the lotus of limitless Great Bliss,
I descended and appeared in the centerless, boundless vast ocean.

"I was born from a lotus without cause or condition,
I was born without parents, family, or clan:
Miraculously arisen, self-manifested,
free from birth and death,
empowered by a host of ḍākinīs.
I practiced and became accomplished
in the most sacred Mantrayāna—
in the highest root teachings,
the explanations and technical instructions
which transcend karma, cause and effect.

"Though you promise to cherish the Dharma
and respect it throughout your life,
though you are a mighty king and rule a great realm wisely,
you cannot barter for the Dharma with material goods.

"Conniving for the Teachings sullies the root commitments.
If I—or anyone else—were to become involved in that,
we would surely fall into hell after death.

"Though you possess all worldly powers,
and have bestowed upon me the gifts of a king,
this is not reason enough to reveal these secret teachings.
The secret teachings require a worthy vessel.

"Consider the rich milk of the snow lioness—
only in a precious vessel of gold will it retain its goodness.
Poured into another bowl, it changes: Its essence is destroyed.
Therefore, I must keep the secret teachings
sealed within my heart."

When Padmasambhava had finished speaking, his body expanded
and grew so that the upper half reached to the heights of the desire
realm, and the lower half extended to the depths of hell. Then he
returned to the shape of a lama and sat down again on the throne.

But the king fell prostrate before him, collapsing like a wall of
bricks, and cried out in despair: "Great Guru! If I am not fortunate
enough to be a worthy vessel for the secret teachings, I am only the
image of a king!" And he lay on the earth, moaning and weeping. Guru
Rinpoche answered him: "Great King, get up and listen to me:

"E Ma Ho!
Why are the secret teachings called secret?
There is nothing sinful in the Mantrayāna,
but it is secret to those of lesser minds on lower vehicles.
You, King, are not so unfortunate,
but a great mind with discriminating wisdom is needed;
one with faith and commitment that will never revert;
one that thoroughly respects and honors
the teacher of the secret doctrine.

"I myself am unsullied by desire or lust;
and such faults as attachment do not exist in me.
But a woman is a necessary accoutrement to the secret teachings:
she must be of good family, committed to the Dharma,
and a keeper of the vows;
lovely of form and complexion,
she must excel in skillful means, discrimination, and learning;
she must be filled with the power of compassion,
and marked with the signs of a Wisdom ḍākinī.
Without such a one,
the maturation and liberation practices are obstructed;

the result, the achievement of the secret teachings
does not occur.

"Though there be many in this land of Tibet under the sun
who practice the Mantrayāna,
those who obtain its fruit are as rare as stars in daytime.
But for you, Great King,
I will open the doors of the esoteric Dharma."

After saying this, he manifested briefly in the form of Vajrasattva,
and then again sat down.

The king, having understood, took the crown from off his head and
bowed low to Padmasambhava. He gave gifts of the five precious
substances, along with other offerings. And he gave Padmasambhava
the Lady mTsho-rgyal.

Padmasambhava was very pleased, and gave mTsho-rgyal special
initiations as the consort of the teacher. Then the two of them went to
mChims-phu dGe'u and engaged in secret practices.

This Concludes the Third Chapter on How
Ye-shes mTsho-rgyal Saw the Nature of Impermanence
and Relied Upon a Teacher

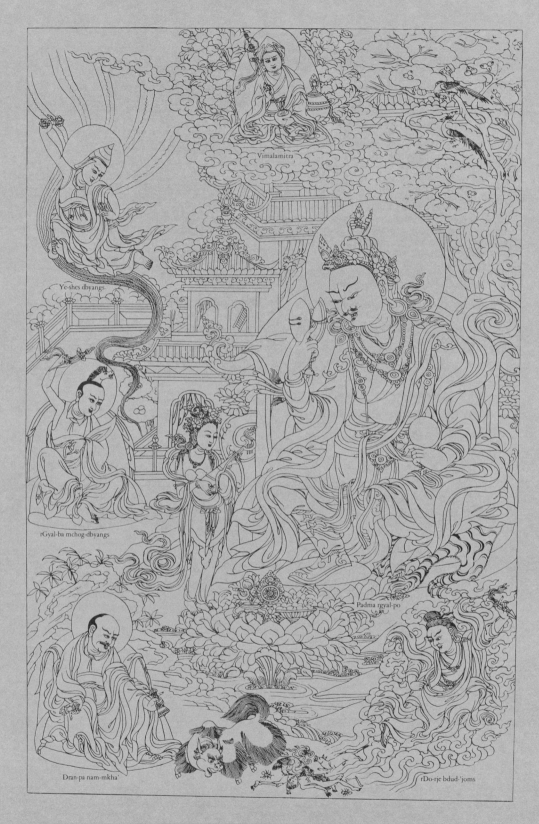

Vimalamitra

Ye-shes dbyangs

rGyal-ba mchog-dbyangs

Padma rgyal-po

Dran-pa nam-mkha'

rDo-rje bdud-'joms

Padma rgyal-po

Ye-shes mTsho-rgyal Asks Her Teacher
for Instruction in the Dharma

Padmasambhava and mTsho-rgyal went first to mChim-phu dGe, as was explained before; later they moved on to the retreat at gYa'-ma-lung. During this time, Padmasambhava advised mTsho-rgyal always to behave in a virtuous manner and to follow the teachings of the Buddha, particularly the Four Noble Truths. He taught her the Sūtras, the Vinaya, the Abhidharma, all the teachings of provisional meaning, including the meaning of cause and effect and karma. Teaching her properly, he explained what must be accepted and what rejected, and ordained her as a novice in the pure Sangha. mTsho-rgyal listened to his instructions in all the six higher Dharma vehicles and took them to heart. Soon she stabilized her meditations, assimilated the explana-tions, and achieved a high degree of spiritual understanding.

At this time the goddess Sarasvatī spontaneously appeared to her in a vision, and mTsho-rgyal found she possessed complete retention of everything she had been taught. She could perceive the entire world through her ordinary eyes, and could keenly distinguish all that deteriorates and all that does not. She also became able to exhibit certain miraculous bodily transformations.

A complete listing of the teachings mTsho-rgyal was given is not set down here because of its great length. But, in short, all the Buddha's teachings were present in Guru Rinpoche as if he were a vessel completely filled. The lady Ye-shes mTsho-rgyal later explained: "After I had served him sufficiently long with material offerings and the delights of body, speech, and mind, thus creating a foundation, I received all these teachings as if the contents of one vessel were being transferred to another.

"I entered a state that was both tranquil and completely wholesome. I clearly distinguished all the nine Dharma vehicles and knew at once what was Dharma and what was not Dharma. I understood the underlying harm implicit in cause and effect. I then felt a desire for the highest, most sublime Dharma which transcends cause and effect and which transcends karma." So she asked Guru Rinpoche in a song:

"Kye Ma!
Jetsun, Incarnate One!
Born in the land of Orgyan,
you surpass all the learned ones of India.
You are the Buddha's successor in the land of Tibet.
As for me, I am young in years, but I have experience:
I have suffered much since the age of twelve.
My father and mother did not follow the Teachings,
but gave me as bride to a man not of the Dharma.
Having no interest in worldly things,
I escaped to the valley of the 'On-phu Tiger Cave.
There, a suitor driven by lust and desire
captured and imprisoned me.
Powerless, I learned about suffering.

"Guru, Lord, by your compassion,
the great Dharma King took me under his protection—
he made me his queen and brought me to bSam-yas.
When I was sixteen, the king offered me to you
as a fit foundation for the three initiations.
Now that I have some understanding
of the harm implicit within cause and effect,
I ask you to teach me the supreme Dharma
that goes beyond cause and effect."

Padmasambhava smiled radiantly when he heard her request. In a rich and beautiful voice, he sang to her:

"Very good, daughter of mKhar-chen bza'.
You are a young woman of sixteen years,
yet you have seen the suffering of eighty.
You realize all this was due to your past karma.
From now on, your karma will have a pure and fine flavor,
from now on, you will always have joy.
Never again will you be burdened
with a bad body due to bad karma.
Now you completely understand
the harm implicit in cause and effect;
it is good that you want the highest teachings
of the Great Vehicle."

Then he brought her to the brink of the Mantrayāna practices by giving her the commitments of the root and branch precepts, and he told her:

"Listen, daughter of mKhar-chen bza'!
Hear me, do not be inattentive, All-good Queen.
These commitments are the root of the great Mantrayāna Vehicle.
If you break them, both of us will suffer.
You must take these solemn vows."

Padmasambhava first taught mTsho-rgyal the fundamental precepts, the root precepts of body, of speech, and of mind, and the twenty-five branch precepts—altogether four areas of instruction.

In this way, mTsho-rgyal studied the fundamental commitments of the enlightened mind, which included a whole series of instructions beginning with the relative enlightened mind and leading up to the ultimate enlightened mind. She learned that from the beginningless beginning of time, one's body is of the nature of a deity, one's speech is the sound of mantras, and one's mind is Being itself, because one can never pass from reality itself.

First mTsho-rgyal studied the commitments concerning the body. These can be divided into three parts: the section on the teacher, the section on the student, and the section on the means of keeping the commitments.

Concerning the teacher, first there is the general lama; second, the guiding lama; third, the lama of the commitments; fourth, the lama as expiator of broken vows; fifth, the lama who liberates the understanding; and sixth, the lama who gives religious instructions and precepts.

Second, mTsho-rgyal learned of the four types of students, or Dharma brothers and sisters: the general Dharma brothers and sisters, all sentient beings; the distant Dharma brothers and sisters, all who follow the teachings of the Buddha; the close Dharma brothers and sisters of one's own lineage; and the interconnected Dharma brothers and sisters of the same mandala.

Third, mTsho-rgyal learned how she should guard the commitments. Externally, one should look upon the commitments of the body as one looks upon one's lord, one's parents, and one's best friend. Internally, one should look upon the commitments as one's eyes, one's heart, one's life itself. Secretly, one should look upon the commitments as one's tutelary deities. Therefore, one must never be dishonest, deceitful, or cunning through the gates of body, speech, or mind.

In short, one should respect all lamas and Dharma friends by all the gates of the body. One should circumambulate them, and spread cushions for them, treating them with the honor a servant shows his master. One should offer them whatever they desire in the way of food, wealth, pleasure, and enjoyment.

In particular, one should respect and honor and make offerings to those close to the lama—his wife, sons, daughters, father, mother, brothers, sisters, other relatives, and even his servants. One should treat them all with the greatest respect, as if they were not different from the lama. This is the way the commitments must be guarded.

Likewise, one must listen well to the words of the lama and never despise those who serve him, his students, disciples, patrons, and so on. In short, one must always honor and make offerings to those whom the lama holds dear to his heart, treating them as if they were not different from the lama. One should treat the lama's horses, watchdogs, and servants in the same way.

Without permission from the lama or from one's Dharma brothers and sisters, one should never use their food, wealth, or possessions, even down to the least seed of sesame. Nor should one even allow such self-indulgent ideas to enter the mind.

Moreover, one should never step over the hat, clothes, belongings, pillows, bed, sitting places, or even the shadow of the lama. It is said that to step over these things is not different from breaking a holy statue or destroying a stūpa. Of course, one should never strike anyone, kill, steal, and so on. Certainly one should never do such things in the lama's presence, but even apart from him, one should not even jokingly suggest inappropriate behavior.

One should never find fault with the teacher, or criticize him to other people. One should not make things up or spread gossip. It is said that one who argues with, or talks back to, or turns against the teacher will surely be born in the Vajra hell. Even should such a one pray to the Tathāgatas of the three thousand realms, he would not be saved.

In summary, the commitments of the body forbid deceit, dishonesty, bad thoughts, abusiveness, wrong views, harmful attitudes, hopelessness, and so on in relation to the lama and Dharma brothers and sisters. If one breaks these commitments for even an instant by just a hair's breadth, one cannot escape retribution.

Next, mTsho-rgyal studied the commitments relating to speech, which concern practices involving tutelary deities. These practices can be discussed in two ways: according to the types of practice, and according to the means of guarding them. The types of practice are as follows:

First, there are three types of mantras: the root mantras which are the infallible cause; the mantras which are the conditions for visualization; and the mantras of activity which are repeatedly recited. The types of mudrās consist of the Samayamudrā, the Karmamudrā and Jñānamudrā, the Dharmamudrā, and the Mahāmudrā.

Second, there are the mandalas of teachers, tutelary deities, and dākinīs, which bear a special relationship to the gates of the body, speech, and mind. The yogic practices involved can be classified as high, medium, and low.

As Ye-shes mTsho-rgyal later explained, Guru Rinpoche gave her 700,000 mandalas of the unexcelled Mantrayāna, and she practiced them as was appropriate, according to the high, medium, and low levels. On the most powerful high level, she practiced the samādhi of Great Bliss which is totally non-conceptual. In the manner of the middle high-level practices, she performed the samādhi which realizes all the appearances of existence to be gods and goddesses. In the manner of the lower high-level practices, she entered the Unbroken River Flow Samādhi.

Also, in the manner of the highest of the high-level practices, she held the mandala of the tutelary deities Hayagrīva and Vajravārāhī firmly in her mind like a continuously flowing river. According to the middle high level, she did the Vajrakīla practices three times each day and three times each night, according to her promise to do them six times each day.

Following the methods of the lower of the high practices, each day she carefully did the eight Heruka sādhanas, making offerings, chanting mantras, and performing the necessary practices. She did numerous other practices relating to the mandalas of other deities, each for an appropriate time and in an appropriate manner, never forgetting to do any of them, not even for a day.

She performed the highest-level practices in their entirety each month, never failing to perform the proper adjunctive practices and making all the offerings at the right times. The middle practices she performed eighty times or more at the time of the new moon and full moon. The lower-level practices she also performed without fail each month. Even the very least of the practices she did once a year, completely and perfectly, without neglecting anything.

Then mTsho-rgyal studied the commitments concerning mind. These can be looked upon in three ways: according to vision, meditation, and action. They can also be discussed according to types of practices and means of guarding them.

First she studied the profound vision; meditation as it operates through the gates of experience; and action as it leads to liberation via the Developing and Perfecting Stages, which can be treated on an outer, inner, or esoteric level.

Second, mTsho-rgyal studied the four outer secrets, the four conditional secrets, the appropriately-held secrets, and the secrets which must not be divulged to anyone.

The four outer secrets are the yidam, the characteristics of deities, the heart mantra, and the signs of realization which may arise.

The conditional secrets are the location of the practices, the time of the practices, the associates with whom one practices, and the substances used in practices.

The appropriately-kept secrets include substances given as offerings: ritual offerings and secret offerings—medicines, tormas, skulls, daggers, staffs, vajras, bells, beads, and other symbolic instruments held in the hand during meditation. They also concern special substances for mandalas, the eight types of cemetery ornaments, bone garlands, and so on, and also any substances used in more advanced Mantrayāna practices. In particular, this includes skull drums, skulls, and thighbone trumpets.

The things one must not divulge to anyone include the private practices of Dharma brothers and sisters, and the purification practices one does to expiate unwholesome behavior. Nor should one gossip concerning the unusual behavior of teachers, Dharma brothers and sisters, or for that matter, about the behavior of any sentient being whatsoever. And one should not discuss with other people any other kind of behavior which is appropriately kept secret.

Thus, there are ten secret commitments relating to body, speech, and mind. The four relating to body concern teachers and Dharma brothers and sisters. The two relating to speech include the three types of mantras and the four types of mudrās. The four relating to mind include the four outer secrets and the four conditional secrets, the four appropriately-kept secrets, and the secrets not to be divulged to anyone.

Once she had received these precepts from her teacher, mTsho-rgyal kept them all without even considering deviating from them, not even in the slightest way for the shortest period of time.

Finally, Padmasambhava taught her the twenty-five branch commitments. The five acts to be symbolically performed: ordinary unity (sexual practices), liberation (killing), stealing, lying, and abusive talk. These are the five practices.

The five substances to be accepted readily by practitioners: human waste, the bodhi mind (semen or other substances), flesh (māṁsa), blood (rakta), and urine.

The five things to meditate upon: the five Buddha families, the five types of Pristine Awareness, the five masculine aspects, the five feminine aspects, and the Five Kāyas, aspects of Being.

The five things not to be rejected out of hand: desire, hatred, ignorance, pride, and jealousy.

The five things to know: the five aggregates, the five elements, the five sense organs, the five sense objects, and the five colors.

Padmasambhava expanded upon these precepts and also gave mTsho-rgyal further teachings so that she would receive the most complete and thorough instructions in their purest form.

mTsho-rgyal never came close to breaking any of these commitments, not even in the least way for even a single moment. She was continually sustained by the compassion emanating from the Orgyan Guru, and therefore entered the mandala of the highest secret teachings, the gSang-ngags bla-na-med-pa.

This thorough description of mTsho-rgyal's training has been included because the door by which one enters the secret teachings is initiation, and the roots of initiation are these commitments.

In the valley of gYa'-ma-lung near bSam-yas, Padmasambhava and mTsho-rgyal opened the mandalas of the secret teaching. In this way, Padmasambhava gave to Ye-shes mTsho-rgyal the Ocean of Accumulated Dharma Teachings.

When the time of the Tibetan New Year drew near, and the populace gathered together to celebrate the holidays, the Tibetan ministers noticed that the Lady mTsho-rgyal was absent. They all wondered where she might be; some thought that perhaps she had come to some harm, but no one seemed to know. So they asked the king. Unable to keep the secret any longer, he told them the details of how he had sent mTsho-rgyal to Guru Rinpoche as the Guru's consort.

Many of these ministers, including such important leaders as Glu Gung-btsan-po and sTag-ra Klu-btsan, Zhang sTong-dbon and rGyud rGyud-ring-mo, Ma Ma-zhang, Bya Rog-rgyung, and Shan Khra-mgo, disliked and resented the Dharma. So with one voice, they said to the king:

"Hail, Great King of Tibet, Lord of all the black-haired peoples! Are you possessed by demons? The royal code is like the cream on milk—don't skim it off! Don't bleed the Tibetans dry! Don't pass wind at your people! Don't treat your ministers like so many dogs! Don't spoil the wealth of our victorious Tibet!

"The traditions and customs are a golden yoke formed by the revered lineage of your god-like ancestors. Now this yokel from the border regions, this 'lotus-born one', this roving doctor, this master of black magic has run away with your wife! If he accomplishes such thievery with no trouble at all, surely terrible things lie ahead for the Tibetan people.

"As for this daughter of mKhar-chen bza': First she brought disgrace to her father's name; then she stirred up trouble all over the place; now she is bringing the whole country to ruin! What kind of behavior is this?

"You must listen! It is said that even if the king's heart were torn from his breast, the ministers have means to put it back. Yet we ministers are suffocating as though we had no air for our lungs! You must consider our advice."

Angered and upset by these words, the king and all his ministers-of-state stood speechless for a time. Then mGos-rgan spoke: "Hail, Lord. We have given you our advice. Since our counsel is now before the king, I suggest we let things be for a while. We will go outside and continue our discussion, and meet with you later."

All agreed to this proposal, so the ministers rose and left the king's presence, intending to continue their discussion elsewhere.

The king himself, upset and disheartened, sent a secret letter to Guru Rinpoche at Red Rock in gYa'-ma-lung. And the Guru replied to him in this way:

"Alas, Lord of Gods, Ruler of Men,
even now obstacles continue to arise!
I myself, the Lotus-born One,
have no fear of birth or death.
My supreme body is like a vajra—
what are the eight fearful things to me?
Even if all the enemies in the world rose up against me,
what would the Lotus-born One have to fear?

"If a few old men make strange faces at me,
am I to be frightened like a small child?
I am the refuge of all sentient beings—
if I could be frightened, whom could I protect?
If I don't protect those who look to me for aid,
how could I impartially guide sentient beings?
So I tell you, Great King,
remove these fears from your mind."

After receiving this message, the king grew calmer and again met with the Tibetan nobles. The statement he gave to them he also transmitted to the country at large:

"Hail! Listen to me, people of Tibet, black, white, and mixed.
I practice the Dharma and I propagate the Dharma.

I am planting the Buddha's Teachings.
You who follow the Bon tradition
had best not try to obstruct the Dharma.
Listen to the words of your King, the Protector of the Dharma.
In this land of Tibet, in this realm under the sun,
I wish to create many retreat centers and Buddhist monasteries,
which will unite the Sūtra and Mantra paths.
If you do not heed me,
if you break the lawful commandments of your King,
you must accept the consequences.
So I suggest you welcome the Lord of Orgyan
and confess your misdeeds to him."

Then sTag-ra and Klu-gong both responded to the king:

"One Lord, Ruler of Men, Son of Gods,
examine all things well.
Look carefully and give counsel carefully—
you are our only Lord.
Don't destroy the customs of your revered forefathers.
Don't destroy the traditional Tibetan government.
Don't destroy the minds of your people.
Tibet is happy and prosperous under the Bon;
without the gods of the svastika, who will safeguard Tibet?

"We hear your queen is unsurpassed—
truly like a daughter of Brahmā.
But where is mTsho-rgyal now?
Perhaps that foreigner, that spiritual charlatan,
has carried her off to kill her!
Your Majesty, are you insane or crazed?
Are you completely out of your mind?
If this is your way of ruling us,
no doubt we will quickly be destroyed.
Please bring mTsho-rgyal back where she belongs,
and punish that heathen!

"It is said that if you let a magician meddle in your affairs, there will be no end of grief. There will be incessant trouble and debilitating

43

disease. Arrest this foreigner and charge him with breaking the law! If he tries to escape, kill him. All you other ministers, take heed of our words, and reach a decision quickly. If we do not assert ourselves in this matter, henceforth we shall be cast aside. If the king destroys his loyal ministers, his pride of lions, he himself will be nothing more than a castrated pig.

"Of course, the king has the right to speak his mind; whatever he wishes to say, let him say. But the ministers have a duty to advise him, and the proper counsel has been determined." All the Bon ministers cried out: "Exactly! This is our advice!"

But the Dharma ministers, Shud-bu dPal-seng and Gru-gu U-be, sKa-ba dPal-brtsegs and Cog-ro Klu'i rgyal-mtshan, Nam-mkha'i snying-po, Lang-gro, 'Bre, gYung, sNubs, as well as others, considered the situation, saying: "Terrible times are upon us. The teachings are in danger of being destroyed. The Bon-pos are promoting evil counsel, encouraging an atrocious attitude toward the teacher who is a second Buddha.

"Even our great Dharma King, our heavenly jewel, cannot remedy this situation, for he cannot possibly follow their advice. By doing so he would prevent the spread of the Dharma. Moreover, it would cause such abominable evil as the five inexpiable sins to come to pass. We ourselves are not afraid to die—why should we be? Even if all Tibet were torn asunder, we would defend what is right. We must support the teacher and his consort in whatever way we can."

Everyone quieted down as the king again spoke: "Those ministers who have no faith or respect, who have not the slightest desire to serve the teacher who is like the actual Vajradhara, propose committing what would be an inexpiable sin. But whatever these ministers plan to do, retribution nine times worse than their deeds shall certainly befall them! The real power in this land resides in me—let no one forget this!" And then he paused.

The reactionary ministers were somewhat subdued; even the Lady Tshe-spong-bza', one of the king's wives who sided with the Bon, had nothing more to say. Yet there was no agreement either, and the situation was becoming increasingly tense.

mGos-rgan pleaded with the great Dharma King:

"Alas! You who are our god,
see how the land of Tibet is breaking apart!
How can it be wrong to accept the counsel of your ministers?"

The king agreed to listen to his ministers, but he also warned them:

"Listen, friends, great ministers of Tibet.
In this world, I am king.
If the king is great, the ministers share his greatness.
If there is no king, what can the ministers do?
So do not try to shame the king;
let us discuss this in a friendly manner."

The ministers agreed. The king then spoke to the Buddhist ministers:

"Even though we are great adherents of the Dharma,
let us stop this fighting.
We cannot justify the accumulation of wrong
on account of the Dharma.
In any case, no one can harm
the diamond-like body of the Teacher.
Better that we all be reconciled,
that the king and all the ministers work together."

Everyone agreed with him, and the ministers gathered about the king to continue the discussion in a more reasonable manner.

"Well," someone said, "up until now this teacher has not actually harmed the king, either by body or speech. Why don't we just give him some gold and tell him to go back to India?"

The consensus was that Padmasambhava should be dismissed, and that mTsho-rgyal should be banished to lHo-brag. Most of the ministers were quite delighted with this decision.

While the ministers were conferring, Padmasambhava and Ye-shes mTsho-rgyal were engaging in secret practices in the cave of gZho-stong near Ti-sgro Rock, a gathering place of ḍākinīs in the district of mThar-byed Dril-bu. There no one could reach them or do them harm.

The great Dharma King sent them both three measures of gold dust and seven bowls of gold and other gifts, asking for blessings and predictions. And so Padmasambhava and mTsho-rgyal set out for gYa'-ma-lung. As they neared the Black Bird Rock, on the side of the mountain, Padmasambhava hid some gter-ma, secret treasure texts, which included many predictions concerning the future.

As soon as he had finished, twelve earth goddesses appeared carrying a white sedan chair that radiated a shimmering light. Guru Rinpoche and his lady seated themselves within it and were carried through the sky. The Tibetan king and ministers, and all those who saw this wonder developed great faith. (Forever after, the mountain was called White Rock or White Light Rock.) The journey took only an instant, and when the Guru and his consort returned to earth, they went at once to the holy cave of Ti-sgro.

mTsho-rgyal prepared an ordinary mandala and, bowing before Padmasambhava nine times, asked for further instruction:

"Kye Ma! Jetsun Lord of Orgyan!
Having obtained a body like a vajra,
you never need fear the demon lord of death.
Having obtained a body like an illusion,
you subdued the army of Māra's demons.
Thus, having the Vajra Body and Rainbow Body,
in one sweep you have conquered
all the demon aggregates of the body.
As you have obtained a body of creative meditation,
the demons of emotionality have become your liberated friends.

"Deathless Guru, Lotus-born One, now I, mTsho-rgyal,
have felt unchanging faith rise in my heart.
May I ask for the highest Mantrayāna teachings?

"In gYa'-ma-lung when the demons attacked,
through your compassion, Lord, we rose to the sky
and came to this place.

Now look upon me with wisdom and compassion,
and please open the mandala that matures and liberates.
Until I too achieve enlightenment,
I ask for your kindness that removes all obstacles."

The great Guru replied:

"Well said, daughter of mKhar-chen bza'!
The mandala of the highest Mantrayāna
is like the uḍumbara flower
that blossoms only once in an age.
It is very rare and does not last for long.
Only the very fortunate can meet
with what is so difficult to find.
But I will give you the secret mandala.
May you delight in the wonder of it!"

And mTsho-rgyal replied: "With joy and respect, with no worldly taint or hint of shame, I have prepared the secret mandala, and I offer it to you."

The Guru smiled compassionately, and five rays of light emanated from his radiant face. All the three thousand worlds were filled by this light which reflected back and shone upon the Guru's face. After he called out "DZA!" and "HŪṀ!" his body was transformed: He rose up in his secret wrathful form as rDo-rje khro-bo, and entered the peaceful lotus-womb of tranquillity.

The male and female aspects moved together in the perfect play of the dance of bliss. Gradually, the mandala of the sun and moon blazed forth in each of their eight root cakras.

Groups of deities appeared as well, circling and making offerings. In each of the eight cakras four deities arose, providing elixir. Sixteen pairs were seen, male and female, facing each other.

Within the expanse of all-pervasive awareness, they experienced the attainment of blissful clarity so difficult to endure. In this way, Padmasambhava opened for Ye-shes mTsho-rgyal the mandala called the mKha'-'gro sNying-gi-thig, Heart Drop of Ḍākinīs.

Within the mandala of the Guru's body arose the male and female aspects of the five Buddha families, ten figures in all, with the great Vajradhara in the center, representing the initiation of the Guru's body. The five male deities represented the five perfectly purified aggregates; the five female aspects symbolized the five elements in their pristine state.

Together with this initiation, Padmasambhava gave mTsho-rgyal various sādhanas involving the Buddha families. "Through the outer vase initiation and the sādhanas of the five peaceful Buddha families in their outer aspect," he told her, "you must realize that the outer world vessel, the external environment, is a heavenly palace, and the inner contents, the beings of the world, are gods and goddesses. You must practice in this way for seven days."

As Ye-shes mTsho-rgyal herself explained: "I did as I was instructed by the Guru, and for seven days I contemplated the outer world as a palace of the gods, and the beings within it as gods and goddesses. Quite naturally and spontaneously, the entire world shone like a heavenly palace. And, indeed, within that palace, I clearly saw all beings who possess form to be the male and female aspects of the five Buddha families, glimmering in many colors before me." Within the field of the five families, there was no awareness of day or night.

Then again, Padmasambhava spoke: "That was the outer initiation. Now the time has come for the inner initiation. Offer a mandala seven times, as you did before."

So once again, mTsho-rgyal, feeling deep respect and great joy, prepared and offered a mandala to Guru Rinpoche seven times, saying:

"E Ma Ho!
The physical body with its head and four limbs
corresponds to Mount Meru and the four continents.
The lotus of Great Bliss is the ground of both samsara and nirvana.
Please accept this mandala, the supreme mandala of Great Bliss,
and bring forth your compassion for the sake of all sentient beings."

The Guru laughed joyously with a deep, rhythmic, resonant voice, making all the three realms shake and tremble, tremble strongly up and down, and back and forth. Arising in the form of the mighty and wrathful Padma Heruka, he cried out in a great voice: "HA HA!" and "HI HI!" The Heruka of the secret symbol entered into the lotus consort.

As mTsho-rgyal recounted: "I was transformed into Vajravārāhī, and Guru Rinpoche into the central deity, a lord of immeasurable wrath—and we manifested within the Mandala of the Heruka Hayagrīva. The empowerment bestowed by the opening of this mandala was called the rTa-mgrin-gi thig-le."

At each of the five cakras of the Guru-Hayagrīva, a pair of ḍaka-ḍākinīs appeared, yab-yum, facing one another, inseparable and multidimensional. This mandala, so sharp and clear, vivid and alive, represented the initiation of the Guru's speech.

When Ye-shes mTsho-rgyal's own body, now that of Vajravārāhī, became inseparable from Hayagrīva, she understood reality in terms of its essential patterning, its primordial dynamic energy, and its manifested vitality.

As the five emotions were transmuted into the five aspects of Pristine Awareness, mTsho-rgyal entered the Indestructible Samādhi of Openness and Bliss, receiving the esoteric initiation and reaching the eighth spiritual level.

Thus, Guru Rinpoche gave to mTsho-rgyal the wrathful means of quickly and certainly realizing the Guru as Hayagrīva and consort, the means of realizing the inner Guru as tutelary deity, and the esoteric inner initiation. When she had opened the mandala of realizing one's own body as deity, and the nature of patterning, energy, and vitality in terms of deities, mantras, and the Mahāmudrā, she was told to practice for three times seven days.

The experience burned within mTsho-rgyal's body like a flaming butter lamp, and she continued to practice until she stabilized the Pristine Awareness which comes from empowerment.

At first, she was overcome by misery, but later she heard within herself the sound which resonates with patterning. mTsho-rgyal's energy flowed naturally and without obstructions, and she completely comprehended the intrinsic vitality whose manifestation is the Mahāmudrā brought to total completion, the perfect creativity of indestructible warmth and bliss.

Thus, mTsho-rgyal brought karmic energy to an end, and the energy of Pristine Awareness entered into the central channel. Many signs of realization occurred.

Then the Guru told her: "Do not harvest barley while it is still green! There are still initiations that you have not completed."

As Ye-shes mTsho-rgyal later recounted, she felt toward the great Guru Rinpoche faith greater than toward the Buddha, and requested of him:

"Jetsun Orgyan Rinpoche,
greater than all the Buddhas of the three times!
Please give this most wonderful initiation
to all of us who are deprived."

The Guru then arose within the mandala of the Red Heruka. Immense light rays, indications of his wrath, radiated from the mantra HŪṀ in his heart. After the rays returned to gather within the Guru's mandala, the Ultimate Heruka formed a mudrā and cried:

"RA HAṀ!
Listen with unswerving attention,
Ḍākinī mTsho-rgyal-ma, benign lady, All-good Queen!
Would you rejoice to enter the mandala of inner clarity?
Then offer the mandala of secret bliss.
If you reveal this teaching,
you will have violated your vows."

She responded: "I, the woman mTsho-rgyal, have caused all worldly appearance to subside—I will set myself free in the nakedness of Great Bliss." Then she cast about her the five precious substances as an offering in the mandala of secret bliss. Again, she asked:

"Hero of Great Bliss, Incarnate Buddha-mind,
Guru, Lord of Great Bliss,

confident and happy I wish to enter
the mandala of Inner Clarity.
I will keep my vows as if my life depended upon them."

Then with nine fingers she formed a lotus with its swirling anther, and performing the dance of the palanquin, offered the mandala to the mandala of the Guru's body. Within the great mandala of the expanse of all that is, the great Lotus Heruka made the gestures of the hook and wheel mudrās with his hands. The radiant Vajra Heruka of the Ultimate, by the waves of his laughter and intense power, by his extraordinary and forceful aspect and fierce facial expression, by his wondrous stance, right foot raised and arms extended, crying out in a loud voice, overwhelmed mTsho-rgyal with the brilliant appearance of Great Bliss and opened the mandala like a blazing sun in the radiant expanse of being. This was the initiation.

As Ye-shes mTsho-rgyal herself explained: "I felt myself caught up in the mandala of the Guru's discriminating wisdom and skillful means, and my four root cakras were transformed into the great realms of the four Herukas. I received the initiation of the Four Joys in the universal mandala which radiated hundreds, thousands, and millions of mystical phenomena, light, and seed syllables.

"When the Lama and I were inseparably joined by powerful waves of blessing from the root cakras of our foreheads, I saw thirty-two realms, gleaming white, and within them radiated the Joy of Pristine Awareness. In each of the thirty-two realms were thirty-two white Herukas in male and female aspect, and within each of them many hundreds of thousands like themselves. The lord and master of all the Herukas, in male and female aspect, revealed to me the Awakened Joy of the Yab-Yum. The emotion of anger was purified, and the taints of habitual patterns of the body were cleansed. Seeing the branches of the path of application, I was able to benefit seven worlds in the ten directions. And I received the secret name, 'White mTsho-rgyal of Great Bliss'.

"Similarly, within the throat cakra, I gradually saw sixteen realms yellow in color, and in them, sixteen yellow Herukas, in male and female aspect. Within these circled, as before, hundreds of thousands like themselves. The master of all the Herukas, the most precious Hero, in male and female aspect, revealed to me the Joy of Limitless Good Qualities. The emotion of attachment was purified and habitual patterns of speech were cleansed. Seeing the branches of the path of accumulation, I was able to benefit twenty worlds in the ten directions. I received the secret name, 'Yellow mTsho-rgyal, Increaser of Good Qualities'.

"Likewise, in the heart cakra, I gradually saw eight realms blue-black in color, and within these realms were eight blue-black Herukas in male and female aspect. In these circled as before hundreds of thousands like themselves. In the center, the Lord of all the Herukas, the Buddha Hero, in male and female aspect, revealed to me the Supreme Joy of the Mahāmudrā. The habitual patterns of mind were purified. Seeing the branches of the path of liberation, I was able to benefit thirty-six worlds in the ten directions. I received the secret name 'mTsho-rgyal Whose Commitment Liberates'.

"In the same way, in the navel cakra, I gradually saw sixty-one realms red in color. Within these realms were sixty-one Herukas, in male and female aspect. In the center was the Lord of all these, the Red Heruka, in male and female aspect, who revealed to me the Spontaneous Transcendent Awakened Joy. The emotions flavored by grasping were purified and with them the habitual patterns tainting the three gates. Seeing the branches of the path of complete purity, I was able to benefit unbounded and limitless worlds in the ten directions. I received the secret name 'mTsho-rgyal of Limitless Pristine Awareness'."

The initiation lasted for seven days, during which time Ye-shes mTsho-rgyal practiced the four empowerments and the four aspects of Pristine Awareness in the Mandala of the Four Joys. An experience of ecstasy followed, and Padmasambhava advised her: "You must now involve yourself in Pristine Awareness in the opposite sequence. But when you assimilate the Pristine Awareness born of empowerment, do not let yourself be distracted by ecstasy or the Four Joys that accompany it. Rather, let the experience little by little rise up within your being. If you lose the impulse toward enlightenment, it is worse than killing the Buddha Amitābha. In no world could you find exoneration; you would fall to the lowest hell."

Padmasambhava taught her how to reverse the energy and cause it to ascend. mTsho-rgyal held the energy as if in a vase, bringing it upward and producing ecstasy. The bliss of continuing awareness was not adulterated by passion; not for an instant did she succumb to laziness while her continuous concentration was maintained.

As mTsho-rgyal concentrated the impulse toward enlightenment in the lotus of the female organs, she purified all ignorance, the first link of dependent origination. Halting the one thousand and eighty motile currents associated with the first link of dependent origination, she achieved the Pristine Awareness of the two comprehensions and reached the Path of Vision. Thus she reached the first spiritual level and developed various kinds of prescience.

As she concentrated the impulse toward enlightenment in the secret cakra and transmuted it, she purified the motivating forces, the second link of dependent origination. Halting the motile currents of the second link, she reached the second spiritual level.

By concentrating the impulse toward enlightenment in the area between the secret and navel cakras, she purified consciousness, the third link of dependent origination. Halting the motile currents of the third link, she reached the third spiritual level.

In the same way, by concentrating the impulse toward enlightenment in the navel cakra, she purified the tendency to distinguish and fixate on name and form, the fourth link of dependent origination. Halting the motile currents of the fourth link, she reached the fourth spiritual level. She purified the mind concerned with samsara and nirvana, Pristine Awareness, and Spontaneously Arising Joy, and she became the Svābhāvikakāya.

By concentrating the impulse toward enlightenment in the area between the navel and the heart cakras, she purified the six sense fields, the fifth link of dependent origination. Halting the motile currents of the fifth link, she reached the fifth spiritual level.

By concentrating the impulse toward enlightenment in the heart cakra, she purified sensation, the sixth link of dependent origination. Halting the motile currents of the sixth link, she reached the sixth spiritual level. Having purified the ordinary, sleeping mind and the Special Joy, she obtained the fruit, the Dharmakāya.

By concentrating the impulse toward enlightenment in the area between the heart and throat cakras, she purified feeling tones, the seventh link of dependent origination. Halting the motile currents of the seventh link, she reached the seventh spiritual level.

By concentrating the impulse toward enlightenment in the throat cakra, she purified craving, the eighth link of dependent origination. Halting the motile currents of the eighth link, she reached the eighth spiritual level. She purified the dreaming mind and Supreme Joy, and achieved the fruit, the Sambhogakāya.

By concentrating the impulse toward enlightenment in the area between the throat and forehead cakras, she purified grasping, the ninth link of dependent origination. Halting the motile currents of the ninth link, she reached the ninth spiritual level.

By concentrating the impulse toward enlightenment in the fore-head cakra, she purified becoming, the tenth link of dependent orig-ination. Halting the motile currents of the tenth link, she reached the tenth spiritual level. The consciousness of the five sense gates which operates at the time of waking from deep sleep was purified, as was the Joyful Pristine Awareness. As a result, she achieved the stainless Nirmāṇakāya.

By concentrating the impulse toward enlightenment in the area between the forehead and crown cakras, she purified birth, the eleventh link of dependent origination. By purifying the motile currents of the eleventh link, she reached the eleventh spiritual level.

By concentrating and reversing the impulse toward enlightenment at the crown cakra, she purified old age and death, the twelfth link of dependent origination. Halting all the 21,600 motile currents of the links, she purified all the four impure occasions—the desire mind, ordinary sleep, dreaming, and waking—as well as the Four Joys and the mind of patterning, energy, and vitality. She reached the twelfth spiritual level and achieved the Buddhakāya and its limitless qualities, taking the shape that benefits limitless beings.

Thus, in a period of six months, mTsho-rgyal completely realized all three initiations. Again, Guru Rinpoche came to her and said:

"O Lady Ḍākimā!
Your beauty matures, youthful one:
Your six senses illuminate your sixteen years.

"Your body, full of vigor and sensitivity,
is a unique occasion, just the right time.
You are the great and wise Sarasvatī!
You are Vajravārāhī who realized the secret teachings.

"Now you must become completely mature for yourself and others!
I will open the doors of the secret teachings
that produce maturity.
Great Bodhisattmā, act heroically!"

Thus he spoke, and mTsho-rgyal answered him: "I, the Lady Ye-shes mTsho-rgyal, having given all worldly pleasures and bodily delights as a mandala offering to Guru Rinpoche, make this request:

"Jetsun Orgyan Thod-phreng-rtsal,
Tree of the Secret Teachings, Vajradhara!
In no way can I repay your great kindness,
but what can I do to most please you?
I would give my body, my life.
Will you now give me the supreme initiation,
that of the Great Perfection?
Now, great Teacher, will you give me
the fourth initiation?"

Thus she asked, and he replied: "This is not yet the time for you to effortlessly enter the Āti Vehicle. For now, you must practice the Dharma of the esoteric Mahāyāna teachings which I have given you."

And so he instructed her: "Now, daughter, there is no way for you to practice the esoteric teachings by yourself. You need a heroic friend to provide the means. Think of it like this: If new pottery is not fired, it will not last for long. Without trees to burn, you cannot make a bonfire. Without seeds nourished by water, you cannot expect sprouts to grow. Accordingly, in the land of Nepal there is now living a native of the Golden Isle, Ācārya Sa-le, who is a manifestation of Hayagrīva. He bears a red mark at his heart and is seventeen years old. Seek him out and make friends with him. You can then quickly reach the stage of Great Bliss."

mTsho-rgyal recounted: "As Padmasambhava indicated, I, the Lady mTsho-rgyal, journeyed alone to Nepal, carrying with me a golden cup filled with loose gold. As I came to the E-rong Valley near the border of Nepal, I was chased by seven bandits with fierce hunting dogs who sought to rob me of my gold.

"I visualized the Guru in my mind and imagined the thieves to be tutelary deities. Thus, as they attacked me, I held in my mind the thought that I was offering a mandala of all my worldly goods, and I sang to them:

"Kye Ma!
O seven yidams of the E-rong border valley,
how wonderful to meet you here today!
I must have accumulated great merit—
may all beings with minds full of arrogance
quickly be purified of evil karma!
How wonderful is the compassion of the Lama!
It has brought you to me today.
My mind overflows with happiness—
may all beings share it and be freed."

mTsho-rgyal brought her hands together in a gesture of offering and spread her sacks and gold before the thieves. Even though the seven robbers could not understand her words, the lovely sound of her voice penetrated their minds, and drew them into the first level of meditation. They stared at her transfixed and asked her in Nepāli: "Most

56

wondrous lady, where did you come from? Who is your father? Who is your mother? Who is your teacher? Why have you come here? Please speak to us again in your beautiful voice."

As they spoke, the bandits' angry faces became calm, their bristling, wild hair lay smooth, and they smiled happily. All seven sat upon the ground and grinned affectionately at mTsho-rgyal.

mTsho-rgyal leaned upon her three-pointed walking stick and answered them, this time in Nepāli:

"E Ma Ho! You seven bandits: We are brought together by past karma. Your fierce and angry minds are themselves Mirror-like Pristine Awareness. The mind full of hatred and obsessed with enemies does not arise from anything but radiance and clarity. Recognition of this is Vajrasattva. Not being attached to what appears before you is the cultivation of openness. My father's country is joy manifested, an open and peaceful realm, land of the Sambhogakāya. I myself am not attached to symbols and forms, but if you wish to visit that fine and perfect land, I will guide you there.

"You seven men brought here by past karma! Your pride and arrogance are themselves the Pristine Awareness of Sameness. The mind which is inflated by ego and passion does not arise from anything but natural meditative composure. Perception of this is Ratnasambhava. Not being attached to concepts of openness is the cultivation of appearance-in-itself. My father is the fulfillment of all needs and desires; the wish-fulfilling gem is my father. I myself am not attached to illusory jewels, but should you wish to have such a perfect old father, I will give you mine.

"You seven men who are linked to me by past karma! The mind full of lust and attachment is itself the All-investigating Pristine Awareness. The mind which desires what lies beyond itself and is attached to pleasant things does not arise from anything but clear understanding. Knowledge of that freshness is Amitābha. Not being attached to radiance is the cultivation of bliss-itself. My mother is the boundless light; the immeasurable Great Bliss is my mother. I myself am not attached to the flavor of pleasure or pain, but should you wish such a perfect mother, I will give you mine.

"You seven brought here today by past karma! Jealousy and divisiveness are themselves the All-accomplishing Pristine Awareness. The envious mind, so jealous and dualistic, does not arise from anything but appropriate activity and realization. Contemplation of this is Amoghasiddhi. Not being attached to subtle or vivid experience is the cultivation of whatever arises. My teacher is complete realization; appropriate activity is my perfect teacher. I myself am not attached to the realm of action, but should you like such a perfect teacher, I will give you mine.

"You seven bandits linked to me by past karma! Bewilderment and unknowing are themselves the Pristine Awareness of the Expanse of All-that-is. Profound ignorance and the mind wrapped in dull confusion do not arise from anything but the holding quality of the Dharma. Contemplating this ignorance is Vairocana. Not being attached to keeping track of everything is the cultivation of whatever arises. My friend is the natural appearance of phenomena; the only friend I desire is this limitless activity. I myself am not attached to the subjective or objective poles of experience, but should you like to learn such a perfect way, I will teach you."

Listening to mTsho-rgyal, the bandits developed unshakable faith, and their minds never again turned toward samsara. They asked her for the Dharma teachings and were soon liberated. Then all seven pleaded with mTsho-rgyal to stay with them in their country and not to return to Tibet.

But mTsho-rgyal left to visit the great stūpa called Bya-rung kha-shor which had been built in ancient times by three Bhutani brothers. As she stood before the stūpa, mTsho-rgyal tossed offerings of gold dust into the air and prayed:

"OṀ ĀḤ HŪṀ!
May the land of Nepal
be the Pure Realm of the Buddhas.

May the offspring of the Dharmakāya
be the protectors of all sentient beings.
Throughout vast ages yet to come
may the Wheel of the highest Dharma continue to be turned,
liberating all beings from the ocean of samsara.
May all sentient beings,
those with bodies and those without, become mature!
And may you, Lord, who have the strength to guide them,
lead those on the isle of bondage
to the wonderful land of liberation."

As she spoke, myriad multicolored rays emanated from the stūpa. In the middle of the sky among clouds and swirling mist appeared the Lotus Guru with the Great Abbot and the Dharma King on either side of him. And ḍākinīs circled round him as he spoke:

"Listen well, daughter of mKhar-chen bza'!
You are disciplined and ethical, patient and free from anger.
With your discriminating wisdom, you have guided many beings;
through your generosity, you have become totally free.
Your vigor is endless, and in your meditation,
you have travelled the five paths and the ten spiritual levels.

"Now remain here for a while and wander no more.
Here you will find the Hero you need.
And then when you bring him into Tibet,
I will open again the gates of the profound Mantrayāna."

After making this prophecy, he disappeared. Ye-shes mTsho-rgyal, having no idea where the boy could be found, at once began a systematic search. She looked everywhere. Finally, while in the city of Kho-khom-han, as she neared the marketplace by the south gate, she came upon a very handsome young man. His complexion was smooth and his cheeks rosy; his teeth were like rows of conch shells, and his four pearly-white canine teeth coiled to the right. His candid eyes were slightly bloodshot; his nose was sharp and his eyebrows dark blue. His curly hair also coiled to the right. His fingers were very slightly webbed, joined like the toes of a bird. He came right up to mTsho-rgyal and said: "Mother, where have you come from? Have you come to ransom me?"

59

She answered him (probably speaking in the language of Ma-zangs-gling):

"Listen closely, captivating boy, brave one!
This is wonderful!
I am from central Tibet,
and I am the consort of Jetsun Padmasambhava.
What is your name? Where are you from?
And how did you get here?"

The boy replied:

"I come from the noble Golden Isle,
and my parents called me Ārya Sa-le.
Abducted from my family by a heretic,
I was sold as a slave to a man in this city.
For seven years, I have lived as a servant here."

The crowd of merchants had by now noticed mTsho-rgyal. At first they were dumbfounded by her beauty, but after a moment, they spoke: "Wonderful lady, please speak again. It would give us great joy and delight!"

So mTsho-rgyal sang this song:

"NĀMO GURU PADMA SIDDHI HRĪ!
In the great all-encompassing expanse of space,
the All-good Lord Samantabhadra,
shines the sun of the Great Perfection.
In the six realms, helpless and in darkness,
live the beings who have all been our mothers.
Is not Padmasambhava their father?

"In the Vajra realm, untouched by change,
dwells the most Compassionate One,
he who has attained Buddhahood,
untouched by karma good or bad, deathless and unborn:
Is not Padmasambhava the father?

"In Ti-sgro cave he dwells, a goodly place,
Akaniṣṭha, most sublime ground of all.

60

Urged on by the compassion of the father,
I, the ḍākinī, met this boy
who holds the conditions for bliss.
Am I not the mother, Ye-shes mTsho-rgyal?

"The great Dharma Mother has come
to Nepal, the land of rains,
compelled by a karmic connection to this boy.
Does not Ye-shes mTsho-rgyal have good reason?"

Even though they could not understand all mTsho-rgyal said, the people gathered around were entranced with her song. They called her 'The Ḍākinī Whose Voice is Like a Melody'.

That evening, mTsho-rgyal went to the house where Ācārya Sa-le was living and stood before the outer door. The lady of the house came out to ask her: "Where have you come from? What do you want here?"

mTsho-rgyal explained in a few words: "Guru Padmasambhava sent me here to ransom Ācārya Sa-le, the boy who is living with you. It is most important that you let me have him."

The mistress of the house replied: "Although this Ācārya is a servant, he has come to be like a son to me. I also paid a great deal of money for him, and I don't want to give him up. But if you want him for yourself, you can live with him here, and then both of you can serve me."

mTsho-rgyal answered her in song:
"When the circle of the sun arises,
darkness is dispelled.
When the sun sets, the stars come out—
yet tomorrow the sun will rise again.

"When a wish-fulfilling gem is at hand,
gold is not needed.
When one is without such a gem,
gold must be counted.
And so tomorrow I will search for that gem.

"Where a perfect Buddha exists,
other means are not necessary.
When the Buddha is gone,
one must rely on other means.
And so tomorrow I will unite wisdom and method.

"If the fruit were mature, I would not need Sa-le.
But on the path to maturity,
I need Sa-le for my friend.
So I ask you to sell him to me."

Mother, father, son, and all the rest of the household gathered round to enjoy her song, and lost their hearts to her. They invited her in and offered her food and drink. The lady of the house then asked: "Do you want this Ācārya for your husband? Is that why you wish to buy him? You are a most fascinating and attractive woman. If a husband is what you want, I will give you this son of mine to marry."

But mTsho-rgyal replied: "The Lotus Guru foretold my meeting Ācārya. I need him as an accoutrement to practice—I have gold, so please sell him to me. How much do you want?"

"How much gold do you have?" asked the mistress. "I paid five hundred ounces of gold when I bought him. You need to give me more than that."

"I will give you whatever gold is necessary," mTsho-rgyal told her. "But you must sell him to me. Let's count how much gold dust I have."

But of course there were not the five hundred ounces. There were not even so much as one hundred ounces. So the lady of the house asked her: "Now what can you do? To buy him you must pay, and to pay you must have gold. There is not even enough here to buy his hand! Unless you have gold, you cannot have him."

Now, at this time the country was in great turmoil. In the very same city where mTsho-rgyal was staying, there lived an extremely rich family headed by a man called Nga-nya-na A-yu, who had a son called

Nāga. This son, only twenty years old, had just been killed in the fighting. The body had been brought to his parents' house, and offerings were being prepared for the funeral. The mother and father were suffering terribly as they sat with their dead child; they wished to die also.

When mTsho-rgyal heard about this family's hardship, a profound compassion arose in her heart. She went to visit them and said: "It is not necessary that you two suffer like this. There is a boy in this city named Ācārya Sa-le. If you give me enough gold to ransom him, I will bring your son back to life."

The parents were overcome with joy and answered: "If you can truly revive our son as you say, you needn't be content with this Ācārya. We will give you enough money to ransom even a prince! If you revive our son, we promise to give you whatever gold you need."

mTsho-rgyal approached the body of their son and placed upon it a cloth of fine white silk which she had folded into four parts. She then sang these words:

"OṀ AḤ HŪṀ GURU SARVA HRĪ!
The ground of everything is the All-good,
pure from the beginning and free from going astray.
But the embodied beings of the six realms
wander on this path and that,
behaving in ways that produce the karma of pleasure and pain.
They create the cause and reap the fruit.
Knowing this, why do likewise?

"I am a yoginī skilled in the secret teachings.
My father is the most compassionate Padmasambhava
who fears neither birth nor death.
He can instantly dispel all evil obstacles—
I ask him now to help me and send his good blessing."

Saying this, she pointed her finger at the boy's heart, and little by little color returned to the corpse. She poured a bit of water into his mouth and spoke ĀYUR JÑĀNA BHRŪṀ! into his ear. Applying a little salve to the great knife wounds in his abdomen, she healed them. Gradually, the boy's awareness returned, and he completely revived.

There was great rejoicing at this wondrous event, and everyone bowed low to mTsho-rgyal with respect and admiration. The boy's father and mother were beside themselves with joy at their son's recovery; the three of them cried and clung to one another.

So it was that they gave many great gifts to the Lady mTsho-rgyal, including one thousand ounces of gold to pay for Ācārya Sa-le. And mTsho-rgyal's fame spread throughout the realm; the king even invited her to visit him and showed her great respect.

Although everyone asked her to remain with them, she did not accept their invitations. Rather, Ye-shes mTsho-rgyal and Ācārya Sa-le travelled to the great Nepāli temple E-yi gTsug-lag-khang where they met another disciple of the Lotus Guru, a Nepāli named Vasudhara. They offered him gifts of gold dust and gold coins, and asked him to share his Dharma teachings with them. Vasudhara understood that mTsho-rgyal was the consort of Guru Rinpoche and treated her with great respect. And so they exchanged various kinds of special practices and Dharma teachings.

mTsho-rgyal and Ācārya Sa-le next went to Asura and Yang-le-shod where Śākya De-ma and Ji-la-ji-pha and other practitioners lived. Ye-shes mTsho-rgyal gave the customary offerings of gold to Śākya De-ma when they met, and said to her:

"O wonderful sister!
We share the same esoteric lineage—
as I am the Tibetan Lady mTsho-rgyal,
please listen to me.

"All we might need or desire
arises unceasingly from Mind-as-Such.
Impartially it provides whatever is wished.
Such is the generosity of the Tibetan Lady mTsho-rgyal.

"The mind itself is stainless, free from broken promises,
its methods and manners always appropriate and correct.

64

Such is the ethical behavior
of the Tibetan Lady mTsho-rgyal.

"The mind itself is impartial,
not leaning toward pleasure, pain, or indifference.
Whatever happens, good or bad, it carries on and endures.
Such is the patience of the Tibetan Lady mTsho-rgyal.

"The mind itself is like a flowing river,
neither accumulating nor discarding—
vigorous and pure, inseparable from bliss and emptiness.
Such is the vigor of the Tibetan Lady mTsho-rgyal.

"Whatever arises in the mind
is the unity of the Developing and Perfecting Stages,
steady and concentrated as Mahāmudrā.
Such is the meditation of the Tibetan Lady mTsho-rgyal.

"Mind itself is the movement
of natural Pristine Awareness, Great Bliss.
Depending on skillful means,
one travels in transcendent wisdom.
Such is the discriminating awareness
of the Tibetan Lady mTsho-rgyal.

"Sister of this good lineage,
what special teachings have you received?
Sister, dear friend,
won't you please offer me equally what you know?"

Śākya De-ma was very pleased and answered:

"E Ma Ho! Wonderful!
Welcome, Dharma sister of one teacher!
I do not have so many special teachings,
but through the compassion of Jetsun Orgyan Sambha,
I know what is necessary for birth and death.
The Developing and Perfecting Stages,
their union, the Mahāmudrā,

the Radiant Light and the Illusory Body— I have all these teachings.
Talk of the bardo or rebirth in a womb is meaningless to me.
These are the special teachings of the Nepālī Śākya De-ma.

"I know what is necessary to die and return.
I can channel the energy of the heart cakra through the central channel.
I have teachings for the gtum-mo practices
for igniting the A-shad within;
I have no fear of death or the disruptions of consciousness.
These are the special teachings of the Nepālī Śākya De-ma.

"I know how to take emotions as the path;
relying on the essence of skillful means and discriminating wisdom,
I practice openness and bliss.
I have the teachings that produce
Pristine Awareness and the Four Joys;
though a whole army of hostile emotions arise,
I am free from fear.
These are the teachings of the Nepālī Śākya De-ma.

"I know what is necessary in the obscurity of sleep;
relying on the Great Perfection, I cultivate the dream.
I have the teachings for entering the Clear Light;
though the whole universe collapse in darkness,
I am free from fear.
These are the teachings of the Nepālī Śākya De-ma.

"I know what is necessary of the nature of reality itself;
relying on the six lamps of the teachings,
I cultivate the Radiant Light.
I have the teachings for reaching the four deep states;
though the Buddhas themselves
should rise up as enemies, I have no fear.
These are the teachings of the Nepālī Śākya De-ma.

"Now I need not, by cause and effect,
pursue the stages of the path;
instantly I can achieve perfect Buddhahood.
How incredible is the most sublime fruit!

"You show all the signs of accomplishment;
what kinds of teachings do you have?
You are an appropriate vessel;
won't you give me equally what you have received?"

So Ye-shes mTsho-rgyal and Śākya De-ma exchanged their many
Dharma teachings and special instructions, becoming of one mind, one
heart. After this, Ye-shes mTsho-rgyal and Ācārya Sa-le went to Tibet.
When the two of them arrived in gTsang province, they went at once
to the meditation caves of Ti-sgro where they stayed at the place of
ḍākinīs. The patrons of that region gave them offerings and showed
them respect, but some thought: "This lady must have been taken over
by demons. She has not been serving her lotus-like Guru as she should;
instead she has gone off and picked up a wandering ācārya." And so
there was a great deal of gossip.

On the tenth day of the month, mTsho-rgyal made the appropriate
offerings and opened the mandala of the Bla-ma gsang-'dus, the Guru
Guhyasamāja. She invited Padmasambhava to come to her, and he
appeared riding upon the sun's rays. She cried out joyfully and with
great fervor: "How long I have sought to prostrate myself before my
Guru!" And she sang:

"Kye Ma! Guru! Compassionate One!
I, a woman, am ignorant, erring, caught in samsara,
wandering in a world of evil actions.
Hold fast to me with compassion!

"Now whatever difficulties I must endure,
may I never part from you, Lord.
Look upon me with compassion!

"I have travelled far across the borders of Nepal
to find the true Ācārya Sa-le.
Now I ask you to permit me
to enter the door of the secret teachings.
Dispel all obstacles on the path.
Look upon me with compassion!"

Padmasambhava was very happy to hear this. Smiling, he said:

"Listen, daughter of mKhar-chen bza':
Be faithful and unwavering.
This ocean of samsara is limitless.
If you want to be freed from this body's restrictions,
you must rely upon the captain, the right teacher.

"You must board the ship
of the oral teaching lineage,
and raise the great sail of profound instructions.

"You must send forth the explorer ravens
of advice and counsel,
and scare off the crocodiles of hindrance
with the sound of the conch.

"You must manage the winds of undesirable action
using weights of lead,
inspire a favorable breeze by the power of your faith,
and fill the pontoons with the purity of your commitment.

"In an instant you will cross
on the waves of maturation and liberation,
and reach the island of the wish-fulfilling gem.
There, all desires for enjoyment are satisfied.
There, all appearance is rich and precious.
There, no dirt, gravel, or decay will tarnish your joy.
Now be happy, for endless bliss will come."

After this song, he asked mTsho-rgyal:

"Daughter, how many difficulties did you undergo?
Was your journey pleasant? Were there obstacles?
How long has it been since you arrived?"

Ye-shes mTsho-rgyal explained all the many difficulties she had en-
countered on her journey, and how hard it had been to obtain gold in
Nepal. She told how she had raised up a dead man and thus obtained
the necessary thousand ounces of gold. After she had clearly and ex-

tensively described her experiences, the Guru said: "Very good! Such difficulties are really very good things; they purify immeasurable karmic obscurations. Although the cost was high, you have done well; you have accomplished a great deal. But reviving those who have been killed and other such practices are just ordinary powers. Do not harbor pride because of such things.

"Your commitment is not due to attachment and desire, nor is it just a woman's desire for a man; moreover, this boy is more noble than any husband you could ever find. Since he cost so much gold, let him be called 'Golden Light'."

Padmasambhava gave Ācārya Sa-le his blessing and opened the mandala of the lama for him. He set him on the course of maturation and gave him initiations similar to those mTsho-rgyal had received. Ācārya Sa-le developed and became mature in his practice. Setting out on the path of liberation, he came to understand the Dharma both in its ordinary significance and in its ultimate sense. Thus he became liberated.

Padmasambhava designated him the trusted friend of mTsho-rgyal and told them both: "Now you must practice until you fully realize the secret teachings." Then the Guru went off to lHo-brag.

So the lady who was Padmasambhava's consort and the boy who was his heart-son went together to an isolated meditation cave, later known as the Secret Cave of mTsho-rgyal. There, where none could find them, they practiced for seven months cultivating the Four Joys. mTsho-rgyal developed the ability to penetrate any kind of barrier; her body became immune to ordinary weakness, disease, old age, and the like. In short, she learned to control the five elements and bring them under her power. The Four Joys manifested in their completeness, and mTsho-rgyal obtained the Four Kāyas. Padmasambhava returned at this time, and the three of them went to a great cave where they stayed while he turned the Wheel of the Dharma.

Now, Guru Rinpoche had previously given the Tibetan king, that great Dharma protector, a number of Mantrayāna practices, including the mandalas of gShin-rje-E, rTa-mgrin dpa'-bo, of Yang-dag mar-me and Phrin-las phur-pa, bDud-rtsi thod and Ma-mo khram, and so on. The king did these practices in an appropriate manner and had certain significant experiences. He felt a profound faith arise in his heart, together with an intense desire for more of the deep esoteric teachings. So he dispatched three of his messengers, Shud-bu dPal-seng, rGya-tsha lHa-nang, and rMa Rin-chen, to invite Padmasambhava and his consort to visit him. Upon arrival at the meditation cave at Ti-sgro, the envoys presented Guru Rinpoche with gold and the message:

"Great Guru and Consort!
We who are skilled in fast-running
are the messengers of the King of Tibet.
The god-like ruler of Tibet, Khri-srong,
yearns for the more profound esoteric teachings
of the supreme vehicle.
He invites you to visit him.
Please, Compassionate One, come quickly!"

So saying, they offered Padmasambhava their presents of gold, and he answered them:

"Attend! You three faithful Fast-runners!
You three worthy and fortunate sons, welcome!
Though I, Padmasambhava, reside in this land of men,
I am one with the Mind of all Buddhas;
Vajradhara is not different from me,
and my manifestations fill the world.

"I am glad that the great Dharma King
has been successful in his practice;
I will now go with you
and give him the secret teachings."

And so all six of them—the Guru, his consort and son, and the three royal messengers—set out for bSam-yas. When they reached gZho-grod, Padmasambhava suggested that the three lotsāwas go on ahead to alert the king to prepare a welcome. The others would follow. So the three scholars hurried off to tell the king how they had seen

Guru Rinpoche, and that he would soon be arriving. They suggested that a great reception be arranged.

When the Tibetan ministers heard this, they thought:

"It would seem this one called Lotus-born
is never-ending like the sky.
Like a river, sharp knives cannot harm him.
Like fire, his brilliance sets things aflame.
Like the wind, he cannot be held down.
Though he appears to be real, it is as if he were not.
Whatever harm we attempt will do no good.
So we will go along with whatever the king says.
The Lady mTsho-rgyal, however, is another matter;
she is hopeless—she won't stay where she belongs.
She flaunts the king's laws and degrades the whole country."

Guru Rinpoche understood their attitude and thought: "I must use the secret teachings, which are so-called because they include many methods and present no difficulties. It is better that the Lady mTsho-rgyal appear in another form; I will transform her into my three-sided staff as I travel in Tibet."

The Dharma King's representatives, sTag-ra and Gung-btsan, along with one hundred other important ministers, went on horseback to meet Padmasambhava at gZho-mdar. Then they proceeded by stages to bSam-yas.

As they came to the gate of the Great Stūpa, they were welcomed by the king, his ministers, and retinue. The Dharma King greeted his teacher; he draped a white silk scarf of welcome over his arm, and offered it to his guru along with a gold vase filled with fresh rice wine.

Guru Rinpoche told him: "Right now, the esoteric doctrine is very fresh and has great power. But in the future, as it spreads, there will be many people practicing it who have not sufficiently matured." As he spoke these words, he touched the vase to the top of his head.

The Tibetan people noticed that mTsho-rgyal was not present, and that Ācārya Sa-le was Guru Rinpoche's sole attendant. The king also noticed this and thought: "I cannot ask for the esoteric teachings without mTsho-rgyal; the way is barred if she is not here. I must inquire of Guru Rinpoche where she might be staying. Moreover, I did invite her and would like to see her again." So he asked: "Great Guru, where is mTsho-rgyal? Why didn't she come with you? Is this Ācārya your disciple? What teachings has he received?"

The great Guru answered him with a smile:

"E Ma Ho! Bodhisattva Dharma King!
This pattern is of the nature of space;
whatever appears is the magical display of the master of space.
The girl mTsho-rgyal has entered the expanse of space,
and now she resides between samsara and nirvana.

"This pattern arose from the Dharma;
there is nothing that cannot occur in the Dharma.
The girl mTsho-rgyal has entered the Dharmakāya realm,
and now she resides in the place of Samantabhadrā.

"This pattern is the bliss of openness;
the magic of openness achieves all desires.
The girl mTsho-rgyal has gone to the realm of bliss and openness,
and now she resides in the palace of bliss, the Three Kāyas."

After he had spoken, Padmasambhava touched his staff with his hand, and it became mTsho-rgyal. The king was astonished. When the others noticed that the queen had arrived, they commented to the ministers: "See what wonderful things this Master can do—he concealed mTsho-rgyal within his three-pronged staff!" While some of the ministers were delighted and amazed, many of the ministers concluded: "mTsho-rgyal could not have done what they say—and besides, the girl in the staff was not necessarily mTsho-rgyal. In fact, there is not enough room in the staff for even mTsho-rgyal's hand. Though you say a great wonder occurred, it was merely an illusion."

So in spite of mTsho-rgyal's miraculous transformation, the ministers plotted against her. But most of the Tibetans continued to honor and love their queen.

The whole procession, which included the king and Vairotsana, twenty-one principal disciples, thirty-two novices, seven ladies of noble birth, and others numbering three hundred and twenty-five, proceeded to the retreat center at mChims-phu dGe-ba. There Guru Rinpoche opened one hundred and twenty mandalas of the highest Mantrayāna teachings, and all were matured and liberated.

In particular, he taught the eight great sādhanas, the Ma-gshin phur-pa, the bDud-rtsi yang-dag, the Bla-ma dgongs-'dus, the Yi-dam dgongs-'dus, the sGyu-'phrul zhi-khro, the Yang-dag zhi-khro, the Padma zhi-khro, and others. He taught the sixty-one practices of the sNying-thig and the seven different dGongs-'dus, the eleven collections of the bKa'-brgyad-rgyas, and the one hundred and twenty-two Thugs-sgrub, the seventy-six special techniques, the one hundred and thirty rGyud-kyi dgongs-pa, and more.

To the king he gave the seven root practices of the bDud-rtsi yon-tan, together with twenty special techniques, and told him to practice them.

To Nam-mkha'i snying-po of gNubs-yul, he gave the nine practices of the Yang-dag mar-me and the twenty special instructions of the bGegs-'dul phur-nag, and so on, telling him to practice them at lHo-brag.

To Sangs-rgyas ye-shes and rDo-rje bdud-'joms, he gave the root practices of the 'Jam-dpal gshin-rje-gshed, the means of realizing the Phyag-rgya zil-snon and the six subsidiary deities. He gave them twenty special root and branch techniques and directed them to practice at Brag Yang rdzong.

To rGyal-ba mchog-dbyangs of Khung-lung and rGyal-ba blo-gros of 'Bre, he gave the rTa-mgrin yang gsang rol-pa, the means of perfecting the three root yogas, the twenty-five special branch techniques, the twelve Tantras, and the Phra-men-ma sādhanas, directing them to practice at mChims-phu.

To Vairotsana and lDan-ma rtse-mang, he gave the means of realizing the dMod-pa drag-sngags and the eight classes of root instructions

73

on the dPal stob-ldan nag-po, and the eighteen mighty branch teachings. He told them to practice at gYa'-ma-lung.

To sKa-ba dPal-brtsegs and 'O-bran dbang-phyug, he gave the inner, outer, and secret root teachings of the Ma-mo, the gNang-dbab-las-'gyed, and so on. He told them to practice at Yer-pa'i-brag.

To both Jñānakumāravajra and Sog-po lHa-dpal gzhon-nu, he gave special instructions concerning the esoteric Yang-phur teachings and the practice of longevity and the Mahāmudrā. He exhorted them to practice at sNye-mo Bye-ma'i-brag.

To dPal-gyi seng-ge and Cog-ro Klu'i rgyal-mtshan, he gave the Dregs-pa rtsa-ba'i sgrub-thabs, the Khro-bo bcus-brgyan-pa, the thirty branch practices, and the Dregs-dpon sum-cu'i bskang-thabs. He gave them special practice techniques, the Las-kyi man-ngag, and told them to practice at dPal Chu-bo-ri meditation center.

To the translators Rin-chen bzang-po and Ting-'dzin bzang-po, he gave the esoteric teachings of the Great Compassion, the means of realizing the Rig-'dzin bla-ma, and the siddha practices of the supreme Mahāmudrā of enlightened awareness. He told them to practice at a meditation center of dBu-ru.

To Lang-gro dKon-mchog 'byung-gnas and rGyal-ba byang-chub, he gave the teachings of the Byin-rlabs bla-ma'i sgrub, the collected esoteric teachings of Hayagrīva, and the means of realizing the powerful sādhanas of rTa-nag dregs-pa. He told them to practice at gYas-ru Shang-gi-brag.

To Dran-pa Nam-mkha' dbang-phyug and Khye'u-chung mKha'-lding, he gave the means of realizing the Padma zhi khro gsang-ba'i sgrub-thabs, the sādhana in which Vajrasattva is the main figure and is surrounded by six subsidiary deities, the practice of dPa'-gcig bsgom-pa, and the oral instructions of the thirty-six Heruka sādhanas. He told them to practice at Byang-gi gnam-mtsho-do.

To both rMa Rin-chen-mchog and rGyal-mo gYu-sgra snying-po, he gave the collected esoteric teachings of Vajrapāṇi, twenty further instructions, one hundred special techniques, and especially the practices involving the yoga of longevity. He told them to meditate at mChims-phu.

As mTsho-rgyal explained: "To me, mTsho-rgyal, Padmasambhava gave the inner, outer, and secret heart practices of the Guru himself, as well as the means of realizing the Root Lotus initiations. He taught me the seven different sādhanas connected with the mandala of the Guru and the means of realizing the three roots, lama, yidam, and ḍākinī, within one mandala. He advised me to practice first at the Tiger Cave of 'On-phu, then at the Tiger Cave of Nepal and the Tiger Cave of Khams, and so forth, and in any place where the image of Guru Rinpoche spontaneously manifested. Especially, I was to practice at Ti-sgro. And he said: 'If you have any difficulties or bad experiences, just call on me, and I will come to you and teach you. But be sure you stay with your companion Ācārya Sa-le.' "

The great Dharma King showed his joy and immense gratitude to Padmasambhava by offering him a great variety of gifts, equal in number to the sādhanas he had received. He heaped mountains of gold, bolts of fine silk, and many kinds of precious worldly substances before the teacher and asked:

"O Great Guru!
This mandala of the highest secret teachings
is difficult to obtain though one search for ages,
but now I possess it!
There is no way to repay your great kindness.
From now until I am fully enlightened,
may your lordly compassion keep me from turning back.
A king such as myself
is subject to infinite diversions and distractions—
always wandering here and there, encountering obstacles.
May you look upon me always with compassion."

Then the king tossed seven handfuls of gold upward over the body of the Guru.

As the assembled lotsāwas who had received instructions from the Guru prepared to go to their various destinations, the king gave them presents to help them on their way. Each received a measure of gold dust and a golden bowl, some fine embroidered silk and fabrics of red, white, and indigo blue, various articles of apparel, and a horse laden with supplies. And they, in turn, vowed to practice until they had perfected their realization.

Padmasambhava was very pleased and said to the king:

"Kye Ma! Wonderful!
You are a great king indeed, a god-like ruler!
And these are the deeds of a king.
I, myself, the Lotus-born One,
have no need of garments and such-like.
But so that the king may accumulate merit,
and the commitments of the secret teaching may be furthered,
I accept them.
These twenty-four disciples of mine,
thus freed from obstacles, will accomplish their purpose.
How good that the Dharma King supports their continued practice—
this is indeed the behavior of a Bodhisattva and most excellent.
With these three things—
persevering faith which produces the heart-bone,
the special instructions of Padmasambhava,
and the support and patronage of the great Dharma King—
endless good qualities will increase.
By the coming together of pure deeds and an altruistic mind,
the ocean of Buddha qualities will be perfected."

To the king and Vairotsana, Padmasambhava gave individual oral teachings which are not included here. Each one received clear and lengthy instructions, and then all of the disciples went to the places where Guru Rinpoche had instructed them to do their practices.

"As for me," mTsho-rgyal said later, "first I went to Ti-sgro and entered the mandala of the unity of the three spiritual roots. I received so many different esoteric teachings, both written and oral, dealing both with overall view and specifics, that it is difficult to describe them all. By merely hearing these teachings, one can be liberated. But there are so many that I fear to put them all down in Tibetan."

This Concludes the Fourth Chapter on How
Ye-shes mTsho-rgyal Listened to the Teachings of the Dharma

Nyi-ma 'od-zer

The Manner in Which
Ye-shes mTsho-rgyal Did Her Practices

Ye-shes mTsho-rgyal practiced in the ḍākinī center of Ti-sgro in the Secret Cave of mTsho-rgyal, and in other retreat centers. In these areas there were many patrons who were happy to support her in her practice.

She first practiced in the cave of the ḍākinīs, and while in that one hermitage, she strove to genuinely invoke Padmasambhava in his peaceful aspect. Her body was completely transformed into that of a deity, and she looked upon the face of her tutelary deity. She understood that her own patterning and energy were the mandala of the ḍākinīs—and whatever she engaged in, she naturally accomplished. She realized that the vitality that manifests was actually her own mind, that her own mind was one with the Guruyoga, and all phenomena were the blessings of the creative play of the Lama. As a natural, spontaneous, and ecstatic devotion for the Lama arose, simultaneously, bright, spectral lights radiated from the borders of her mandala. Ḍākas and ḍākinīs flashed in and out through the translucent radiance.

Within that visionary experience of rich and vivid light, she saw the land of the Orgyan ḍākinīs. This is how she described it: "The trees were like keen razors, and the earth seemed made of flesh. All the rocky hills were bristling skeletons, and small loose bones strewn here and there served as pebbles.

"In the midst of that land stood a great castle formed of three types of skulls—freshly severed, partly rotted, and totally dried up and free of flesh. Its roof was covered with a sheath of skin; the doors as well were made of skin. All around, for a distance of hundreds of thousands of miles, mountains of fire burned fiercely. A vajra formed a kind of tent above it all, and sharp weapons fell from the sky like lightning.

"Eight cemeteries formed a ring, rimmed by walls of beautiful lotuses. Predatory flesh-eating birds and wild blood-drinking animals wandered about, and demons and demonesses, roaming in great numbers, stood out vividly against the landscape.

"Although the beings there did not attack me or threaten me, neither did they make friendly overtures. As I advanced upwards, I passed along a path that circled in a zigzag fashion three times, and ended at a door. Within were many ḍākinīs whose external appearance was that of women, but they were of many different colors. They were carrying offerings to present to the principal ḍākinī.

"Some of the ḍākinīs had cut their bodies into small pieces with razor-sharp knives and prepared offerings of their own flesh; others were giving their streaming blood. Some were giving their eyes, some their noses. Some were giving their tongues, still others, their ears. Some were giving their hearts, others were giving their viscera. Some were giving their outer muscles, some their inner organs. Still others were giving their bones and marrow.

"Some were giving their life energy, others, their breath, and still others, their heads. Some had cut off their limbs, and so on. They had cut up their own bodies and had prepared offerings of them for the principal ḍākinī, who appeared Yab-Yum before them. The offerings were then blessed as signs of their faith.

"Then I asked the ḍākinīs: 'Why do you suffer in this way? To what purpose? If one lives in accordance with the Dharma until death, is that not sufficient?' And they answered me:

'Dear woman of irresolute mind!
The compassion of a great teacher who has all the qualifications
may only be available briefly.
If you do not offer whatever he wishes when he looks upon you,
later nothing you do may lead to fulfillment.
If you procrastinate, obstacles will multiply.

'Your insight and certainty may last only a moment;
natural and spontaneous faith may not stay long.
If you do not make the offering when Pristine Awareness arises,
later nothing you do may lead to fulfillment.
If you procrastinate, obstacles will multiply.

'Now, at least, you have a human body – you may not have it long.
The chance to practice the Dharma seldom arises;
if you do not make offerings when you meet the qualified teacher–
if you procrastinate–obstacles will multiply.

'The teacher may only be here briefly;
only now can you be certain to enter the door of the secret teachings.
If you do not offer yourself
when you have access to the highest Dharma –
if you procrastinate–obstacles will multiply.'

"Thus they spoke, and I felt ashamed. Then, as each ḍākinī presented her offering, the Vajra Yoginī appeared before her, snapping her fingers. Instantly, each supplicant was healed and became as before. After requesting a regular Dharma practice from the principal ḍākinī, each one returned to her own meditation place. They did twelve sessions of meditation each day.

"Next, a gatekeeper appeared at each of the gates, and the Vajraḍākinī appeared in the very center in the midst of flames, her guise so brilliant it was difficult to look upon her.

"I saw many other different lands such as this, but as they are described elsewhere, I will not transcribe them here for fear of making the text too long."

As mTsho-rgyal later explained, she then met with Guru Rinpoche and told him the story of her visions. She asked him the significance of such experiences, saying: "As I wish to do such difficult practices, would you please give me the necessary vows?"

Guru Rinpoche replied: "What you saw were merely symbolic experiences. It is not now necessary for you to do such arduous practices, offering your flesh and so forth. Just follow the disciplines I will give you now:

"Listen, Goddess mTsho-rgyal-ma!
Watch and listen undistracted, Irresistible Lady.
Seek to attain the Golden Tree,
the precious jewel-like human body.
If you understand how to use it, you will have food forever—
if not, you may not have even one day's breakfast.
Without understanding this, you will starve to death.
But if you can do as you promise, all will go well.

"Take the healing essence of herb, nectar, and mineral,
and then eat the food of air:
This is the discipline of food.

"Wear cotton cloth, wear bone ornaments,
and then go naked without adornments,
relying on the gtum-mo breathing:
This is the discipline of dress.

"Practice invocation, sādhanas, Dharma activity, mantras,
energy flow, and silence—abandon idle talk:
This is the discipline of speech.

"Do prostrations and circumambulations,
purify your body, and adopt the lotus position—
remain calm and composed:
This is the discipline of body.

"Practice vitality, bliss, and openness,
the Developing and Perfecting Stages—

meditate upon their unity:
This is the discipline of mind.

"Adhere to the Buddha's teachings, guard the doctrine,
practice skillful means—teach, debate, and write:
This is the discipline of teaching.

"Benefit others, be benevolent,
hold to the Mahāyāna aspiration of immeasurable compassion
without regard for your own life:
This is the discipline of benefitting others.

"Regard your enemies as your sons—
look at gold as if it were clay,
love others more than you do yourself:
This is the discipline of compassion.

"When you act like this, you practice the Buddhadharma:
You will perfect the most sublime wonder—Great Bliss.
If you do not act this way, you cast your lot in with the heretics:
Your discipline will be the same as theirs.

"Daughter of mKhar-chen bza',
understand this and use it well."

So he spoke, and mTsho-rgyal vowed to fulfill the eight great disciplines as taught by the Guru:

"What a great wonder!
To this unhappy land came the Buddha's teaching;
to this land of darkness came the clear burning crystal lamp.
To Tibet, land of demons, came the Lord of Orgyan,
and beings who lacked the Dharma
felt the rain of the pure teachings.

"I feel the same wonder
as when the troubled looked up and found good fortune,
when the actual Buddha appeared
and performed his deeds at Vajrāsana.
How can I repay the Guru's kindness
which liberates us from samsara?

"Now I, the Lady mTsho-rgyal,
have entered the door of the esoteric teachings—
yes, even the door of the secret mandalas.

"I would rather die
than break my promises to you in any way,
or disgrace the eight great disciplines.
I will disregard my body, my fate, my life;
I will consider only the teachings of the Jetsun Guru.

"I would rather die
than compromise my commitment to the Dharma.
I will disregard food, drink, and clothing;
with body, speech, and mind,
I will care only for what benefits the Buddha,
the Dharma, and sentient beings.

"I will care for others more than for myself,
and fulfill the eight compassionate tasks.
I will certainly not take this practice lightly,
or neglect the essential teachings."

She made the gesture of promise three times and solemnly vowed to practice the eight disciplines. Padmasambhava was most pleased and gave some final instructions and prophesies. Then he returned to the king's sanctuary.

The Lady began by practicing the discipline of dress with gtum-mo exercises. She climbed to the mountain heights near Ti-sgro and found a cave lying between the icy glaciers and the forested mountain slopes. Wearing only one piece of cotton cloth, she settled down to practice for one year.

At first, the heat of gtum-mo did not arise in her body. Outside, the icy winds of the new year were blowing; snow fell heavily and hoarfrost blanketed the world. mTsho-rgyal could barely continue. Ācārya Sa-le had gone with Guru Rinpoche to serve him, and she was absolutely alone. But the promise she had made strengthened her resolve, and she continued to meditate.

Her whole body became covered with blisters from the cold, and sharp, stabbing pains ran through her. Her breath came in short, choking gasps; she was near death. But mTsho-rgyal visualized the Jetsun Guru in her mind and prayed to him:

"Orgyan Dharma Lord, Protector of Beings,
look upon me with the sunlight of your compassion!
Your daughter is naked, friendless, all alone.
This terrible cave is dark, and freezing winds blow through it.
When the blizzard rages outside, whose daughter am I?

"My stone bed is hard and cold as ice.
Like a rock, I cannot do anything.
Inside or outside the cave, there is no difference—
this white cotton cloth is useless.
Bless me with the warm sunlight of your compassion!
Please help me kindle the gtum-mo heat!"

As she prayed, her karmic energies became slightly altered, and this small change was enough to allow the gtum-mo heat to rise. mTsho-rgyal felt an overwhelming and spontaneous confidence toward her teacher and prayed:

"When the teacher with all the qualifications
bestowed upon me the pure essence—
the powerful grace of the Vajrayāna, the esoteric teachings—
I felt the pristine wisdom of Vajrasattva,
and the Four Great Joys danced in my heart.
Then the White-dressed One, the Fire Ḍākinī, rose up within me,
and sublime warmth and bliss came forth.
Now I am wondrously happy!
Please continue to show your kindness!"

Just as these thoughts occurred to her, the Orgyan Lama himself appeared before her in the form of a Heruka, handed her a skull cup of beer, and disappeared.

As Ye-shes mTsho-rgyal later explained: "I continued to experience ever-increasing warmth and bliss. I felt joyful and happy. My body, before so cold and miserable, changed as completely as a snake losing its skin.

"Now I decided the time had come for donning the bone garlands, so I set aside my cotton cloth and put on garments of bone. I integrated the three facets of meditation for this stage, and practiced this discipline for one year. At this time, all my food supplies were gone; not even a grain of barley remained. For sustenance I relied upon mineral substances and drank only water. And I continued to meditate.

"Sometimes I had powerful visions of past lives and other striking experiences, but I became weaker and weaker. My legs could no longer support my body; my body could no longer support my head. I could barely breathe, and even my mind became weak. Growing worse, I came to the brink of death. But then again I called upon my teacher, propitiated my yidam, and continuously visualized a stream of offerings to the ḍākinīs. I prayed:

'From the beginning I have given my body to the Lama;
whatever will happen, happiness or misery,
the Lama knows.

'From the beginning I have given my speech to the pure Dharma;
whether my breath will continue to flow or not,
only you now know.

'From the beginning I have directed my mind toward virtue;
whether it is virtuous or not,
only you now know.

'From the beginning my body has been a citadel for the yidam;
whether he wishes to abide there or not,
only you now know.

'From the beginning my patterning and energy
have been a conduit for the ḍākinī;
whether she wishes to enter this path,
only you now know.

'From the beginning my vitality
has been the essence of the Sugata;

will I pass beyond misery or turn the Wheel of the Dharma?
I have watched sentient beings, my mothers,
unceasingly wander in confusion.
Whether I, your daughter, find samsara or nirvana, you decide.'

"When I had spoken these words, a red lady, completely naked and lacking even bone ornaments, appeared before me. She placed her bhaga to my mouth, and blood flowed from it, which I drank of deeply. Then it seemed that all the realms were filled with bliss! Strength equal to that of a lion returned to me. I experienced a meditation of complete transcendence without any attributes at all.

"Now I felt the time had come to sit naked and rely on the food of air. Thus I practiced for one year, wearing no garments and no ornaments, nourished only by the pure air.

"At first, bliss accompanied the coming and going of my breath. I had various kinds of clear and visionary experiences, and creative and penetrating awareness arose unimpeded.

"But after a while, doubts assailed my mind. My breath became unstable, and I could not control it. My throat became dry and rough, my nose and throat felt as if they were stuffed with cotton; my stomach, growling and filled with gas, gave me great pain. Once more, I came close to death.

"Collecting myself with great effort, I called upon Guru Rinpoche, singing: 'Innumerable times your daughter has assumed bodily form and wandered in samsara. I have suffered in the harsh states of being, surrounded by birth and death, distraught with heat and cold, hunger and thirst, yet I have endured.

'The most important possession is a human body.
The shortest path is the esoteric teachings;
the quickest method is difficult practice.
Although this is almost unbearable, what else is there to do?
There is no end to my vow:
I will still continue to practice the disciplines—
I will be mTsho-rgyal of the Heart-bone!

'Wonderful magically lotus-born Tulku,
Self-arisen Lama, Teacher of Orgyan,
compassionate and mighty one!
Your wonderful diamond body is a mandala of the Rainbow Body.
Please look with compassion on beings with ordinary bodies!
Will you help my poor inferior body?
Whatever happens to this physical form, wherever you may be,
please look upon me with love and compassion.'

"As soon as I spoke, Padmasambhava appeared to me in the midst of shining light, smiling radiantly. He sat down in the air itself, only an arm's length away, and said to me:

'Listen well, daughter of the lineage,
daughter of mKhar-chen bza'!
When you were the daughter of a king,
you cared only for finery and pleasure,
and could bear no misfortune at all.
Now is the time to be unconcerned
whether you meet happiness or misery on the path.
Whatever comes, suffering or Great Bliss, carry on!
Do not crave bliss.
Be devoted, virtuous, and humble.

'Listen well, daughter of mKhar-chen bza'!
When you were the young wife of a king,
how proud you were—
you were fettered by your own desires.
Now is the time to give up all activities and needs.
Meditate on impermanence
and think about the suffering of the lower realms.
Do not have great desires.
Be devoted, virtuous, and humble.

'Listen well, daughter of mKhar-chen bza'!
When you were the consort of the Lama,
how egotistical you were—
your position meant so much to you.
Now is the time to reject your old faults;

do not hide them but constantly tear them out.
Do not wish for fame.
Be devoted, virtuous, and humble.

'Listen well, daughter of mKhar-chen bza'!
How proud you were of following the Dharma,
how crafty and deceitful you were—
before you were only a hypocrite.
Now is the time to reject all artifice and sham;
do not hold back, but show your perseverance.
Do not dwell on what you have done.
Be devoted, virtuous, and humble.'

"Then Padmasambhava came down to earth and sat upon a large rock. He continued: 'Now, there is something more for you to do. Carefully extract the essence from plants and herbs, and use these to cleanse your awareness, stimulate your creativity, and restore your body.

" 'I, Padmasambhava, exist only for the benefit of beings. From beginningless time, I have hidden many precious and sacred Dharma teachings. These are inexhaustible and will continue into the future until samsara is completely emptied of beings. Later, I must go to the rNga-yab Ḍākinī Island. You, my lady, must take pains to procure all my profound treasures, so tomorrow I will open for you the many mandalas of the highest Mantrayāna. The time has come to work for the benefit of beings; make such preparations as I direct you.' He gave me many detailed teachings, and then departed."

As mTsho-rgyal later explained, after meeting Ācārya Sa-le and his friend, the girl named bDe-ba-mo, she led them to the three Lion Lair Caves of Bhutan to practice. First, they went to the Lair of the Lion's Mouth and extracted the essence from medicinal plants and minerals. Then mTsho-rgyal sought for just the right minerals, especially the white cong-zhi 'essence of all minerals', and distilled its healing properties. Her body became as strong as a vajra and impervious to weapons. Her speech became clear and melodious, its sound so soothing it calmed even the proud tigress. Her mind entered a meditation like the indestructible vajra.

mTsho-rgyal now felt in her heart that the time had come to practice the arduous discipline of speech. First she prayed over and over again to purify all obscurations involved with speech. She practiced a very long time, doing Dharma sādhanas uninterruptedly, day and night, with never a break in the sound of her chanting.

In the beginning, she practiced the one-hundred-syllable mantra and other mantras of the Rig-sngags, as well as those of the gZungs-sngags. She also took up the expiatory and purification practices of the Krīya, Caryā, and Yoga Tantras.

Next, she practiced the teachings of the five Buddha families and the three deities, Avalokiteśvara, Vajrapāṇi, and Mañjuśrī, and the related teachings, chanting the gZungs-sngags of the Upa and Yoga mandalas.

Finally, she recited the Sūtras by heart and recited confessions and vows. She behaved in the manner set forth by the Vinaya, and practiced the teachings of Amitāyus. In order to make her mind sharp and clear, she strove to completely master the Abhidharma, logic, epistemology, and so on.

At first her voice stammered. Her throat was torn so that great quantities of blood and pus frothed forth; she felt a searing pain in her esophagus, and it became twisted, hard, and dry, swollen with blood and pus. Again she came close to dying.

But in the end, at whatever length she wished to speak, she felt no discomfort. The sound of her voice was always beautiful, the words clear and appropriate, the rhythm musical and pleasing. She could speak at any pitch, high, medium, or low; she could talk very fast or very slow or at a moderate rate. She thus developed complete control over her voice, and it responded exactly as she desired. In short, she developed all the sixty different fine qualities of voice. She also perfected the seven powers of complete retention.

mTsho-rgyal opened the eight Heruka mandalas in the manner of the Mahāyoga Tantras and practiced until she clearly saw the faces of all the deities. When the practice was perfected, mTsho-rgyal and the deities were no longer separate entities but had become one. As she sat cross-legged in the lotus position, her hands placed for meditation, many different deities appeared before her. Rays of light flashed above her, and other auspicious signs occurred.

After a time, her yidam came to her and made the prediction: "You will develop both the ordinary and the eight great siddhis. Your accomplishments will be as indestructible as the vajra, and you will attain the dPa'-bar 'gro-ba'i ting-nge-'dzin, 'the Heroic Samādhi'. In the end, you will be completely liberated and enter the expanse of the All-good. This is my prophecy."

Then mTsho-rgyal opened the mandala of the Bla-ma dgongs-pa 'dus-pa and practiced according to the instructions of the Anuyoga Tantras. Having prepared herself through proper meditation, mantra, and breathing, she considered her own body the central figure of the dGongs-pa 'dus-pa mandala. Thus meditating, she perfectly understood the essence of patterning, energy flow, and vitality, and took it to heart.

At first, there was great agony from the inversion of the energy flow and the stiffening of the vitality. The pain in the pattern of energy channels brought her near to death. But though her suffering was enormous, mTsho-rgyal still practiced without judging the experience as harmful.

And after a time, many different deities appeared before her. She developed complete control over the pattern, energy, and vitality of her life and severed forever the four currents of birth, old age, sickness, and death. She became a great and powerful siddhā indeed. "I will never be able to repay the Guru's kindness," she thought, and sang:

"Wonderful! Guru, Lord, Padmasambhava, I bow to you.

"You, Guru Rinpoche, turned this pile of atoms
accumulated since time began
into a king of mountains!
I am that Sumeru.
Now I think perhaps I can help others—
come, virtuous Indra, and be my patron!

Perhaps some, living deep in ravines, have not the karma,
but the great Guardian Kings
and those residing in heaven realms
will find happiness, satisfaction, and bliss!

"You, Guru Rinpoche, transformed all the drops of water
fallen in the ocean since time began
into seven enchanted lakes!
I am that ocean.
Now I think perhaps I can help others—
come, happy virtuous ones, and be my patrons!
Perhaps a few fish and frogs in murky ponds
have not the karma, but the eight nāgas
and those residing deep in the nāga palaces
will find happiness, satisfaction, and bliss!

"You, Guru Rinpoche, have taught
inconceivable qualities to the powerful Munis
who have accumulated merit since time began.
I am one such powerful Muni.
Now I think perhaps I can help others—
come, lordly men and Dharma Kings, and be my patrons!
Perhaps some beings in barbarous regions
have not the karma, but the Śrāvakas
and those residing in this realm
will find happiness, satisfaction, and bliss!

"You, Guru Rinpoche, transformed
all the fruits of virtue gathered since time began
into a wondrous human being!
I am that girl.
Now I think perhaps I can help others—
come, lucky children, and be my patrons!
Perhaps some with wrong views and evil ways
cannot follow the Dharma, but those with faith,
the Tibetan folk and all others in the world, will find bliss!"

Then mTsho-rgyal went on extracting medicinal nectar from the
hundred and eight healing plants and herbs. Representatives of the

four types of siddhas and the four medicine goddesses circled round her, one hundred and eight in all. Each of the medicine goddesses held a vase with healing nectar of singular power, and they offered them to mTsho-rgyal, praising her in this song:

"Wonderful!
Though a human girl, you bear the marks of excellence!
You were our sister in a former life, in a time of gods.
Your pure aspirations were a sufficient cause
to bring you great Pristine Awareness.
You led the gandharvas with sounds of lutes,
and so we praise you,
wondrous mTsho-rgyal, Sarasvatī!

"Then when the Dharma Wheel of the Great Muni turned,
your purity was sufficient cause
for you to become a Śrāvaka nun.
You led all beings with the eye of compassion—
and so we praise you, mTsho-rgyal, Goddess of the River Ganges.

"Now the great Vajradhara has arisen from a lotus,
and the Dharma Wheel turns by his methods,
opening the secret doors that combine all Mahāyāna teachings.
You practiced the disciplines for the sake of all beings,
and so we praise you, mTsho-rgyal!

"All things come from the expanse of the mind.
Distilling the essence of poisons and herbs,
you drank deeply of the nectar;
and now you bear the marks of eternal youth.
Praise to you, enlightened mother of all beings of the three times!

"Driving out disease and evil,
you cure beings with the best medicine,
the nectar of deathlessness.
Mother of all good qualities, goddess of healing,
is that not you, mTsho-rgyal?"

Then they all rose up into the sky. Shortly afterwards, a young human girl, Khye-'dren, arrived and offered mTsho-rgyal a large amount of honey. Thus she was blessed with the power of both inner and outer good omens.

After eating the honey, mTsho-rgyal began the discipline of the body. First she did circumambulations, then she did prostrations. She practiced day and night, until her forehead, the palms of her hands, and the soles of her feet developed open sores and were worn to the bone. A great stream of blood and pus flowed from the sores, yet mTsho-rgyal continued to do these and countless other physical practices as indicated in the texts.

At first her body was painful and unresponsive; she felt completely exhausted. The joints of her hands became inflamed and swollen, twisted and painful as if diseased by arthritis. Her veins became distended and varicosed, and various symptoms spread and increased so that she was terribly weakened.

But eventually, mTsho-rgyal did cleanse her body; all conditions due to impurity dispersed, and she rejoiced. Her vitality supported the natural flow of Pristine Awareness. The knots in her veins and channels were untied, her joints became straight, her crookedness was cured, her sores healed and covered over. Every part of her body worked in an orderly and healthy fashion. She had established the foundation for realizing the esoteric teachings.

mTsho-rgyal continued to practice in isolated wilderness caves, such as the one at Seng-ge Ne-ring. Having made the commitment to meditate, without speaking, without moving, she sat erect in the full-lotus posture, her gaze never wandering, her posture never slouching.

The brilliance and power of mTsho-rgyal's meditation was unbearable to the regional gods and malignant spirits. They flocked to her in peaceful and wrathful forms, with and without corporeal bodies, and taunted her with strange visions. At first, all kinds of food appeared before her, one thing after another; then clothing, horses, and even elephants appeared. All sorts of worldly goods manifested apparitionally before her.

But mTsho-rgyal subdued them all by the power of her meditation. Some of these things disappeared as soon as she saw their illusory nature, others disappeared merely because of her indifference to worldly things. Some she transformed by her meditation into earth and stones and the like. Some things, such as food and riches, she wished to be hidden away for the country's future use, and this was accomplished.

On another occasion, there appeared before her a group of attractive young men—youths with beautiful faces and smooth skin, sweet-smelling, wonderfully formed, quite tangible and thoroughly enticing. First, they respectfully addressed her as 'Mother' and 'Lady'. But soon they began to talk of sex and spoke to her by name, saying 'mTsho-rgyal, girl', as they tried to seduce her, sometimes being passionate, sometimes merry and playful.

Gradually they revealed themselves, saying: "Girl, wouldn't you like this for yourself? Wouldn't you like to milk it?" and that sort of thing. "Wouldn't you like me to embrace you? Or stroke your breasts or between your legs? Wouldn't you like me to kiss you?" So they went on, suggesting various acts of passion, trying to excite her.

The brilliance of her meditation overcame some of them, and they disappeared. Some of them she meditated upon as illusory—and as they were deceptive creations, they disappeared when she told them to. Some of them she contemplated as hindrances to the Bodhisattva mind, and then they changed into black corpses. Some became old and crippled, while others became lepers. Some turned blind or lame or mute or fiercely ugly. Finally, they all vanished.

Then very wrathful forms appeared. The earth shook back and forth, and there was a noise greater than one thousand thunderclaps sounding at once. Lightning, flashing through the total darkness, sent bright streaks darting across the sky. Moving white lights blazed; red lights flickered on and off; yellow lights whirled about; smoky blue lights drew them all together, and iridescent lights zigzagged here and there. This dizzying display was hard to endure.

Next, mTsho-rgyal saw weapons—daggers and spears of many kinds, keen and shining. Sharp translucent blue blades stabbed and crossed and darted around in a most unbearable fashion. But all these manifestations mTsho-rgyal controlled by the power of her meditation, thinking that though she be cut to pieces or killed, she would not be afraid. Finally, because of the power of her mind, they all disappeared.

A few days later, packs of tigers and leopards, bears and hyenas, and all sorts of other wild animals came prowling. Growling ferociously they stalked around the cave and blocked the entrance. Then, howling and screaming, they advanced into the cave—filling the passageway, prowling to the left and right and in front of her. Some, driven by hunger, widened their mouths to show their fangs. Threatening mTsho-rgyal, they twitched their tails upon the ground and clawed the dirt, their bodies trembling, their hair bristling and standing on end. But she considered how terribly attached these animals were to their physical bodies and felt great compassion for them, and they all disappeared.

Then, like a great army converging upon that place, millions upon millions of worms and insects and other crawling things, such as spiders and scorpions and snakes, swarmed over everything. Some of them filled her sense organs; some bit and stung and scratched her as they crawled onto her. Some jumped upon her; others attacked each other, tossing bits of their bodies about as they ate. All sorts of strange and magical forms appeared. But mTsho-rgyal just trembled a little and felt compassion rise up in her mind. As the forms became more and more angry and frightful, raging around her, mTsho-rgyal thought:

"Many times I have vowed to be unattached to anything associated with body, speech, or mind. All these sentient beings, worms and other crawling things, arise continuously, increasingly, and abundantly from karmic forces. Why should I tremble with fear before such magical manifestations of the elements? I must remember that all activity is the result of good and bad thoughts. Therefore, whatever may arise, either good or bad, I will recognize as dualistic mental activity and be unconcerned." Having come to this profound realization, she said:

"All phenomenal existence
is merely the magical manifestation of mind.

96

I see nothing to fear in all the expanse of space.
Therefore, all of this must be self-arising luminance.
How could there ever be anything other than this?
All these activities are only ornaments of my own being.
Better that I rest in meditative silence."

After saying this, she entered a meditative state that was completely quiet, without any discrimination of good or evil. And all the apparitions disappeared.

But later, more strange forms appeared, ugly, vague, and fearful visions, moving here and there. Disembodied arms and hands whirled about. A great bodiless head appeared, its upper jaw in the sky, its lower jaw resting on the ground. Its tongue curled and darted in the space between, and its sharp, white, tusk-like teeth advanced closer and closer.

Within a palace as small as a mustard seed, she saw many men arguing and fighting. A great fire was raging, water was rushing forth, rocks were avalanching, and trees were falling in a hurricane wind. But mTsho-rgyal entered the Vajra-like Samādhi and remained unmoved, and all these forms disappeared.

Next, from E in lower Nepal up to 'Ja' in upper Bhutan, a great army of gods and demons of the border tribes of Klo-yul, Kha-khra, and rKang-khra raged. Some wept, and others howled. Some were wailing, others screaming. Above mTsho-rgyal's head, thunder roared, and below her feet, fires burned. In between, a great flood of water rushed forth, and sharp weapons swirled about like a strange blizzard. All sorts of hindrances and obstacles arose.

But mTsho-rgyal meditated intensely, expanded her awareness, and sharpened her wisdom. Again, she felt imperishable faith arise and sang:

"How wonderful!
I have reached the stage of realization —
realization of the Dharmakāya,
the Enlightened Mind of the Great Mother,

Essence of the Ten Perfections.
Acting within the deepest discriminating wisdom,
I have no fear of phenomenal appearances.
Whatever arises is the magic play of Dharmakāya,
and these manifestations are the compassion of the Lama.
So stir up some more of these creations!

"How wonderful!
I have reached the stage of realization—
realization of the All-good, the Lama,
Essence of vision, meditation, and fruit.
Acting spontaneously with whatever arises,
I have no fear of divisive concepts.
Whatever arises is the magical play of cognition,
and discursive thoughts are the compassion of the Lama.
So stir up some more of these creations!

"How wonderful!
I have reached the stage of realization—
realization of the Lotus Lama,
Essence of the profound, far-reaching Āti.
With the unblemished activity of my own mind,
I do not dwell on defilements.
Stains and such are the magical play of reality itself,
and all ways of seeing are the compassion of the Lama.
So stir up some more of these creations!

"How wonderful!
I have reached the perfect place—
the practice of the girl mTsho-rgyal,
the essence of the supreme Mantrayāna vehicle.
Pleasure and pain have the same taste,
so why should I choose good or bad,
rejecting this or that experience?
All appearances are the compassion of the Lama,
so stir up some more of these creations!"

As she finished her song, great armies of gods and demons gathered from Tibet, China, and Nepal. Their generals took the fore—black, red, and blue they were. Again and again, using many different means, they manipulated the environment, creating all kinds of obstacles. They incited the human inhabitants, insulting and sneering at them. The smoke created by these gods and demons darkened all of Bhutan so that no one could tell day from night. Disorder reigned, and chaos prevailed—lightning, hail, and rain descended, disease and pestilence spread, confusion ruled, and great misery pervaded the land. Everyone was asking what could be the cause of such disaster.

"Why is this happening?" the people asked. One Bhutani who had seen mTsho-rgyal spoke up: "In a distant cave on a rocky site sits a Tibetan woman as if deaf and dumb. Perhaps she has been doing improper practices, and that has caused all this trouble."

After some discussion, they decided that she must be killed and set off in a group. Upon arriving at the cave, they called out to mTsho-rgyal: "You corpse-like Tibetan demoness! Thanks to your evil mantras, chaos and gloom hang over Bhutan! Thick darkness covers the country, lightning and hail descend upon us, sickness and misery of all kinds prevail. It is because of your evil practices that all this has happened. If you don't do something about these conditions right now, we will kill you!"

mTsho-rgyal considered: "The wrath of the gods and demons has struck these people, but there is nothing I can do to help. Therefore I will carry on. Whatever happens, I will concentrate my mind on the practices. Whatever occurs, I will not break my commitments." So she gave no answer and remained as before, sitting still, her gaze steady.

At that, some of them said: "She is ashamed!" Others said: "She is deaf and can't hear us." They threw dust in her eyes and pricked her ears with a knife. But mTsho-rgyal remained in a state of concentration, not engaging in discursive thoughts.

"Demoness!" they cried, and then began to shoot arrows at her. Some beat her with sticks, some tried to run her through with their spears. Others stabbed at her with knives. But wherever they attacked her, however they tried, they were unable to harm her. The Tibetan lady sat fearless and unharmed.

"Nothing we do has any effect on her," they said, and so they all returned home.

At this time, the girl Khye-'dren, who had previously given mTsho-rgyal the offering of honey, was staying in the area. She was the daughter of the king of Bhutan and thus was very influential. Because of her great faith, she came often to pay her respects to mTsho-rgyal and to offer her buffalo milk and honey. Delighted with her young patron, mTsho-rgyal remained to meditate in that area quite a long time.

Not long afterward, the gods and demons, local spirits, and nāgas called upon mTsho-rgyal, offering her their hearts and lives. In particular, the demons, local spirits, and nāgas who had magically tormented her before promised to support her teachings and drive off all her enemies. They sang to her:

"E Ho Ho!
This is the lady who pleases Padma Thod-phreng!
Who can conquer this heroine, this Herukā?
We who came first to insult you, now make amends.
Now we will be your subjects—we offer heart and life.
We promise never to break our vows
and from now on to follow all of your teachings."

Likewise, all the great and wild Tibetan gods and demons became mTsho-rgyal's defenders and guardians. They offered her their hearts and lives, promised to uphold and guard the teachings, and then they departed. Finally, all those in that land, both male and female, who had thought to harm her, came together and made atonement for their actions.

Ham-ra, the king of Bhutan, developed particularly great faith in mTsho-rgyal and her attainments. mTsho-rgyal spoke to him of his daughter Khyi-'dren, the beautiful young girl of thirteen who possessed all the marks of a ḍākinī. So great was the power of the king's faith that he presented his young daughter to mTsho-rgyal, and mTsho-rgyal accepted her. She gave Khyi-'dren the name bKra-shis spyi'-dren and took her with her to sPa-gro Tiger Cave.

There mTsho-rgyal practiced the final discipline for her own development, the discipline of the essence of vitality, the unity of bliss and emptiness. Together with her friends Ācārya Sa-le, Mon-bu Sa-le, and Ācārya dPal-dbyangs, she practiced healing techniques using medicine and nectar. Night and day they practiced without interruption, clarifying their creative awareness.

At first, their bodies were disturbed and upset, their minds shaken. Pus streamed from both upper and lower extremities, and they were sick and feverish, aching and trembling to the point of death. But finally the unhealthy conditions were transformed into the essence of vitality, and their bodies were filled with bliss. Although at first this bliss was mixed with emotional instability, it gradually acquired the flavor of Pristine Awareness, until this joyful awareness became a steady state.

Then, little by little, the white and red energy intermingled; as a result, the dichotomy of subject and object vanished, for its cause had been destroyed. mTsho-rgyal's body became a presentation of the Buddha mandala. By the offering of bliss, her body became great bliss, and the world partook of great bliss.

Lovely she was then, radiant with the vitality of youth, her complexion like roses and cream. Her body, now that of a confident and heroic Herukā, looked much like a beautiful sixteen-year-old girl. At that time, she looked upon the mandala of Amitāyus and achieved the Vajra Body, as well as the power of long life without decline. It was prophesied that she would live two hundred and twenty-five years in this world.

The Lord Hayagrīva and Vajravārāhī exorcised all negativity. The five ḍākas and ḍākinīs became her shadows and aided her in charismatic activities. Bodhisattvas wished her good fortune. mTsho-rgyal became a Knowledge-holder, capable of controlling the duration of her life, and was given the name 'Radiant Blue Light Master of Longevity'.

Then mTsho-rgyal and her five students went back to 'On-phu Tiger Cave where Guru Rinpoche was staying. mTsho-rgyal bowed before him, and Guru Rinpoche asked: "Has a splendid Herukā arrived? How are you? Aren't you a bit tired?

"Wonderful yoginī, practitioner of the secret teachings!
The basis for realizing enlightenment is a human body.
Male or female—there is no great difference.
But if she develops the mind bent on enlightenment,
the woman's body is better.

"From beginningless time,
you have accumulated merit and wisdom.
Now your good qualities are flawless—
what an excellent woman you have become, a true Bodhisattmā!
Are you not the embodiment of bliss?
Now that you have achieved what you wanted for yourself,
strive for the benefit of others.

"Lady, could any other as wonderful as you exist in this world of men?
In the past there were none; there are none at this time;
and I have not heard of one to come later.
Ah! Are you not Ye-shes mTsho-rgyal?

"From now until the end of future time,
you will have five incarnations—
thirty times you will prolong the Buddhadharma.
In particular, in the land of Dvags-yul,
you will be known as Lab and appear as a woman
bearing the signs of Tārā.

"Great Lady, listen to the essence of my instructions:
You will spread the profound teachings of the gCod,
a teaching most beneficial to beings.
At that time, Ācārya Sa-le will be Thod-pa, the priest,
and with him as your consort you will open the esoteric gates.
The Bhutanī girl, bKra-shis khyi-'dren, will be your daughter,
and Mon-bu Sa-le will be your son, a crazy yogi.
The Ācārya dPal-dbyangs
will be the monk Grva-pa mNgon-shes, your secret consort,
and you will practice for the supreme benefit of self and others.

"At that time, I, Padmasambhava,
will be an Indian by the name of Dam-pa.
I will spread the zhi-byed teachings
through the border areas of La-stod.
Lady, you and I will meet then.
Wonderful omens will herald the esoteric doctrine.
Because of the skillful means of that profound path of zhi-byed,
for a while humanity will find joy.
But we will not stay for long.
You and I will return to the wonderful Lotus Light,
and not part again.
We will benefit beings through the Sambhogakāya."

After singing this, Padmasambhava gave various other predictions, creating comfort and ease. mTsho-rgyal was very grateful for Guru Rinpoche's kindness and answered him thus:

"Wonderful!
Tree of the Secret Teachings, Vajradhara,
Deathless Amitāyus, free from causal circumstances;
able, vigorous, and mighty Lord Heruka,
you are the unique and unequalled Lotus-born One!
There is no other like you.
Because of your kindness, great guide,
I have achieved the esoteric mantric power;
I have achieved the eight great siddhis;
I have mastered both the Sūtra and Mantra paths.
Though my birth is low, my qualities are great.

"My body has now become the deity,
and ordinary phenomena have no hold on me.
The samādhi where all is illusory has arisen,
and I hold sway over the five elements.

"My speech has now become Mantra,
and ordinary senseless talk has no hold on me.
The Vajra-like Samādhi has arisen,
and I understand completely
both Sūtra and Mantra Dharma.

"My mind has now become Buddha,
and ordinary divisive thoughts
have passed into expansiveness.
The samādhi of Heroic Being has arisen,
and I am one with the mind of Vajradhara.

"Lama, Lord, most kindly one, from this time forward
for however long and in whatever guise I am to live,
if your Lotus Being were ever to leave me,
how could I find another lord?

"Look upon me with compassion and never leave me.
There is no way I can return your kindness.
I confess whatever wrong I may have done you
through the power of unknowing in all times past,
with regard to your body, speech, or mind,
your qualities, or your actions.

"I promise never to transgress in the future,
with even the slightest wrongdoing.
Now, Guru of great kindness,
I ask you to turn the wheel of the esoteric teachings
for the benefit of all beings."

After she had spoken, Padmasambhava asked her to explain how she had practiced the disciplines, what realizations she had attained, and what gods, demons, and men had appeared before her. He also wished especially to know how she had practiced the secret Mantrayāna practices at sPa-gro Tiger Cave and in what manner she had seen the deities related to Amitāyus.

Padmasambhava was very pleased with her explanations. He put his right hand upon mTsho-rgyal's head and said: "Now, girl, the time has come for you to practice the yoga of longevity. Your experiences while you were at sPa-gro were an indication that, with the teacher's compassion, if you act as directed, specific results will occur. Now I will open for you the mandala of Amitāyus and give you his empowerment. You will need to find another spiritual hero to support you in the longevity practices.

"The girl Khyi-'dren from Bhutan has all the marks of a Vajrakarma ḍākinī of Pristine Awareness. Send her to me, and she will be my assistant in the Vajrakīla practices. I must give her many technical instructions of rDo-rje gzhon-nu. Otherwise, the secret teachings will not spread in this foolish land of Tibet. Yogis will be confused and they will not even be able to take care of themselves and their own lives. In border regions, hostile gods and demons will create obstacles to the Dharma. Without this teaching, though the esoteric Dharma may extend slightly, it will decline immediately."

mTsho-rgyal bowed before the Lama and thanked him for his kindness. She offered him a mandala of gold and turquoise, and the girl bKra-shis khye-'dren. Then she asked:

"Great Guru!
I, the woman mTsho-rgyal, am very grateful
for these instructions on the yoga of longevity.
What kind of associate do I need for these practices?
Is Ācārya Sa-le not suitable?

"There could be no greater gift
than the mandala of the esoteric Kīla teachings.
As I have offered you the girl Khyi-'dren,
please, in your compassion,
open the gates of this secret teaching for me.

"I am a woman—I have little power to resist danger.
Because of my inferior birth, everyone attacks me.
If I go as a beggar, dogs attack me.
If I have wealth and food, bandits attack me.
If I look beautiful, the lustful attack me.
If I do a great deal, the locals attack me.
If I do nothing, gossips attack me.
If anything goes wrong, they all attack me.
Whatever I do, I have no chance for happiness.
Because I am a woman, it is hard to follow the Dharma.
It is hard even to stay alive!
Therefore, I beg you to be compassionate.
Give the Vajrakīla practices to me as well."

Padmasambhava reflected a moment and then spoke again: "The yoga of longevity is like a ship captain; the Kīla is like a protective escort. At first, whatever esoteric practices you do, you must remove obstacles. The Kīla Sādhanas are very important—they are especially important for you as your personal deity is the Heruka Kīla. But for the Kīla and longevity practices, you must have an associate. You should go to dBus in central Tibet. There you will find a fourteen-year-old boy from the Rlangs clan. His father is lHa-dpal, his mother is Cog-ro-bza'. He will be your associate for these sādhana practices."

As mTsho-rgyal later explained: "I proceeded to find the boy, as Padmasambhava instructed, and when I returned with him, Guru Rinpoche told him: 'You are the Knowledge-holder for the Kīla practices. Once you have realized the Vajra of Longevity, others will find you very difficult to subdue. It was prophesied by the gods that you would be a heroic demon destroyer. This practice will give you the strength of a lion. I will call you lHa-lung dPal-gyi seng-ge, God-prophesied Lion Lord.' And upon entering the mandala of the esoteric teachings, dPal-gyi seng-ge spiritually matured."

Later lHa-lung dPal-gyi seng-ge, Nam-mkha'i snying-po of lHo-brag, rMa Rin-chen-mchog, the Lady mTsho-rgyal, and rDo-rje bdud-'joms, the five root offspring, along with the girl bDe-ba-mo, now called dPal-gyi mchog-gnas, and others gathered together for the Vajrakīla Sādhanas.

bDe-ba-mo was appointed Vajra attendant. Ācārya Sa-le and Ācārya dPal-dbyangs were both appointed Vajra drummers, and renamed Karma don-grub and Karma mthar-byed. Mon-bu Sa-le, renamed Byams-pa dpal-bzang, was appointed Vajra performer. With mTsho-rgyal first as the principal attendant, and then bKra-shis khyi-'dren as the liberating attendant, the Guru and his two attendants practiced the forty-two E-khram mandalas associated with the Byi-to-ta-ma Tantra of the Vajrakīla.

For seven days they practiced, opening the mandalas of the seventy-eight Kīla, perfecting all the marks and signs, and beholding all the Kīla deities. The daggers which had been used as accoutrements flew up into the air, gliding, floating, flame-encircled, emitting fine perfumes. And as evening came, more amazing signs such as these occurred. Padmasambhava himself rose up in the form of rDo-rje gro-lod. mTsho-rgyal appeared as Ekajātī and Khyi-'dren became a tigress. Together, they established dominance over the gods and spirits of Tibet, the four continents, and the three thousand realms.

The Guru and his consort, mTsho-rgyal, mounted the back of the tigress who was Khyi-'dren, and entered the samādhi of Vajrakīla. In his right hand, the Guru brandished a nine-pointed vajra, and in his left hand he spun a kīla of bronze. From all parts of his splendid wrathful body came innumerable emanations. One of these, the blue-black rDo-rje khro-phur, went to sPa-gro Tiger Cave and established dominance over the gods and the eight classes of spirits throughout Bhutan, Nepal, India, and all the southern regions and border regions near and far, binding them by oath.

A dark brown rDo-rje khro-phur went to the region of the two Tiger Caves in Khams and achieved dominion over all the gods and the eight classes of spirits in Khams, 'Jang, China, Mongolia, and all the border regions near and far, binding their lives and hearts by oaths to serve the Dharma.

At this time there dwelt in the great lake of Manasarowar a very evil nāga. Magically he transformed himself into a red bull and went before the Dharma King, begging for refuge. His limbs were bound in chains, blood and brains dripped from between the cracks in his skull; his tongue lolled in and out, and his eyeballs protruded down onto his face.

The king asked him: "How did you come to such a state?" The bull replied: "This heathen son of barbarians, Padmasambhava, the one born from a lotus, is attempting to completely destroy both the men and gods of Tibet. Even now he is tormenting the innocent Tibetan gods and spirits, though they have done nothing wrong. And so, great Dharma King, I have come to you for refuge."

Feeling great compassion for the bull, the Dharma King said: "You can remain here for now." But as soon as he said this, the bull disappeared. As the Dharma King was wondering what had happened, he heard the voice of Guru Rinpoche:

"Great Dharma King, your compassion is misplaced.
Now your future lives and your lineage will be mixed:
Obstacles will mingle with achievements.
Though in the future
some of your descendents may live by the Dharma,
their lives will be short and evil conditions will abound.
Three generations from now,
the red bull will manifest as a king named Glang.
He will kill his brother
and establish evil laws and wrong behavior.
Both Sūtra and Mantra vehicles will be nearly destroyed
so that even their names will not be heard.
This will be due to karmic consequences;
and nothing can be done to prevent it."

So he spoke. But dPal-gyi rdo-rje prayed: "May I be the one to subdue this evil king."

And the Guru said: "Good! You will be the one to subdue him!" He then gave dPal-gyi rdo-rje various empowerments as well as exact instructions on the practice of the Kīla Sādhanas. He also gave him the twenty Kīlaya Sādhanas of great power, and told him to practice them.

As the Lady mTsho-rgyal later explained: "The boy dPal-seng and I both practiced the Vajrakīla Sādhanas, and in a short time, we looked upon the faces of all the associated deities and achieved the siddhis. We also studied the original texts of the rDo-rje gzhon-nu and the other associated Kīla practices, the empowerments, and the great sādhanas. From the first section, we did the Bodhicitta practices for the enlightenment of all sentient beings, the peaceful sādhanas associated with the deity Vajrasattva. From the later section, we learned the practices associated with killing and so forth, the means of cutting the karmic link which involve the black poison Kīla Sādhanas for liberating the consciousness, connected with the Sras Kīlāya practices.

"The Guru told us: 'I, Padmasambhava, have no teaching more profound than this Vajrakīla cycle. You must do these practices and bring forth the powers connected with them. Transmit one part as an oral lineage, and hide one part as a gter-ma.' Then he made various predictions.

"He gave us the teachings of the Tshe-dpag-med 'Chi-med 'od-kyi phreng-ba, the gSang-ba kun-'dus, the rGyal-ba kun-'dus, the lHa-cig bum-gcig, and the mandalas of the sixty-two gods of long life.

"dPal-gyi rdo-rje and I practiced together like brother and sister, never even for an instant giving in to laziness. As we practiced, we saw the faces of the associate deities and easily achieved the knowledge of immortality."

At about this time, the heretical Bon-pos were brought under control, and mTsho-rgyal finished the final and ultimate disciplines, but these will be spoken of later on. mTsho-rgyal practiced meditation in various places on the borders of Tibet: at Ti-se-man and Byams-gling-yan, at the twenty-five snow mountains and the eighteen great fortresses, at the one hundred and eight gNas-phran and the twelve great hidden valleys, at the seven places of miracles and the five secret places, at the seventy million places were gter-ma were hidden, and so forth. Some of these will be described later on; but others will not be explained in detail for fear of making the text too long.

 སམཡཿ རྒྱ་རྒྱ་རྒྱ༔ དྲི་པན་ཆིཏྟ༔ རཱཿ

This Concludes the Fifth Chapter on How Ye-shes mTsho-rgyal
Did the Sādhana Practices and the Disciplines.

Rong-bu guhya

Prince Mu-tig btsan-po

Ye-shes mTsho-rgyal

Guru Śākya seng-ge

mKar-chen dPal-gyi dbang-phyug

dPal-gyi seng-ge

Guru Śākya seng-ge

A Summary of the Auspicious Signs Which Occurred as Ye-shes mTsho-rgyal Practiced and the Siddhis She Manifested After Achieving Realization

Ye-shes mTsho-rgyal summarized her experiences in verse, omitting the details which were explained previously:

"At Ti-sgro, spurred on by the ḍākinīs' words,
I practiced the eight disciplines
and developed the signs of siddhi.

"On icy peaks I kindled the burning gtum-mo heat
and was freed from worldly needs.

"In meditation caves I gained
the warmth of the four empowerments
and ordinary phenomena became the Lama's pure appearance.

"In the land of Nepal, I raised a dead man,
in order to ransom Ācārya.

"I obtained the essential siddhis of the profound path,
and my speech became as sweet as Brahmā's,

my body became the perfect Rainbow Body, unfettered in space,
and my mind became the Enlightened Mind of the three times.

"At Seng-ge rdzong I gathered healing nectar,
and the medicine gods surrounded me.

"At Ne-ring I conquered hordes of demons,
and siddhis rose in the heat of inspiration.
I beheld the faces of the yidams
and developed the bliss of siddhi.

"At sPa-gro Tiger Cave I practiced the profound path—
with my three friends, I performed
the Heruka Sādhanas of Great Bliss
and developed control over patterning, vitality, and energy.
The five elements became the powerful lords;
body, speech, and mind became the Three Kāyas.
Assured of boundless life, inseparable from Vajravārāhī,
I became the mistress of all mandalas.

"At 'On-phu Tiger Cave I practiced the Kīla—
gods and spirits from three thousand realms
pledged to me heart and life.
I gazed upon the deities associated with Amitāyus,
and held the knowledge of life without death—
I became a Vidyādhara,
a Vajra unconquerable and indestructible.

"In this land of Tibet,
in the highlands and lowlands of this world,
and in innumerable other places, I practiced.
Nowhere could you find two handfuls of earth not blessed by me.

"In the future, hidden treasures bearing the mark of truth
will be revealed and brought forth.
In obscure places beyond imagining,
I have left the imprints of my hands and feet upon the rocks
and carved images of mantras and letters.

In the future these will represent my faith—
a measure of the efficacy of merit and prayer.

"My charismatic power destroyed demons and heretics,
but this will be told in detail later.
By controlling the five elements,
I covered the earth with treasure.
By gaining the power of complete retention,
I became the receptacle of the Lotus Words.
By fearlessly spreading his teachings,
I preserved them, as was prophesied, for the future.
I became the same as all the Buddhas,
and accomplished the charismatic deeds
of the Tathāgatas of the three times.

"Now I am adorned with all the ordinary siddhis:
I can control worldly phenomena and move by fast-running;
I can heal with my gaze or with medicinal ril-bu;
I can transform my body
and travel in the sky or anywhere on earth.

"I possess the wonders of the three meditations,
the realized mind of the expanse
of the All-good, Samantabhadrā,
the adorned playfulness of the Dharmakāya,
unhidden, unfearing, unstraying.
Yet I am no nihilist with restricted views,
for I have realized the profundity of total openness—
the fruit of the Great Perfection, free of incidental action.
I spontaneously realized the encompassing Āti,
and merged with the openness of the enlightened mind.

"My compassion is more radiant than the sun;
my blessing more profoundly full than clouds heavy with water;
my power swifter than the sudden shower.

"Thus, in the future, those with faith, those who ask,
will receive the great key instructions,

which come from having seen
how the links of Dependent Origination fit together.
Even in places of evil, I will be guide.
If I forsake this vow, I forsake all Buddhas—
I will hold fast to compassion,
knowing that suffering endures because of wrong views.
I shall continue to train myself
until karma comes to an end."

This was the Promise Spoken in Verse by the Lady
Ye-shes mTsho-rgyal, Concluding the Sixth Chapter
on Her Realization and the Signs Thereof.

Prabhāhasti

lHa-lung dPal-gyi rdo-rje

rMa Rin-chen mchog

Seng-ge sgra-sgrog

'O-bran dPal-gyi dbang-phyug

dPal-gyi seng-ge

Seng-ge sgra-sgrog

The Manner in Which Ye-shes mTsho-rgyal Acted to Benefit Sentient Beings

Benefit to sentient beings is the only purpose of the Buddha's teaching, and so the Buddha's activities can only bring benefit. In Tibet these benefits manifested themselves in a threefold way. First, a firm foundation for the precious teachings was established, and the demonic and human opposition was removed. Then, comprehensive teachings of both the Sūtra and Mantra paths were spread, and the Buddhist community developed and increased. Finally, to ensure the successful growth of the Buddha's teachings, boundless Dharma treasures were concealed. These will last far into the future, until the world comes to an end, until samsara is emptied.

Long ago, when the Bon religion was widespread in the land, a descendent of the Indian Śākya clan by the name of gNya'-khri became ruler of all Tibet. Generations passed, and finally, in the reign of lHa-tho-tho-ri, last of the elder kings, the Buddhadharma appeared. Indications of the Indian Śākyamuni spread to the four corners of Tibet, and many Tibetans heard and practiced the ten Buddhist virtues.

At this time, the Inner Bon teaching was also prevalent and existed harmoniously side by side with the Dharma. The Bon maintained that the Buddha Śākyamuni and the Bon spiritual forefather, sTon-pa gShen-rab, were really the same in essence, though different in aspect. According to descriptions, depictions of gShen-rab, who was believed

117

to have come from Zhang-zhung, were similar to depictions of the Buddha.

During the long life of the Dharma King Srong-btsan sgam-po (who was a manifestation of Avalokiteśvara), two famous statues of the Lord Buddha were brought to Tibet and placed in special monasteries which the king built for them at lHa-sa and Ra-mo-che. The king also constructed 108 temples throughout Tibet which served to teach and subdue the outlying regions. Depictions of all the Holy Ones in engravings and paintings, styled in both Nepalese and Chinese fashion, also multiplied. A statue of Tārā spontaneously appeared at Khra-'brug, and the amazed and delighted king had a special temple built there for it. The names of the Three Jewels, the six-syllable mantra, OṀ MAṆI PADME HŪṀ, and the influence of Avalokiteśvara filled Tibet, Khams, and even China.

The Dharma and the Bon had both spread, and no great distinction was made between them at that time. The Dharma practitioners walked clockwise when they circumambulated; the Bon practitioners walked counterclockwise. Both called prostrations 'dBu-ma chen-po', and each group did them the same way.

The king established laws based on the ten Buddhist virtues, and Thon-mi Sambhoṭa, his minister, translated from Sanskrit many of the Avalokiteśvara Tantras—long, medium, and short. The king and his queens, the ministers and the people, all engaged in pure and proper practices.

About twenty-five years after this godly king had passed away, a heretical sect, the rGyu-bon, began to spread in Tibet. They tried to destroy both the Inner Bon and the Dharma. Even today, the Inner Bon are unable to withstand them, and many Inner Bon have been banished, some to Khams, some to Kong-po, some to gTsang. Others have become inactive or left the country altogether.

The rGyu-bon tried to root out the Dharma, but the kings and ministers-of-state did not agree among themselves about how to go about this. So the Dharma was never completely suppressed. But the

Dharma did cease to spread, and the Dharma's position in Tibet remained more or less as it had been before the rGyu-bon.

The rGyu-bon had very perverted views and followed evil practices which corrupted the country. Because of this, later, at the time of the Dharma King Khri-srong lde'u-btsan, many circumstances made it difficult for the Dharma to take hold.

These are some of the perverse customs and philosophies of the rGyu-bon: They had no conception of heaven realms or worlds other than this one. Their deities consisted of non-humans, 'kings', sorcerers, and the eight types of spirits; they worshipped local spirits, foundation lords, gods of action, gods of luck, and so forth. They believed that these spirits 'were' the world.

Their customs were such that they sent their daughters away and kept their daughters-in-law at home. They were malicious. They liked to tell ancient stories of their traditions, to sing and dance and rejoice in order to bring about good fortune.

In the fall, they killed the wild ass and used its flesh in bloody sacrifices. In the spring they carved up does for burnt offerings. They believed that one could ransom the dying by the killing of animals. In the winter, these Bon-pos made red offerings to their gods, and in the summertime they held fire ceremonies which also entailed sacrifice. Thus, they followed the ten non-virtuous ways and indulged in the inexpiable sins.

Their world view held that everything is insubstantial mind, and as the mind is nothing but the manifestation of gods and spirits, the gods and spirits are mind. Their greatest hope was for birth in a place where nothing exists; next they wished for birth in an infinite place; following that, they wished to be born in the citadel of neither existence nor nonexistence.

They sought power in strange ways: If a god manifested in physical form, they felt the most appropriate response would be to kill sentient beings and eat their flesh; failing that, one should drink blood; at the very least, one should inflict pain. This was their teaching.

119

Ordinary, simple-minded people took such things as the truth and believed the rGyu-bon teaching; as a result, many became involved in all sorts of evil practices. The malevolent rGyu-bon spread throughout Tibet, supported especially by the Zhang ministers.

They destroyed many holy paintings and statues, and none would listen to the Dharma teachings. The great monasteries at lHa-sa and Khra-'brug fell into ruin, and the many monasteries built throughout Tibet were destroyed. The country itself became divided.

But then Mañjuśrī himself manifested in Tibet in order to reestablish the system of the Buddhist teachings, taking birth as the great Dharma King, Khri-srong lde'u-btsan. This king welcomed many learned men from India and invited Śāntarakṣita, the Bodhisattva of Zahor, to Tibet. He repaired the holy temples of Ra-mo-che, Khra-'brug, and lHa-sa (built by the Dharma King Srong-btsan) and had these temples reconsecrated. But when he began planning to construct bSam-yas, the gods and Bon-pos of Tibet began creating obstacles.

The Learned One, Śāntarakṣita, predicted: "Both the men possessing form and the formless gods and demons are unsettled and restless. Unless you invite to Tibet the Indestructible One, the Lotus-born Teacher of Orgyan, he who has the Vajra Body, you can be sure of all kinds of obstacles for both of us, patron and teacher."

So the king dispatched three lotsāwas, Tibetans of great wisdom and learning, of great purity and faith in the Dharma, to invite the Orgyan Guru Rinpoche to come to Tibet from India.

The three lotsāwas easily found Padmasambhava, who then travelled to Tibet upon their invitation. Feeling unhesitating faith in the Guru, the Tibetan king, as well as some of the queens and ministers, sent a delegation to gZhong-mdar to greet him. They also prepared great ceremonies for his arrival in lHa-sa. The king met Padmasambhava at 'Om-bu'i tshal, and he himself took the bridle of the Guru's horse. The devotee and the object of devotion met and mingled their hearts and minds. The king, queens, ministers, and people all felt great faith in the Guru, and so great was Padmasambhava's charisma that none could gainsay him or resist him in anything. Even the Learned One, Śāntarakṣita, bowed before the Guru, and for a long time, these two discussed the Dharma together.

Later they all went to the future site of bSam-yas—the king, his ministers, and retinue in one group, and Padmasambhava, Śāntarakṣita, and the lotsāwas in another. Padmasambhava examined the earth, searching for the most auspicious place to build, and made various predictions.

At this time, the king said: "My ancestor Srong-btsan sgam-po built 108 temples during his long life, but they were all widely dispersed, and it was not possible to maintain them. So they have all gone to ruin. I would like to built one great temple within a strong-walled compound. Is this possible?"

"Yes!" Padmasambhava replied. "That is indeed possible. We should build a temple like the cosmos. It should have four outer sections resembling the four continents, each with its two subcontinents, twelve in all. And in the center should be a temple like Mount Meru, with an outer wall surrounding and ornamenting it." Padmasambhava went into meditation and manifested a vision of this temple complex for the king to see, saying: "Great King, if a temple like this were built, would it please you?"

And the king replied: "It would give me great pleasure, though it is truly beyond my powers of conception. Can this really be done? If we could construct such a temple, I would call it bSam-yas, 'Beyond Conception'."

"Great King, do not be small-minded!" the Guru replied. "There is no reason we cannot do this. You are the king of all Tibet! You have power over all who possess form, and I have power over all formless gods and spirits. What could be the problem?"

So they created bSam-yas, first completing the outer structure and then filling it with statues and texts and heart symbols, representing the body, speech, and mind of the Dharma. Next they brought together the practitioners who would make up the Sangha. At this time, Padmasambhava predicted that there would be 108 special lotsāwas. From thirteen thousand Tibetans, three thousand would be selected, and from these three thousand, three hundred would be chosen to form the first Sangha. Śāntarakṣita would ordain them, Padmasambhava would teach them, and the lotsāwas would translate.

But the Bon ministers resisted the Dharma. The rGyu-bon created obstacles so that a number of lotsāwas had to be sent away several times, disrupting the continuity of their teaching three times.

Eventually, however, the Buddhists and Bon-pos each developed their own Sangha. The Bon decided to establish their seat at Yar-lung, and the king and ministers agreed to this.

The Buddhists invited twenty-one great Masters from India. The 108 lotsāwas who had dispersed to all corners of Tibet gathered again at bSam-yas. Now, three thousand of the thirteen thousand Tibetans supporting the Dharma were ordained as young monks. Even important Bon-pos were invited—seven learned scholars from Zhang-zhung and the surrounding area, and seven powerful Bon leaders from 'Om-bu.

At this time, Padmasambhava and his consort had been residing at 'On-phu Tiger Cave. The Dharma King sent the great lotsāwa, Dran-pa nam-mkha', with three others to invite Padmasambhava to bSam-yas. They brought the Guru his great black nine-gaited garuda-horse, and leading pack horses and other animals, they all set out quickly for bSam-yas.

Padmasambhava predicted: "In a little while, I shall perform seven ceremonies for the foundation of the Mantrayāna, which will center at lHa-sa. Śākyamuni himself gave me this prediction."

They travelled by stages, being welcomed first at the stone sepulchre at Zur-mkhar, and then at bSam-yas.

At bSam-yas, Padmasambhava sat upon a throne erected for him under the medicinal trees. The twenty-one scholars from India and the Tibetan lotsāwas approached and bowed to him, and the great Master

Vimalamitra, together with these learned ones, sang to him in one voice:

"Only now have we been able to meet the Orgyan Guru
in bodily form! Only now can we meet Padmasambhava!
Merit accumulated through many ages has borne this fruit!"

Tears streaming down their faces, they gazed upon the wonderful face of the Guru.

Padmasambhava and Vimalamitra were especially pleased to meet one another; like long-lost father and son, they clasped each other's hands and sat together in the highest gallery.

The Dharma King, his nobles, and the scholars bowed to them from the middle level and sat down. Three times they repeated special consecratory blessings for the temple, praying for the propagation of the Dharma. Padmasambhava declared that three separate fire ceremonies were necessary to conquer the demonic forces, and he performed the first one, planning the others for later. But the king was distracted and did not ask for the others to be done, so Padmasambhava did no more. He predicted that though the Dharma would spread in the future, difficulties and demons would increase as well.

The king invited both Buddhists and Bon-pos to bSam-yas for the ceremonies at the last month of the year. Five learned Bon-pos came to participate in the ceremonies, but they did not understand the forms, sounds, or symbols of the Dharma. The images, texts, and religious implements meant nothing to them; nor did they comprehend the ten virtues. They did not join in the salutations or the circumambulations, but rather stood in a row at the back, leaning against the images of deities. They did not rejoice with the common people, the ministers, and the king.

The next day, the king and the Bon-pos met in front of the statue of Vairocana. The Bon-pos asked: "O Lord, God-like One, here at the center of the topmost gallery is the figure of a completely naked lord surrounded by eight other naked men. What are they for? Where did they come from? Are these the Indian paṇḍitas?"

The great Dharma King answered: "This master in the center is a representation of Vairocana. Surrounding him are eight Bodhisattvas. These are statues of the Buddha, and we pay homage to them. If you make offerings to them, you accumulate merit and counteract previous bad karma."

The Bon-pos asked again: "Over there by the door are two very fierce and wrathful beings. What are they? Are they man-killers? Why were they made? Why do you need them?"

The Dharma King answered: "Those two by the door, like all wrathful forms, are beneficial—powerful and splendid and good. They are destroyers of evil and obstacles, and they aid all followers of the Dharma. They represent Mahākāla and were made from many precious substances by great Indian artists. Padmasambhava and the learned Indian masters have blessed them. Their purpose is to spread and increase the Buddha's teaching and cleanse the obscurations of sentient beings. That is why we need them."

But the Bon-pos replied: "They are just made of clay—some clever men have tricked you with fakes. They are nothing special. King, you have been cheated. Tomorrow we will show you some truly marvelous things! Our worship is indeed wonderful and complete; we Bon-pos have incredible power. We will delight you with our miracles, which are beyond belief."

Then they all strolled outside to see the stūpa. "What is this—this sheath over the top, these wrinkles in the center, this bottom that looks like a pile of dog shit? What is this?" the Bon-pos asked.

The Dharma King responded: "The top is a symbol of the Tathāgata lineage, representing the Dharmakāya. Should you want to know what it does not represent, it does not represent the Sambhogakāya. It is called a 'mchod-rten', support of worship, because it supports the worship of beings of the Nirmāṇakāya realm. The umbrella and ornaments around the pinnacle represent the thirteen parts of the Dharma wheel. The central part resembling a vase stands for the expanse of the Dharmakāya and represents the Four Immeasurables.

124

The base is a richly decorated lion-throne holding a treasury of wealth—whatever one desires."

"If you practice the disciplines, what do you need with such images and structures?" the Bon-pos asked. "This is unbelievable! The brave cannot use them for fighting, the cowardly cannot use them for hiding. These Indians have very evil hearts—they are cheating our king."

The king, ministers, and the rest did not believe a word of this. So the Bon-pos went to stay at Island Eight near the Third Continent of the Lady and prepared for the sacrificial ceremonies for the king. The paṇḍitas went to stay at the Continent of Hayagrīva.

After a while, the Bon-pos sent a message to the king that they needed one thousand full-grown stags and does for their sacrificial ritual, as well as hinds in halters of turquoise, yaks, sheep, and goats. They requested a thousand of each, male and female, and also some of the king's clothing. The king quickly gave them whatever they asked for and whatever types of material substances they needed: clothing and the eight types of alcoholic beverages, the nine types of grain, and all else they wanted.

The Bon-pos then called the king and his retinue to come and meet with them. So the king and queens and lords and the rest of the retinue all went to see the Bon-pos.

Nine learned Bon-pos stood in a line in the center, flanked on the left and right by rows of nine strong men. Many men called 'Oblation Helpers' carried sharp knives. Those called 'Bathers' carried water in great golden ladles to wash the beings awaiting sacrifice. Those called 'Black Bon-pos' scattered all types of grain about the animals. Those known as 'Questioners' asked questions of the gods and spirits who surrounded them and received their answers.

Next, the 'Oblation Helpers' cut the throats of the stags and wild asses and offered the remains as sacrifices. They did the same with the yaks, sheep, goats, and other animals—three thousand were sacrificed at one time. They seized the does and cut off their legs as offerings. They took another three thousand female animals, yaks, sheep, and goats, and, after first cutting off their legs, skinned them alive for the sacrifice. They killed horses, oxen, cows, mules, dogs, birds, and swine, all in different ways. When they had finished, all bSam-yas was filled with the stench of burning flesh.

Then those called 'Separators' separated flesh from bone. The 'Dividers' divided up the remaining parts and spread them all over the place, and the 'Numbering Bon-pos' counted it all. Many kettles were filled with blood and covered with skins which were then heaped high with piles of flesh. At this point they chanted the Bon rites. Such was the Bon practice.

The king and queens and the ministers were not pleased at having to watch all this. Steam rose from the blood, and in the waves of steam they could see strange rainbows and hear noises unconnected with any form—evil sounds, sad sounds, screeches, and mad cries of HU SHU! and HA HA!

"These are the sounds of the svastika Bon gods, sounds of luck, sounds of prosperity! Wonderful sounds!" the Bon-pos cried. And they offered all the dripping red flesh and blood to the king, and asked him if he were happy with this evil ceremony. "Your Majesty, isn't this fine? Aren't you just a little pleased with the Bon? Great King, do you not feel faith rising up in your heart? Isn't this wonderful?"

But the king was not at all pleased in his heart. The others did not know what to think, and so, full of indecision, they went back inside.

The paṇḍitas and lotsāwas had seen it all, and they said to the king: "You cannot have two doctrines where there should be one. If the East is low, then the West must be higher. To mix the Buddhadharma with the teachings of heretics makes no sense. Fire and water can never meet as friends—you must send these allies of evil far away! Not even for a moment can we associate ourselves with such misguided ones. This malicious teaching contaminates everything; we will not drink of such impurity. If they stay, we will arrange to practice far from here, in bliss and peace. Should the king so desire, the Dharma can remain in the land of Tibet. But only if the Bon-pos are not allowed, even for a moment, an equal footing with us."

Nine times they sent this strong message to the king. The last time, the king called together all his ministers and lords and said: "Lords and ministers of Tibet, hear me. The Bon-pos have one system of doing things—the Buddhists have another. They are like the palm of the hand and the back of the hand; like accepting and rejecting; like giving and receiving. Who could believe both at once? The learned Indians, the Tibetan lotsāwas, and the three thousand young lamas have made known to me their position. What is to be done?"

In reply, the Bon-po Zhang ministers said: "Lord, our god! It is best that the river and its bank be separate but equal. In the past, many lotsāwas had to be sent away. But if the Bon-pos stay in their place, and the Buddhists keep to theirs, there will be peace."

'Gos-rgan disagreed: "If the Bon spreads, the king will be very upset and disturbed. If the Dharma spreads, the ministers will not be happy. The king and ministers are being pulled in two different directions. If the Dharma and the Bon remain in one place on equal footing, they will be like fire and water, natural enemies. Therefore, the time has come to end this disruption. Let us disentangle truth from falsehood: Let us cast the die to resolve which is the truth. We need to distinguish the true teaching from the false. The one shall succeed, and the other shall end.

"Tomorrow we will hold a debate. The king will sit on the highest level; the ministers and lords will sit in front. The Buddhist monks will sit on the right and the Bon-pos on the left. There will then be a debate which will examine the distinguishing features of their philosophies. The king, ministers, lords, queens, and the rest must stand behind their own teaching. Each must support the teaching they feel is true.

"We will cut down what is false and accept the truth—which will show itself by miraculous signs. We will summon forth each other's skill. If the Dharma is true, we will support the Dharma and destroy the Bon down to its roots. If the Bon is true, we will destroy the Dharma and follow the ways of Bon."

The king and his retinue agreed to this, promising to comply with the final decision. Even the Bon-pos agreed to the debate, for they were convinced that the Dharma was no equal to the Bon in power and magic. The Dharma King then consulted the Indian paṇḍitas:

"E Ma Ho!
O Learned and Accomplished Ones,
God-like Lords, Enlightened Beings!
When the Buddhists and Bon-pos face each other
they are like killers—neither will accept the other.
The king is distressed, as are the ministers and queens.

"Buddhists and Bon-pos alike
find this situation unacceptable.
Therefore, tomorrow they will engage in debate—
they shall vie with each other,
using philosophy, signs of true realization, magic powers.
The king and ministers will then decide which teaching is true.
We will know which one to follow—
we will have confidence and faith.
The teaching which is untrue will be wiped out,
its supporters banished to the wild borderlands.
The king and ministers will know what laws to follow.
They will see what path to promote."

The paṇḍitas were quite delighted and answered the king:

"Excellent, Formidable One, Lord of the Gods!
This is indeed the proper way to proceed,
truly the way of a Dharma King.
Dharma will surely conquer non-Dharma,
and the demons and misguided ones will surely be subdued.
Gathered here are all the learned and accomplished Buddhists—
even in Bodh Gayā there were none higher.
Many times we have conquered heretics with the truth.
What have we to fear from these ones called Bon-pos?
They shall be defeated and banished to other lands,
and good laws will then be instituted."

This answer pleased the king enormously. He went immediately to explain the arrangement to the Bon-pos. They also agreed, saying: "If our nine learned leaders debate, we will surely win. They have great ability and power, and we will be victorious!" And so they gathered together to make preparations.

And so the New Year arrived. On the fifteenth day of the lunar month, on the plain surrounding the great hill of bSam-yas, a great throne was prepared for the king. A platform for the Buddhists had been built on the right where the lotsāwas, paṇḍitas, and Buddhist followers would sit, and a platform for the Bon-pos and their followers was constructed on the left. The ministers and lords sat in the front rows, surrounded by a large and diverse crowd of people from all parts of Tibet.

First the Dharma King spoke: "Listen well! I am lord over all the land of Tibet! I am lord over gods and men, Buddhists and Bon-pos. All are under my dominion. Ministers, queens, and nobles, listen to me.

"The previous kings of Tibet supported both the Buddhists and the Bon-pos. But since then, the Bon have spread. I myself, like my ancestor Srong-btsan sgam-po, would like the Bon and the Dharma to coexist. But they face each other like murderers. I have tried to be equitable, and so have the ministers, but our attempts have been frustrated. Now, we must decide between the tenets of these two systems.

"Whatever the outcome of this debate, all must accept it—he who does not will feel my wrath. I decree that whichever doctrine is deemed false, be it Buddhism or Bon, must be banished; even the sound of its name shall not be heard in the land of Tibet. The losers must accept defeat. The winners will be greatly praised, and all will follow them."

Nine times the king made this proclamation, and also had it written down to be distributed far and wide. As the crowds of people settled down, waiting for the debate to begin, the Great One from Orgyan, Padmasambhava himself appeared, sitting in space at the height of a palm tree above the ground. "Listen well!" he said. "This is a great opportunity to distinguish between the tenets of Buddhism and Bon.

"First, there should be a light debate to begin the event; next, for edification and enjoyment, an explanation of religious customs and beliefs. We will turn them inside out! Finally, we will distinguish the systems by debate, examining basic philosophies and purported results. We will clarify what is true and what is false. Skill, wisdom, and psychic power will be tested until the king and ministers are convinced, and signs show themselves."

When Padmasambhava once again seated himself, his body was the image of Śākyamuni, and the king and ministers were overcome by his majesty and beauty. His speech remained that of Padmasambhava, Lord of Paṇḍitas, and all the lotsāwas and paṇḍitas took courage. His mind manifested as rDo-rje gro-lod, subduer of the erroneous and heretical, and even the Bon-pos who felt his remarkable power developed impenetrable faith and praised the one from Orgyan.

First, Ācārya dPal-dbyangs and the Bon-pos engaged in a contest of wit as a prelude to debate. The Bon-pos won the play; they waved their flags and shouted praise to their gods. They received many great prizes, and when they were given drink by the king himself, the Bon-po ministers rejoiced.

In his heart the king was not happy, but Śāntarakṣita said to him: "He who eats first is first to suffer—although the Bon-pos won the game, the Dharma is not lost. Now the nine learned Bon-pos will debate the teachings with the great paṇḍitas."

The great and wise Vimalamitra rose and spoke:
"All things proceed from a cause.
The Tathāgata has explained the cause,
and he has explained its cessation also.
These were the words of the great ascetic:
'Cease to do evil; perfect what is good.
Completely train your own mind.' "

As Vimalamitra spoke, he rose in space and sat cross-legged in a halo of light. Three times he snapped his fingers, and the nine learned Bon-pos were struck dumb and could give no answer.

In a like manner, the twenty-five scholars from India and the 108 lotsāwas each explained their understanding of the scriptures with acute perception. They held their ground in debate and manifested their realizations and the truth of their teachings. Again, the Bon-pos were tongue-tied. They could not manifest any signs of truth. They just sat there, dull and befuddled.

The Bon ministers countered: "Yes, you have won the debate, but the contest of magic is still to come. The Bon-pos will make such magic that all Tibetans, gods and men alike, will be filled with wonder! We will present sweet and wonderful discourses—we will amaze you all! We will manifest gifts to delight you! We will transfix you all! We will show such signs of realization, such power, such dark mantric abilities, that you will quickly withdraw!"

The Bon-pos burned inside and spoke harsh words born of their wrath: "These Indian barbarians are so ignorant that they create a dense obscuring cloud which hurt our Bon svastika gods. We will not debate the paṇḍitas now. After we restore our power, we will kill them. For now, we will debate only with the lotsāwas, not with foreigners."

The Dharma King, after offering each of the great paṇḍitas a measure of gold dust and a beautiful silk robe, praised all of them highly. Buddhist banners waved, music played, and flowers fell from the sky. Deities appeared high in the air singing with joy. Thoroughly amazed, the Tibetan people developed such great faith in the Dharma that they were moved to tears.

But on the Bon side, hail fell like stones. "The gods have spoken!" they said, and the Bon ministers had to bow to the Dharma. They showed deference to the paṇḍitas and apologized to the lotsāwas. Mañjuśrī manifested to the Dharma King, who now knew in his heart what was Dharma and what was not. At once most of the Tibetans cried out: "The Dharma has won! The Dharma is great and wonderful! Now all will follow the Dharma!"

The Dharma King spoke: "Now the lotsāwas and Bon-pos must debate with each other." The great lotsāwa Vairotsana debated with the

Bon-po Thang-nag, and Nam-mkha'i snying-po debated with sTong-rgyus. Each lotsāwa debated with a Bon-po, but none of the Bon-pos were a match for the lotsāwas. After each contest, the Dharma King gave the winner a white 'truth' stone and the loser a black stone.

When Vairotsana had accumulated nine hundred white stones, and Thang-nag one thousand and five black ones, all the lotsāwas waved flags of victory and cheered. When sNubs Nam-mkha'i snying-po had won three thousand white stones, and sTong-rgyus thirty thousand black ones, again the lotsāwas waved their flags. Even mTsho-rgyal and the Bon queen Cog-ro-bza' debated. mTsho-rgyal won, for the Bon lady was unable even to speak. But we will explain the miraculous things that occurred later.

So the 120 lotsāwas won, and the nine learned Bon leaders lost. Completely tongue-tied, they could not even reply. Their mouths became twisted, their faces perspired, and their knees shook, but words would not come.

Then the time came for the contest of signs of realization. Vairotsana held all three realms in the palm of his hand; Nam-mkha'i snying-po rode the rays of the sun and manifested many fine and wondrous deeds. Sangs-rgyas ye-shes drew demons together on the tip of a dagger and killed them by impalement. Then he thrust the dagger into a rock. rDo-rje bdud-'joms flew as fast as the wind and circled all four continents in a moment. To prove he had done it, he gave the king seven types of stone found only at the ends of the earth.

rGyal-ba mchog-dbyangs manifested Hayagrīva on the crown of his head—Hayagrīva then neighed three times, filling all the three thousand realms with the sound. Beings of the three realms, the heaven realms and others, were instantly subdued. As a sign of proof, he offered the nine-spoked golden wheel of Brahmā.

rGyal-ba'i blo-gros walked upon water. lDan-ma rtse-mang completely subdued the Bon-pos by his exposition of the Dharma. He could present all the translations of the Buddha's teachings from memory; he even was able to show the very vowels and consonants in space.

sKa-ba dPal-brtsegs brought demons under his control, and 'O-bran gzhon-nu moved underwater like a fish. Jñānakumāra removed nectar from rocks, and rMa Rin-chen-mchog ate rocks as if they were bread. dPal-gyi rdo-rje moved freely back and forth through stone. Sog-po lha-dpal forced the tigress of the south to come to him, merely by using his iron hook mudrā, command mantra, and meditative concentration.

Dran-pa nam-mkha' called the wild ox from the far north, and Cog-ro Klu'i rgyal-mtshan invited the Lords of the Three Families to appear in the sky. Lang-gro dKon-mchog 'byung-ldan brought down thirteen thunderbolts at one time, and directed them where he chose, like arrows. Khye'u-chung attracted dākinīs to him and held them by the power of his meditation. rGyal-mo gYu-sgra snying-po subdued everyone by means of grammar and logic. Ting-nge-'dzin rtogs-sa-pa outshone all others with many poetic translations. rGyal-ba byang-chub sat cross-legged in the sky, and Ting-nge-'dzin bzang-po flew through the air, and was able to see four continents and more at one time.

The twenty-five great siddhas from mChims-phu, the one hundred powerful psychic ones from Yer-pa, the thirty mantric practitioners from Shel-brag, and the fifty-five with understanding from Yang rdzong, as well as others, each showed different signs of realization such as these. They turned fire into water, and water back again into fire. They moved in the sky and penetrated rocks and mountains. They stayed afloat on water, made many things into few, and few things into many—these are just some of the marvelous deeds they performed.

The Tibetans couldn't help but have faith in the Dharma. And the Bon-pos couldn't help but give in. The Bon ministers were speechless.

The culmination came when the Lady mTsho-rgyal debated with the Bon-pos, and the Bon-pos lost. At that point, they cast murderous spells, demonic black magic spells, using weasels and dog meat, butter lamps and blood. They cast nine such evil mantric spells, and nine young monks suddenly died. But with mTsho-rgyal's blessing, the monks all came back to life. In fact, the nine she saved became even sharper and wiser, so the Bon-pos were thoroughly confounded. Making the great and powerful Finger-pointing Mudrā at the nine men, mTsho-rgyal said PHAṬ nine times, and they fell down unconscious. Then she said HŪṀ nine times, and again they rose up. They gained such control over the five elements that they could sit in the sky in the lotus position, and do other wondrous things.

She brought forth flames of different colors from each of the five finger tips of her right hand, each colored flame spinning like a wheel. The Bon-pos were terrified. Five different colored streams of water poured forth from the five fingers of her left hand and flowed together into a lake. She cut the great boulders at mChims-phu with her hand as if they were butter and made the rocks into different shapes. Such wonderful things mTsho-rgyal did! She even made twenty-five manifestations of herself, each performing a different extraordinary feat.

The Bon-pos said: "We will not associate with this woman; any Tibetan of breeding considers her beneath contempt." And the next day, when nine powerful men were struck down at once, the Bon-pos threatened to turn bSam-yas into dust. They climbed the hill of Has-po-ri and threw thunderbolts down upon the temple. But mTsho-rgyal caught them on the tip of her finger, and threw them all to 'Om-bu, the land of the Bon, where they caused great devastation.

The Bon hurled thirteen more thunderbolts at bSam-yas, but mTsho-rgyal sent them all back to fall upon the Bon-pos. Thus, the Bon lost both the competition and their power. By rights, they should have been banished, but sTag-ra and Glu-gong and the others were such powerful ministers that they could not be eliminated so easily. They went to 'Om-bu where they threatened to destroy all Tibet by casting many powerful spells—the nine cycles of the Power Goddess, the nine cycles of Great Deeds, as well as fire spells, water spells, earth and air spells.

The Dharma King asked the lotsāwas and paṇḍitas for advice on what means were available to control the Bon-pos. But in reference to this, Padmasambhava merely told mTsho-rgyal: "Lady, you protect the king." mTsho-rgyal meditated at the highest gallery of bSam-yas, opening and practicing the Vajrakīla mandala. For seven days she practiced, beholding large numbers of deities and developing the signs of great power.

She then caused the force of the Bon-po spells to turn upon itself so that the Bon gods of vengeance attacked their own supporters, in one stroke killing sTag-ra, Klu-gong, and five other Bon ministers who despised the Dharma. Of the nine most powerful Bon-pos, eight were now dead; only one remained. The ranks of Bon-pos were decimated and their power weakened.

Immediately the Dharma King called all the Bon-pos together at bSam-yas and made certain laws concerning them. Padmasambhava advised him: "The Inner Bon are in harmony with the Dharma, so let them be. But these perverse Bon are no different from the most evil and wrong-minded heretics. You cannot kill them, for if you do, people will hear of it—but you can send them out of the country."

The Dharma King did as the Guru advised, treating the Inner and Outer Bon differently. The Outer Bon texts he burned in a fire, but the books and such of the Inner Bon he treated as treasures, putting them away for safekeeping. The Outer Bon were banished to Mongolia, the country of the monkey-faced men, while the Inner Bon were sent to Zhang-zhung and the border countries surrounding Tibet.

Under laws instituted later, it was decreed that those under the sovereignty of the Dharma King (including ministers, nobility, Tibetans, and non-Tibetans) should follow the rule of the Dharma and not that of the Bon. The king declared:

"The Tibetan realm from China to Khri-sgo will be filled with the Buddhist doctrine, with the Sangha, and with adepts who will teach the Dharma."

To celebrate this decree, the king had the great Dharma bell rung at bSam-yas. The Dharma conch shell was blown, Dharma flags waved, and the Dharma throne was made ready. The Great One from Orgyan, Padmasambhava, along with the most learned Zahori Bodhisattva Śāntarakṣita, and the wise Kaśmīri Vimalamitra, sat on great golden thrones. The twenty-one scholars from India and the great lotsāwas

Vairotsana and Nam-mkha'i snying-po sat on seats formed of nine brocade pillows piled one upon another. The other lotsāwas were given seats formed of two or three cushions.

The king offered everyone many gifts of gold and other precious substances. Each of the great Indian masters received nine bolts of brocade, three gold ingots, three measures of powdered gold, and a mountain of other gifts. The three masters from Orgyan, Zahor, and Kaśmīr were given mandalas of gold and turquoise, bolts of fine silk, and innumerable other wonderful things. Then, as a special request, the king urged these three masters to remain in Tibet and spread the scriptures of both Sūtra and Mantra throughout the land. All of the paṇḍitas were most pleased at this request, and exclaimed: "Wonderful! Wonderful!" At this time Śāntarakṣita, Padmasambhava, and Vimalamitra each promised to remain in Tibet and give Dharma teachings for as long as the king wished.

Training then began at bSam-yas for seven thousand scholar monks and at mChims-phu for nine hundred practitioners. One thousand students studied at the scholastic center of Khra-'brug and one hundred at the practice center of Yang rdzong; three thousand studied at the scholarly center of lHa-sa and five hundred at the practice center of Yer-pa. In one year's time, the students at the three main Dharma centers at lHa-sa, bSam-yas, and Khra-'brug, as well as at the six secondary centers, had finished the course of instruction.

Many other Dharma centers were now built: at Glang-thang in Khams, Rab-gang in Me-nyag, rGyal-tham in 'Jang, Bya-tshang in sMar, and all through the four eastern valleys and the six eastern mountains. mDong-chu was built in sPo-bo, Rong-lam in Bar-lam, Bu-chu in Kong-po, and mChims-yul and Dvags-lung in Dvags-po; temples were erected in the four central regions: Jo-mo nang sTag-gdan in gTsang, at La-phyi, gTsang and gTsang-rong, in mNga'-ris-man, and so forth. So the Dharma spread widely throughout Tibet.

How the Lady Ye-shes mTsho-rgyal Continued
to Protect the Sangha and Benefit Beings

The doctrine of the Buddha, the community of the Sangha, tantric study centers, and the practice of the Dharma spread without friction throughout Tibet. The learned masters from India, China, Nepal, and other lands were filled with satisfaction. Showered with kindness and a great deal of gold, they then returned to their respective homes.

But Śāntarakṣita, Padmasambhava, and Vimalamitra remained to turn the Wheel of the Sūtra and Mantra Dharma, bringing joy to the heart and mind of the great Dharma King. The king's power and might reached unsurpassed heights. The perverse Bon were conquered, and the king's enemies in all four directions were subdued—all he wished was accomplished, even his slightest whim. So King Khri-srong lde'u-btsan gave over control of the country to his son Mu-ne btsan-po.

Not the least hint of emotional turmoil remained to trouble the Dharma King, not the least bit of pain or sickness. He went from bliss to bliss. Then, one evening, he called together his wives and sons, nobles and ministers-of-state, and gave them various instructions. At midnight he performed a ceremony in the temple and made offerings of flowers. Early the next morning he attained high spiritual realization, and at dawn he merged with a ray of light and was absorbed into the heart of Mañjuśrī, never to be seen again.

Some time later the new king, Mu-ne btsan-po, was poisoned by one of his father's wives, and another of Khri-srong lde'u-btsan's sons, Mu-khri btsan-po, took the throne to become ruler over Tibet.

At that time, the queens still resented the Dharma, and were attempting to create divisions between the two religious communities by encouraging competition and contention. But the Lady mTsho-rgyal, using all her compassion and skillful means, eventually reconciled them so that such disorder did not arise again.

Near bSam-yas, at Has-po-ri, lived the Inner Bon queen known as Cog-ro-bza' or Bon-mo-mtsho. She had been acquainted with mTsho-rgyal since they were both quite young, but, inspired by jealousy, she now gave mTsho-rgyal some nectar containing poison. Though mTsho-rgyal knew this, she took the drink anyway, saying to Cog-ro-bza':

"Kye Ma!
Listen dear friend, this nectar is wonderful,
the very essence of goodness;
my body is the Vajra Body, unsullied and indestructible.
It has transmuted this nectar
into the wondrous essence of immortality.
Though this purpose of yours has not been fulfilled,
I have turned it to great fulfillment.

"Because I have not developed jealousy,
I have cleared away the discord
between the Buddhists and Bon-pos.
You should pray to the gods and yidams,
develop pure intentions toward spiritual brothers and sisters,
feel compassion toward the helpless,
and humble devotion toward the teacher."

Then mTsho-rgyal's body became filled with many rainbows; shimmering and moving lights extended even to the tips of her hair: She became of the Vajra essence.

Cog-ro-bza' was very much ashamed; she would not stay anywhere close by and left for another country. The Tibetan queens were very upset at this incident and banished mTsho-rgyal to gTsang.

First mTsho-rgyal went to Kha-rag gangs where about three hundred disciples gathered to practice with her. (Later this place became known as the Kha-rag of the Lady.) Thirty-nine of these disciples developed remarkable magic powers and signs of realization; twenty became great teachers; seven became equal to mTsho-rgyal herself; and they all benefitted beings in immeasurable ways.

Then mTsho-rgyal practiced at Jo-mo nang, named in her honor. There, one thousand and one nuns gathered; one hundred became great teachers able to help others; five hundred developed remarkable powers; and seven became equal to mTsho-rgyal herself.

When mTsho-rgyal practiced the secret teachings at 'Ug-pa-lung, her fame spread throughout gTsang, and one thousand male and thirteen hundred female practitioners came to be near her. They all engaged in the highest Mantrayāna teachings, uniting the maturation and liberation practices. Not one of them ever returned again to samsara. mTsho-rgyal gave her special lineage practices to eighty special siddhas and to seven practitioners of particularly pure karma so that her oral lineage spread widely. As her teachings became well-established at Jo-mo nang, many aspirants appeared at 'Ug-pa-lung, and many siddhas appeared at Kha-rag and Jo-mo nang.

When mTsho-rgyal went next to Sham-po gangs, seven bandits raped her and stole her possessions. But as they were joining with her, she sang them this song of the Four Joys:

"NĀMO GURU PADMA SIDDHI HRĪ!
Today, my sons, you meet with me, the Great Mother—
this is due to the power of merit gained before.
Now is the time—the conditions are right for the Four Empowerments.
Listen, my sons, and be attentive;
I will move with you through the Four Joys.

"Gazing upon the mandala of the Mother,
you will clearly see the feeling of desire arising,
and gain confidence from the Vase Empowerment.
Explore the pure fact of your own desire—
merge inseparably with the deities of the Developing Stage.
Turning all into deities and yidams,
contemplate your desire mind as the deities' manifestation, my sons.

"Join with the space of the Mother's mandala;
Great Bliss arises from that root.
Pacify the angry mind; the loving mind replaces it,
and power is gained from the Secret Empowerment.

Explore the pure fact of joy—
merge joy with breath and let them circulate a little.
There is no turning back from the Mahāmudrā.
Explore the bliss of Mahāmudrā, my sons.

"Join with the expanse of the Mother's Great Bliss.
Let your vigor take on a life of its own;
you and I will merge hearts and minds,
and gain blessing from the Wisdom Empowerment.
Guard unwavering the pure fact of bliss—
merge with the Great Bliss which is openness.
There is no turning back from indestructible bliss and openness.
Explore the Bliss of the Supreme Joy, my sons.

"Join with the root of the Mother's Bliss—
make the 'two' of duality the 'one' of enlightened mind.
Stop the appearance of self and others,
and gain Pristine Awareness from the Creativity Empowerment.
Guard its spontaneity within the world of appearance.
Merge masterful desire with openness,
and there is no turning back from the Great Perfection.
Then explore transcending the Joy of Spontaneity, my sons.

"These instructions are especially sublime.
Thus wondrous liberation comes from our meeting,
and instantly, with lightning speed,
you receive the Four Empowerments,
and reach maturity by realizing the Four Joys."

During this song, the seven bandits achieved maturation and liberation. They developed power over their patterning and energy, and became great masters of the Four Joys. Without abandoning their bodies, the seven bandit siddhas went to the land of Orgyan and gave great aid to innumerable sentient beings.

Having trained these seven masters, mTsho-rgyal returned to Nepal where the patrons from her previous visit as well as the Nepāli king, Ji-la-ji-pa, again offered her their support. In return, she gave them many of the Guru's instructions on meditation. While she was there, she met a fourteen-year-old girl whose father was called Bha-da-na-na and whose mother was called Na-gi-ni. The child was a ḍākinī in human form, and mTsho-rgyal took her with her. She called the girl Kālasiddhī, for in the future, this girl would gain great mantric attainment and become a great siddha of the Ming-du-sku'i ḍākinī lineage.

After leaving Kho-shod, mTsho-rgyal travelled slowly through many lands. For one whole year, she opened the mandala of the Lama's secret teachings with Kālasiddhī, Blo-gros-skyid, bDe-chen-mo, gSal-bkra, and others of her students. She gave them many teachings, and they attained siddhi. She established the Dharma in far away borderlands where it had not yet spread, gathering as many as two hundred Dharma followers about her at one time and teaching them the nature of cause and effect.

Finally, the Dharma King Mu-khri btsan-po sent three of his nobles to invite the Lady mTsho-rgyal to return. So mTsho-rgyal appointed the Lady Blo-gros-skyid to act as her regent while she was absent, and then returned to Tibet with thirty of her students, including Kālasiddhī. On the way, she visited Kha-rag, Jo-mo nang, and 'Ug-pa-lung, receiving offerings and homage from many people.

Upon her arrival at bSam-yas, the king held a great welcoming ceremony for her and presented her with many gifts. He led her to the topmost gallery of bSam-yas where the ministers-of-state, nobles, and lotsāwas greeted her with joy as great as if she had returned from the dead.

But while mTsho-rgyal was away, the great and learned Śāntarakṣita had died. She at once went to his tomb and offered seven handfuls of gold, nine silken scarves, and many mandalas. There she expressed her loss, lamenting with this song:

"Kye Ma Kye Hud!
Great and Holy Teacher!
Though the sky is vast and filled with many stars,

if the sun's seven fire horses are absent,
who will light up the darkness?

"Who will brighten the dark land of Tibet
now that the stainless crystal mandala is gone?
Without the protection of your compassionate rays,
who will lead us, who are like the blind?

"Though we may possess a king's treasure of jewels,
if the wish-fulfilling gem is gone,
who will give us what we need and desire?
Whose shining love will clear away the suffering
in this Tibetan land of hungry ghosts?
Precious Wish-granting Gem, where have you gone?

"Dear Treasure, who satisfied all our needs and desires,
if you do not continue to help us, who will?
We are as cripples, unable even to stand; who can help us?
Though the three thousand worlds be filled with powerful lords,
if there is no one to turn the Wheel of the Dharma,
who will protect us?
Where can we now go for refuge in barbarous Tibet?

"Wheel-turner, Most Victorious One, Lord, where have you gone?
If you do not continue to protect us with the law of the Dharma,
in whom can we take refuge, we who are stupid and mindless?
Though this world has many siddhas and learned ones,
without you, Great Master,
how can we grasp the teachings?
Most excellent successor of the Buddhas, where have you gone?
If you do not continue to protect us with Sūtra and Mantra,
who is left to help us,
we who are like corpses, without movement or understanding?

"Kye Ma Kye Hud!
The Most Excellent One, Master of Peace,
Lord of Bodhisattvas, Leader of Gods, Protector!
By your compassion, I and other beings in many places
entered the door of the teachings.

By the Dharma of both the Sūtra and Mantra,
we obtained the maturation and liberation practices and bliss.
By the four means of conversion, we are able to benefit beings.

"Father, when I have perfected all great acts of the Buddha-sons,
may I become a leader of teachers and teachings!
May the victory banner of the teaching be raised
and never lowered!
May all embodied beings cross the ocean of samsara
on the ship of this teaching!
And may I attain realization and become the teacher of beings!"

When mTsho-rgyal had finished, a song was heard coming from the top of the stūpa, though no one could be seen:

"OṀ Ā HŪṀ!
All your actions are the deeds
of the Buddhas of the three times;
your charismatic deeds increase boundlessly, like space.
The Buddha's teaching, root and branch,
fills all the ten directions,
for you are the Great Mother of the Jinas,
the Protectress, filling the three times
with your auspicious deeds."

All who had gathered with mTsho-rgyal at the tomb heard these words and rejoiced.

For a while, mTsho-rgyal stayed at the temple of the great Dharma King, and then she went to mChims-phu where she remained inseparable from Guru Rinpoche for eleven years. Together they promulgated the teachings, both philosophy and practice, and Guru Rinpoche revealed all his secret heart treasures, philosophy, and technical instructions to his lady. It was truly as if the contents of one vessel had been completely emptied into another, leaving nothing behind.

At this time, Guru Rinpoche said to her: "Soon the time will come for me to go to rNga-yab Ḍākinī Island. Before I go, we must fill Tibet with great, profound, and inexhaustible Dharma treasures. For this, I need a girl named Siddhī, who is of the lineage of the Conch Shell Ḍākinīs, to be my assistant in esoteric mantric practices. Thus I will spread many profound instructions not heard of in any other esoteric teaching and conceal many treasures for the future."

As mTsho-rgyal later explained: "I did as instructed by the Guru and sent the ḍākinī Siddhī to him. Together they opened the mandala of the Bla-ma dgongs-pa 'dus-pa. They gave maturing and liberating practices to the King Mu-khri btsan-po, who ever afterwards guarded and supported the Dharma teachings in the tradition begun by his ancestors."

Guru Rinpoche instructed his students in all the many teachings to be hidden as gter-ma, after first giving them instructions in the proper way of transcribing the treasures. He gave Nam-mkha'i snying-po instructions in rapid writing and gave Ācārya dPal-dbyangs instructions in beauty of style. To lDan-ma rtse-mang he gave instructions in three different types of rapid and stylish writing; he also gave instructions on the flowing writing to sKa-ba dPal-brtsegs. To Cog-ro rGyal-mtshan, he taught cleanness of style. He taught grammar, logic, and philosophy to gYu-sgra snying-po; to the brilliant Vairotsana he taught everything. To mTsho-rgyal he taught the siddhi of Never Forgetting.

His twenty-five disciples and many apprentices acted as scribes, using many different languages and styles. Some used Sanskrit, some Ḍākinī writing, some Nepāli. Others wrote in fire, water, or wind letters. Some used Tibetan letters of various types: dBu-chen and dBu-med, lCags-kyu long and short style, Bon letters, 'Bru and 'Bru-tsha scripts; Khong-seng or Khyi-nyal, rKang-ring or rKang-thung; some wrote using different forms of shads, and so forth.

Padmasambhava wrote down the cycle of the ten million Thugs-sgrub-skor practices, and the ten thousand cycles of the sNying-thig, root text, explanations, and technical instructions, extensive and profound. Though large in number, these teachings were pithy, concise, and easily understood, great blessings of bliss. Even the short texts were profound, clear, and complete, providing whatever was needed and desired. Then, in order to establish confidence in his gter-ma, he established a system of sequential proofs of their validity. He set forth the kha-byang, yang-byang, snying-byang, lung-byang, and so forth, and sealed them for the future.

The Guru and his consort, having become of one heart and mind, benefitted beings by their great wisdom and means. Having become one in the charismatic communication of speech, they revealed the expanse of Sūtra and Mantra teachings. Having become one in the magical manifestation of body, they demonstrated power over all the world of appearance. Having become one in enlightened wisdom qualities, they benefitted beings and the Doctrine. Having become one in enlightened activity, they manifested power over the four aspects of action. As the absolute, the All-good and the Lotus-born, the Yab and Yum of the essence of bliss, they filled the sky with the dance of their body, speech, heart, quality, and action.

Then, from mChims-phu they gradually passed through the outer reaches of Tibet, giving blessings and teachings. First they visited the three Tiger Caves. When they came to sPa-gro Tiger Cave of Bhutan, Guru Rinpoche prepared all his individual treasures and gave the lung-byang, predictions concerning their future discovery. He said: "Whoever practices here, because it is my heart place, will receive the Mahāmudrā siddhis. At the same time that I, the Guru, was abiding in the Akaniṣṭha heaven, these representations of my body, speech, and mind appeared spontaneously—a statue of rDo-rje gro-lod, a stūpa, the six-syllable mantra, and other things." He then recited prayers and gave blessings.

When they went to 'On-phu Tiger Cave of Tibet, Guru Rinpoche designated all the gter-ma masters, future gter-ma repositories, and gave the snying-byang, the predictions concerning the entrusting of the treasures. He said: "Whoever practices here, because it is my body place, will develop the siddhi of longevity. At the same time that I was born on the lake of Dhānakoṣa, these symbols of my body, speech, and mind appeared spontaneously—the three-syllable mantra, the Ra-lu-'bru-dpu, stūpas, and vajras." He then recited prayers and gave blessings.

When they went to the Tiger Cave of Khams, Guru Rinpoche concealed many individual treasures and proclaimed the oaths, vows, and oral instructions to be used by future gter-ma masters, as well as the kha-byang, the predictions concerning their revelation. He said: "Whoever practices here, because it is my speech place, will be blessed with great renown. Even those who break their vows, if they practice here, can develop both the ordinary and great siddhis. At the same time that I sat upon the Vajra Throne and turned the Wheel of the Dharma, subduing demons and those with wrong views, there spontaneously appeared these representatives of the Three Kāyas—the six-syllable mantra, the three-letter mantra, the twelve, and so forth." He then recited prayers and gave blessings.

In like manner, they visited many other places, the details of which can be found in such other texts as the Life Story of Padmasambhava.

Finally the Guru and his consort returned to the great temple of the king in the land of Tibet and stayed within its lofty citadel. The king, his ministers, the queens and the nobility, and all the lotsāwas gathered before Padmasambhava, receiving instructions and prophecies. Soon, on the tenth day of the month of the monkey, in the year of the monkey, Guru Rinpoche would ride upon the sun's rays to the Isle of rNga-yab in the Southwest. But mTsho-rgyal was yet to remain in order to benefit beings—to give the teachings of the Dharma's six divisions to the king and his people, and to conceal the Guru's treasures in all the designated places.

The Dharma King and his retinue accompanied Guru Rinpoche to Gung-thang la-thog. Then, after asking for and receiving many predictions and instructions, they sadly turned back.

But not the Lady mTsho-rgyal, who later explained how she continued on with Padmasambhava, riding upon the sun's rays to Tsha-shod rong on the border between Tibet and Nepal. There they descended into the secret cave of Tsha-shod where they remained for seventy-three days, opening the mandala of the all-extensive Great Perfection Āti teachings and giving initiation.

However, the ceremony proved inauspicious (due to an assistant who harbored various doubts), causing the Guru to declare: "For now, the esoteric teachings will spread in this land of Tibet, but eventually a time will come when the Mahāyāna Āti teachings will be held in question, when only a few will be liberated by the oral transmission or by the hidden treasure transmission. The benefit of these teachings for beings will be limited. According to the way in which events are linked, though there will be the outer appearance of the esoteric teachings, their power will have little influence. Sometimes these teachings will spread, but at other times swiftly decline. Such is the unhappy effect of this ceremony.

"Yet to you, mTsho-rgyal, I will give my complete teachings, comprehensively and withholding nothing. This is not the ordinary path —this is the doctrine which causes the dualistic mind to disappear. Now this teaching will come to you in full measure.

"If you had received these teachings before, you would not have sown the seeds of your previous acts, and as a result, there could have been no harvest of their good fruits. For a great length of time, the world would not have seen these teachings.

"With this teaching there are no good or evil actions. There are no higher or lower births. There is no lifetime, no youth or old age. There are no sharp or dull senses—for this teaching gives passage into an expanse where all entities have ceased. If I had given this teaching to you as you were before, certain benefits would not have ensued for embodied beings. It would have been difficult to teach them the most profound treasures of the Buddha's doctrine. And why is this? Because this teaching instantly transforms the transitory physical body.

"Now meditate continuously until you are not for an instant separate from the Chos-nyid mngon-sum, the first of the Āti realizations. Though you will remain in possession of a physical body, you will quickly become a Buddha.

"From here, you will go to Zab-bu and Ti-sgro and other places, continuing to practice for three years. After three years, you will obtain the next higher Āti realization, the Nyams-snang-gong. After six years, you will achieve the Rig-pa-tshad, the third of the Āti realizations.

"At this time, you will prepare all the gter and work to benefit others by giving specific and technical teachings. You will go to lHo-brag in mKhar-chu to practice, where you will manifest extraordinary feats and miraculous physical transformations, such as making parts of your body invisible. For approximately two hundred years, you will retain a physical body and benefit beings. Then you will meet me at rNga-yab Ḍākinī Island in the Great Pristine Awareness. You will benefit beings without discrimination and become a Buddha."

After making this prediction, Padmasambhava rose upon a ray of light and prepared to leave. mTsho-rgyal, weeping, bowed before her teacher and cried desperately:

"Kye Ma Kyi Hud! Orgyan Lord!
Now you're here, now you're gone.
Must there be this birth and death?
How can birth and death be changed?

"Kye Ma Kyi Hud! Orgyan Lord!
For a time we were inseparable:
Now, suddenly we part.
Must there be this meeting and parting?
Is there no way for friends to remain together?

"Kye Ma Kyi Hud! Orgyan Lord!
For a time all Tibet was filled with your blessings;
now only your footprints remain.
Must there be this impermanence?
Is there no way to reverse the winds of karma?

"Kye Ma Kyi Hud! Orgyan Lord!
For a time Tibet was protected by your teachings;
now they are but a story once told.
Must there be this change?
Is there no way for you to stay?

"Kye Ma Kyi Hud! Orgyan Lord!
Until now, you and I have been inseparable;
now you leave me for the sky.

This woman is stricken with evil karma;
who will give me empowerments and blessings?

"Kye Ma Kyi Hud! Orgyan Lord!
Though you have given me many profound teachings,
now you go into deathless space.
This lady is wretched;
who will clear away obstacles now?

"Kye Ma Kyi Hud! Orgyan Lord!
Now, please—give me your promise:
Forever gaze upon me with compassion,
forever look upon Tibet with eyes of blessing."

Then mTsho-rgyal threw thirteen handfuls of gold over the Guru
and recited his mantra. Mounted on the ray of light not far away,
Padmasambhava answered her:

"Kye Ma! Listen, lady, Lake of Good Qualities,
Padmasambhava is leaving to overcome the cannibals.
The activity of the Three Kāyas
is perfect, powerful, and creative,
not at all the scattered froth of ordinary beings.
If you fear birth and death, hold tight to the Dharma;
practice the Developing and Perfecting Stages,
bring patterning and energy under your control—
this is the means to reverse birth and death.

"Kye Ma! Listen, faithful and virtuous lady,
Padmasambhava is departing to benefit beings.
Undiscriminating compassion pervades everything,
not at all like the bewildered confusion of ordinary beings.
Make the meditation on the Guru Yoga your inseparable friend—
everything that arises is the pure manifestation of the Teacher.
This is the best teaching:
that meeting and parting do not exist.

"Kye Ma! Listen and look closely, irresistible lady!
Padmasambhava is departing to teach and train others.

149

This supreme and indestructible body destroys destruction,
not at all like the evil karma that pursues ordinary people.
All of Tibet is filled with my children, my siddha disciples.
Meditate on the Mahāmudrā as you watch impermanence,
for samsara and nirvana are inherently free—
there is no better way to reverse the winds of karma.

"Kye Ma! Listen, faithful young lady,
Padmasambhava is departing to turn the Dharma Wheel
in the land of savages.
This is an unchanging, supreme Vajra Body,
not at all like the sick, suffering body of ordinary beings.
The Dharma fills Tibet from top to bottom:
If you study and practice,
you will never lack the wealth of the Dharma.
By listening, examining, and meditating,
you protect the Buddha's teachings;
both you and others become perfectly realized.
There is no more profound way to reverse change.

"Kye Ma! Listen, faithful daughter of mKhar-chen bza',
Padmasambhava is departing for the Lotus Light.
The Tathāgatas of the three times have asked me to do so.
This is not at all like ordinary beings
driven on by the Lord of Death.
Lady, you have a wondrous body, a siddha's body;
ask the Lord, your own mind, for blessings and empowerment.
There is no other regent of the Lotus Guru.

"Kye Ma! Listen, Ye-shes mTsho-rgyal-ma,
Padmasambhava is going to the place of Great Bliss.
I will reside in the Dharmakāya, the deathless divine state.
This is not at all like the parting of mind and body
which afflicts ordinary beings.
Already, mTsho-rgyal, you have been liberated
by the profound teachings.
Meditate on the Great Perfection of the Āti
which destroys corporeality;

meditate, pray, practice, and clear away obstacles.
The compassion of the Lama clears away all hindrances.

"Kye Ma! Listen, auspiciously marked Radiant Blue Light—
many times I have given you oral instructions.
Practice the Guru Yoga and understand the meaning
of collection and cessation.
Let your head be anointed with rainbow light—
visualize there the moon and lotus,
and Padmasambhava himself, teacher of beings:
having one face and two hands, holding a vajra and skull cup,
wearing layers of multicolored robes, religious garments
that symbolize the complete perfection of the vehicles.
His hat is a snyan-shu with an eagle feather on top;
earrings and necklace are his ornaments.
He is seated in the lotus posture.
Endowed with radiant light, the auspicious signs and marks,
ḍākinīs of the five rainbow colors surround him,
and brilliant lights flash back and forth.
Continue to meditate
until the radiance of this image pervades your mind.
When that clarity comes, absorb its power with equanimity,
and until that radiance appears, practice with great effort.
Repeat the Vajra Guru Mantra:
the essence of the essence of the Guru.
Finally, merge your own three gates with mine,
and receive the Lama's blessing and dedication.
Rest within the actionless creativity of the Great Perfection.
mTsho-rgyal-ma, there is nothing more sublime.

"Padmasambhava's compassion does not rise and fall;
the light of my compassion will never cease to brighten Tibet.
One need only ask, and Padmasambhava will appear before him.
I am never far from those with faith;
or even far from those without it,
though they do not see me.
My children will always be protected by my compassion.

"Thus, in the future, on the tenth day of the month,
Padmasambhava will appear on the sun's rays.
As the four seasons change, so shall I,
from peaceful to wrathful forms,
and I will give my children the siddhis they desire.
It is especially important to practice
on the tenth day of the month
when all the siddhis of the wrathful deities
and empowerment can be attained.

"On the fifteenth day, I will come on moon rays,
with blessings and compassion, shaking the world;
I will empty all the lower realms,
benefitting all beings with my perfect charismatic action.

"On the eighth day, night and daybreak, dawn and dusk,
mounted on the magical horse Cang-shes,
I will wander the world giving aid and strength to beings.
In the country of demons, I will turn the Dharma Wheel.
In twenty-one distant lands across the sea,
and in thirty even more distant,
I will manifest without distinction
in peaceful and wrathful forms,
as fire, water, air, space, and rainbows—
my vibrations passing everywhere,
my many manifestations leading to bliss.

"For the same reason, girl, to benefit countless beings,
you must remain in the land of Tibet
for more than a hundred years yet to come,
to lead beings to bliss.
In one hundred and one years, come to rNga-yab Island,
and together we will protect and educate, as one.
You will be called Knowledge-holder, Radiant Blue Light.
Until then, you will remain one with my body, speech, and mind.
You have cut the stream of birth and death,
you have stopped the winds of karma.
In the future you will manifest only to benefit beings.

"We two will continue to manifest in Tibet—
without weariness or restraint we will help beings.
We are now the same, mTsho-rgyal,
not for an instant will we ever really part—
only for a little while, only in a relative sense,
so be happy!
May my blessings and compassion rain upon all Tibet!"

As he finished, the sky was filled with light, and with hosts of ḍākas and ḍākinīs; music poured forth, unimaginably wonderful sounds from shells and drums and damarus, from horns and harps and violins, from gongs and cymbals and drums, and more.

Flags and banners appeared, streamers and ribbons, parasols, victory banners, standards, colored powders, medicinal powders, musical instruments, fans of all kinds, canopies, curtains, cymbals, conch shells, thigh bone trumpets, hand drums, large drums, lutes, wind bells, and more, all in the midst of great, truly inconceivable clouds of offerings. Brilliant lights flashed back and forth, passing overhead. Gradually, the Guru and his retinue disappeared into the southwest.

As Ye-shes mTsho-rgyal later explained, she was utterly desolate and called out:

"Guru Rinpoche!
You are the one Buddha-teacher;
you are the one father of beings;
you are Tibet's only eyes;
you are my only heart . . .
O what little compassion you have!
O what a terrible thing you have done!
Kye Hud, Kye Hud!"

Thus she cried and fell down in full prostration. Once more Guru Rinpoche looked back and gave his first testament. And again, music played and lights blazed and darted. In the midst of this light, mTsho-rgyal could faintly see the host in the distance, disappearing into the southwest, and then they were gone.

Again she threw herself down and pulled at her hair, scratching her face, beating her body, and cried:

"Kye Ma Ho! Kye Ma Hud! Orgyan Lord!
Has the land of Tibet been left empty?
Has the light of compassion gone out?
Are the Buddha's teachings abandoned?
Have the Tibetans been left with no conscience?
Has mTsho-rgyal been left with no refuge?
Look upon us with compassion. Look now!"

Loudly she cried, and in reply, a clear, sonorous, and majestic voice gave a last call, though no one could be seen. And so he gave his second testament. Suddenly, the sky blazed forth with light which spread to all four corners of the world; briefly, dākinīs could be seen darting back and forth through a radiant net of light. Then darkness fell again, and all disappeared.

Again, she collapsed onto the stones. Bleeding and aching all over, she called out to the Guru in her terrible pain:

"Kye Hud! Sphere of Compassion!
Your charismatic deeds are equal to all space—
but today your life in Tibet has ended.
Though each of the black-headed ones has his own destiny,
today the fate of Tibet has been sealed.
All beings experience both pleasure and pain—
now is my turn to feel pain.
Alas! Look quickly upon me with compassion!"

And as she called out, an invisible voice spoke: "mTsho-rgyal, look here!" As she looked up, there appeared before her in space a ball of light the size of her head, inside of which was the first of Padma's bequests. Lights filled all Tibet and then coming together, rushed into the southwest and disappeared.

mTsho-rgyal was inconsolable. She cried out: "Orgyan Lord, Compassionate One, don't leave me! Look at me. How can we part?" There came the same sounds as before, and in front of her appeared a ball of

154

light the size of her hand. Within it was a box containing the second of the Guru's bequests. A light bright as the sun blazed briefly, and then closing into itself, dissolved into the southwest, leaving a darkness deep as midnight. The Guru and his retinue of ḍākinīs had completely disappeared. It seemed as if she had awakened from last night's dream.

mTsho-rgyal was greatly distressed and sat crying as she thought upon her Guru. Through her tears, she sang this song:

"Kye Ma! Jetsun Orgyan Rinpoche!
You are the one father who protects Tibet.
Now you have gone to the Isle of Ḍākinīs,
and Tibet has become a lost and empty place.
Where has the finest of treasures gone?
Even though nothing ultimately goes or stays,
today you have gone to the realm of Orgyan.

"That sun which warmed the land of Tibet,
shining over both gods and men, has set.
Now who will warm us, who are totally naked?
The luckless Tibetans have lost their eyes.
Now who will lead us, who are blind and alone?
Our hearts have been torn from our breasts.
Now who will guide these mindless corpses?
You came here to benefit beings.
Why couldn't you stay just a little while longer?

"Kye Hud! Orgyan Rinpoche!
A time of thick darkness has come to Tibet:
a time when hermitages are empty;
a time when the Dharma throne is vacant;
a time when vase initiations are no more.
Now we can only guess as to the nature of things;
now we must look to books for teachings;
now we can only visualize the lama;
now we must use images as his substitute;
now we must rely on dreams and visions;
now a grievous time has come!

155

Alas! Jetsun Orgyan Lord!
Look upon me with compassion!"

And as she prayed, from the southwest a light radiated forth and halted right before her. Within the tip of the light ray was a box about an inch long. This was the third bequest of the Guru. Its arrival created a profound confidence in her heart—all inner insecurities and emotional instability were cleared away. She realized how meaningless is the concept of being together with or apart from the Teacher. With great respect, she opened the mandala of the Bla-ma gsang-ba 'dus-pa and practiced for three months. Six times during the days and nights of this period, Guru Rinpoche appeared before her, giving advice, teachings, and predictions.

Feeling filled with the Guru's blessings, mTsho-rgyal then went on to practice the Yang phur Sādhanas, together with their related prayers and expiations. She cleared away all the obstacles which plague the advanced teachings, and practiced the rDo-rje gzhon-nu Sādhanas Padmasambhava had given her. When she was done, she gave these teachings to bDe-ba-mo and to others blessed with faith. mTsho-rgyal left both the oral and treasure lineages at that place.

After this, mTsho-rgyal went to Mang-yul, to the great joy of all those with faith, especially those who had previously been her students there. They presented her with many offerings and asked her to remain with them always. But she stayed only one month, clearing away her students' obstacles, developing their potential to the utmost, and spreading many instructions on reaching enlightenment. Then she took the road to gTsang.

For a time, mTsho-rgyal wandered through the borderlands between gTsang and Mang-yul and all the people there welcomed her, saying: "The Guru has gone to the Demon Land, but the Lady is with us!" They were confident mTsho-rgyal was one with Guru Rinpoche and crowded about her so thickly that she could scarcely walk. She gave them all instructions and benefitted them greatly.

Then she went to the region of Zur and remained for one year, teaching gNyan dPal-dbyangs, sBe Ye-shes snying-po, La-gsum rGyal-ba byang-chub, 'O-bran dPal-gyi gzhon-nu (the later one), Lang-lab Byang-chub rdo-rje, and 'Da' Cha-ru-pa rdo-rje, a seven-year-old boy who showed great promise. Seeing them to be worthy vessels, she gave them the maturation and liberation teachings.

mTsho-rgyal went on to Shang and stayed in the caves of sPa-ma gang for three years, doing much to benefit beings. After that she visited Zab-bu, where she remained one year in a meditation of the effortless Āti vehicle, experiencing the ever-growing compassion and extreme joy which comes with higher realization. She hid thirty great gter-kha there.

She went on to gZho-yi Ti-sgro, remaining there for six years; she experienced the Rig-pa-tshad, the third realization of the Āti, impressing the Great Perfection on her mind. She benefitted many ḍākinīs and visited sixty-two heaven realms. This account, however, is found in other texts.

At this time, mTsho-rgyal took upon herself the sufferings of others. For example, the evil minister Śānti-pa, who had caused mTsho-rgyal such great suffering earlier in her life, had been reborn in one of the hot hells. By great effort and the power of her compassion, she drew him out of hell. Without making distinctions, she freed many other hell-beings as well. But you must look elsewhere for that story.

She gave her body to wild animals, clothing to those who were cold, and food to the hungry. To the sick she gave medicine; to the poor, riches. To the powerless, she gave protection, and to those with great desire, she gave her own body. She gave of her body and life in whatever manner would be of use to other beings. Without regard for herself, she even gave her own sense organs where they could be of use. Śakra and the nāga king Nanda both kept watch over her.

Once, when she was at Ti-sgro, three men approached her carrying a cripple. She asked them what had happened, and they explained: "We have come from 'On-phu in Tibet. The king ordered this man punished by having his kneecaps removed. A great and learned Tibetan told us that only the kneecaps of a woman could help him, otherwise there is no hope. Lady, it is said that you will give anything to those who have need. Thus, we have come to you. Could you possibly give us what we ask for?"

Looking at the cripple, mTsho-rgyal saw the long oblong scars on his legs and felt great compassion arise within her heart. "You may take from me whatever you need," she told them, "for I promised my teacher always to act for the benefit of beings by my body, speech, and mind."

So they took up a knife. "We need to make great incisions in your body. It will be very painful . . . can you stand it?" "Whatever must happen, let it happen," she replied.

First, they cut across the top of the knees and then pulled out the knee caps with a loud popping noise. When they set the red objects down in front of mTsho-rgyal, for a moment she lost her breath. But she recovered and told the men to take them. They rejoiced and left. After a time, her knees healed.

Another man came to her, a leper in a terrible state—his body decomposing, blood and pus spewing forth, his nose and mouth nothing but a deep wound. He reeked with the odor of decay, and he was weeping.

"Why are you crying?" asked mTsho-rgyal. "This is your karma; it is useless to cry. It would help you more to do some spiritual practices."

"Yes, illness is everywhere in this world," he answered. "But this sickness is not my only problem."

"What is the trouble?" she asked.

"This illness came upon me all of a sudden, and very strongly. I had a beautiful wife like you; she looked like a goddess. When I caught this terrible disease, she would not stay with me, but ran off and took another husband. I have heard that you live only to help living beings, and so I came here to ask you to be my woman. Do you think you could stand it?"

Again, mTsho-rgyal felt great compassion, and she answered: "Do not weep. Whatever you say, I will try to do." And so she served him.

In like manner, mTsho-rgyal sacrificed herself many times. Once seven Bon-pos came, saying: "We need your skin for a ransom ceremony." So she gave her skin to them. Similarly she was asked many times for her eyes, head, arms and legs, tongue, and so forth. Many beggars came to her, and she always gave, joyfully and with blessings.

Then Indra came and offered her the wealth of the gods: the five kinds of heavenly garments, the vessel full of the nectar of immortality, and the seven kinds of heavenly jewels. Praising her, he said:

"Amazing Lady, adorned with auspicious marks,
your deeds are those of the great Bodhisattvas of the past.
Without regard for body or life, you devote yourself to others.
Heroine, Queen of Compassion, I take refuge in you.

"Wondrous and supreme, I praise you above all others—
I will stand by you from now until the kalpa ends.
Please, Lady of Initiation,
stay and turn the Wheel of the Dharma—
I exhort you, stay and teach sentient beings!"

Thus Indra spoke and then disappeared. At the same time, all of mTsho-rgyal's infirmities were cured, and she was quite as before.

Then the leper turned into the nāga lord, Nanda, and heaped immeasurable nāga wealth in front of mTsho-rgyal. Clasping his hands in faith, his eyes filled with tears, he said to her:

"Kye Ma! Guru Ye-shes mTsho-rgyal-ma!
You are the secret key of Padmasambhava.
In your compassion, you take up others' sufferings.
You neither judge nor grasp at clean or unclean;
you care only for the benefit of others,
and conceal any love you might feel for yourself.
Buddha Consort, Queen of the Teaching, to you I bow.

"Padma Thod-phreng was our teacher.
O Dharma Sister, look upon me with compassion.
In you lies the ocean of secret Dharma teachings!

You hold the profound meaning
of the treasures of the Lotus teachings.
Because of your comprehension,
his teachings do not decline but continue to spread.

"As long as you remain, as long as I live,
I will follow you, protect you, and guard you.
May the good succeed, and the wrong be overturned!"

Thus he spoke and disappeared.

When Khri-srong lde'u-btsan's son heard that mTsho-rgyal was at Ti-sgro, he sent her an invitation. And so she went to bSam-yas and stayed at mChims-phu for six years. The great Dharma King Mu-khri btsan-po, the principal lotsāwas, the ministers-of-state, the nobles and queens, as well as the Tibetan people, all treated her with great honor and respect and requested her blessings.

The practitioners who had first practiced at mChims-phu had long since accomplished their own good, achieved their purpose, and dispersed to benefit others. Some had since passed into nirvana, some had grown old, and only a few remained. But again, new monks were being ordained by order of the Dharma King: Fifteen hundred were ordained at one time, and the learned Kamalaśīla came from India to become abbot. mTsho-rgyal continued to meditate at mChims-phu, giving teachings and helping students to develop siddhi and mature in their practice.

At this time, a dispute was going on over the validity of the ston-min view versus the rtsad-min view. A monk called Hva-shang, teacher of the ston-min, had been propounding wrong views; these were refuted, and the defeated group declined. The debate between the two philosophies had been held at bSam-yas with the teacher Kamalaśīla defending the rtsad-min at the temple of Hayagrīva, and the Hva-shang arguing his position from the temple of Maitreya.

As mTsho-rgyal explained later, she came down from mChims-phu with one hundred followers in hopes of reconciling the dispute, but no one would listen to her. Through demonstrating siddhis and miraculous manifestations, she tried to bring the followers of ston-min and those of rtsad-min together by a show of faith. But this failed, and the Dharma teachings and the tenets of the teacher Kamalaśīla were established as being correct. Hva-shang and his followers were given gold and escorted to the boundaries of their own country, China.

After that, under the influence of the great Dharma King, the Dharma centers at lHa-sa, bSam-yas, Khra-'brug, and elsewhere continued to expand. Thirteen thousand novices entered the Sangha.

mTsho-rgyal then spent some time at mChims-phu and mNga'-ris, Mang-yul and Pu-rang, Mon and gTsang, Byar and Lo-ro, the four parts of dBus and gTsang, the four of Byang-kha, the six mountain ranges of mDo-khams, in rGya, 'Jang, Hor, and Me-nyag, and so forth, all-the places where previously Guru Rinpoche had given teachings and ordained students. The Lady mTsho-rgyal did likewise, teaching old students and newly ordained monks, and anyone who came with faith in Guru Rinpoche. She benefitted beings immeasurably, and her lineage filled all the land.

In order to fulfill her duties concerning the Dharma treasures, and to help all beings without distinction, mTsho-rgyal visited many small holy places and secret shelters. She explained in her own words how she travelled about and hid the Dharma treasures:

"I did my best to benefit the teachings and to benefit beings. According to the Guru's predictions, half my lifetime was over. I had achieved the Rig-pa yang-tshad realization, achieving the sPyod-pa yang-tshad. I then decided to go to all the places which Guru Rinpoche had himself blessed, and in these places to put Dharma treasures and add my blessings and do practices.

"First, I went to Ti-sgro where I remained for one year and seven months. There I concealed ten gter-kha and practiced and prayed for the benefit of beings. Then I went to the border regions and hid five gter-kha in the crystal cave at Yar-lung. I remained there in meditation for thirteen months. Having blessed that place, I went on to Yang rdzong where I remained for one year and concealed thirteen gter-kha. At Yer-pa I stayed one month and hid ten complete kha-gter.

161

"Gradually I travelled on to the Tsa-ri snow mountains in the east where I stayed one year and four months and hid thirty great kha-gter. After that I went on to the land of Kong-po and hid one hundred and fifty kha-gter. I went to the great mountains of Nepal to the south where I remained for thirteen months and hid thirty-five kha-gter. Then I went to the great mountains and passes of the western border, staying four months and seven days, and hiding eight gter-kha. I went to the great mountains in the demon lands near the northern border and stayed three months and five days, hiding three gter-kha.

"I went to the Valley of the Kings in the southeast mountains where I stayed one year and fifteen days and hid ten gter-kha. I travelled to the Gra-phu valley in the southwest, stayed five months and ten days, and hid seven gter-kha. Then I went to the 'Jag-ma valley in the northwest, stayed one year and five months, and hid nine great gter-kha. Then in the Gro-ma valley in the northeast, where I stayed eleven months, I hid five kha-gter. I spent one month and ten days at the snow mountain of Yar-bu and hid three kha-gter. I spent a year at the great snow mountains of gSal-rje and hid ten gter-kha. In the mountains and valleys of gYu, I stayed for three months and hid three gter-kha. In the mountains and valleys of 'Brong-rje, I stayed ten days and hid three gter-kha. In the mountains and valleys of gYul I stayed three months and hid four gter-kha.

"At the great mountains and valleys of Jo-mo, I spent five months and hid ten gter-kha. In those of sNye-bo I stayed five months and hid four gter-kha. At rDza-yul mountain I stayed twenty-one days and hid one gter-kha. At the mountains of sNa-nam I spent seven months and hid five gter-kha. In the lHo-rong mountains I stayed three months and seven days and hid thirteen gter-kha. In the mountains of Rong-btsan I spent seven months and hid fifteen gter-kha. In the mountains of Shel-dbrang I spent two months and ten days and hid five gter-kha. In the mountains of sGam-po I spent one year and one month and one day, and hid twenty gter-kha.

"At the mountains of Bye-phu I spent one month and hid fourteen gter-kha. In the mountains of Bu-'bol I stayed twenty-one days and hid three gter-kha. In the mountains of Seng-phrom I stayed seven days and hid two gter-kha. In the mountains of mTsho-nag I stayed twenty-four days and hid one gter-kha.

"Similarly, in the valley of Ma-kung in the east, I spent one month and hid thirteen gter-kha. And at rBa-lcags-śrī in the south I spent one year and hid seven gter-kha. In the valley of sBrang-sman in the west I remained one month and hid three gter-kha. At Se-mo-do in the north I stayed three months and hid four gter-kha.

"I placed gter-kha in other places as well: in the upper Tsā-ri rdzong and the middle Kha-rag rdzong and the lower Ge-re rdzong, at Phag-ri rdzong in Bhutan and the Bu-chu rdzong in Kong-po, and Bag-yul rdzong in sPu-bo. At the lDan-gyi rdo-rje rdzong and the Phyams-kyi Na-bun rdzong, and at the Ne-ring Seng-ge rdzong, and the gYa'-ri Brag-dmar rdzong, the Ka-ling sPin-po rdzong, the lHa-ri gYu-ru rdzong, the lTo-la'i dPal-'bar rdzong, the Re-kha'i Bu-mo rdzong, the Brag-dmar rdzong in Gling, the lHa-brag rdzong in 'Bri, the Brag-dkar rdzong in lower Kong-po, and so forth, I remained for a month and a day, giving teachings and concealing gter-kha.

"And at the eight great repositories: 'Bras-mo gshongs in Nepal, Padma-bkod in Klo-yul, Zab-bu valley in Shangs, mGo-bo ljongs in sMad, rGyal-mo rMu-rdo ljongs, lHa-mo dngul-khang ljongs, rGyal-lung 'jog-po valley, and the Bu-ldum valley in Bhutan, I stayed for one year giving teachings, making preparations, and concealing many gter-kha.

"At twenty-five great snow mountains and four places of blessing, at the eighteen great fortresses, and at one hundred and eight power places of Guru Rinpoche, I practiced for one year, one month, and one day, hid gter, and prayed for the well-being of the region.

"In particular, in the border regions of mDo-khams, at the eight places of the eight signs of the Guru's blessing, at the five places of the five classes of Thod-phreng-rtsal, at the twelve places of wonderful charismatic deeds, at the three places of the blessings of the oral teachings, and so forth, in the regions where the Guru's pure teaching extended, I gave blessings and hid gter-kha."

And beyond that, throughout Tibet, at the 105 great sacred places and the 1070 smaller sacred places, at many millions of other locations, mTsho-rgyal practiced and prayed and hid gter-kha. But these names are not included here for fear of making the text too long. In the outer reaches of Tibet as well as the central locations, bSam-yas, lHa-sa, Khra-'brug, and so forth, she hid gter-kha, but one should look in the various gTer-kha-byang and the life story of Guru Rinpoche for further details.

ཐ་སྐལ་ལ༔ རྒྱ་རྒྱ་རྒྱ༔ སྨྲ༔ གུ་ཧྱ༔ ཁ་ཐམ༔ ༔ རྒྱ༔ ཟབ་རྒྱ༔ གཏེར་རྒྱ་རོ་ཉིས་ཐམ་བཏ༔ ས་རྒྱ་རྒྱ་རྒྱ༔

This Concludes the Seventh Chapter
Concerning Ye-shes mTsho-rgyal's Deeds
For the Benefit of Sentient Beings.

Śāntigarbha

rGyal-ba byang-chub

Vairotsana

rDo-rje gro-lod

lDan-ma rtse-mang

Ka-wa dPal-brtsegs

rDo-rje gro-lod

How Ye-shes mTsho-rgyal Reached Her Goal, Achieved Buddhahood, and Entered the Expanse of All That Is

Thus mTsho-rgyal blessed important sacred places throughout the land and concealed many gter-kha, as has been explained. She then returned to dBus province in central Tibet and stayed some time at the sanctuary of the Tibetan sovereign at mChims-phu. She continued to aid and protect sentient beings, even surpassing what she had accomplished before. In the temple of sKar-chung rdor-dbyings, she gave many extensive, profound, and supreme Dharma teachings for maturation and liberation to seven worthy vessels, including the Dharma King Mu-khri btsan-po, Prince Mu-rum btsan-po, and Ngang-chung dPal-gyi rgyal-mo.

In particular, mTsho-rgyal revealed the Bla-ma bka' gsang 'dus-pa, the Lama's Oral Teaching of the Guhyasamāja, the Yi-dam dgongs-pa 'dus-pa, the rDzogs-chen Āti 'dus-pa, and so forth, and set forth the maturation and liberation practices related to them. Then she opened the mandala of the Bla-ma gsang 'dus-pa and practiced.

At dawn on the seventh day, after beginning the service, she invited the Guru:

"In the northwestern land of Orgyan,
within the flower of the lotus,

the renowned Padmasambhava,
the Lotus-born One endowed with wondrous realization,
appeared amidst a host of ḍākinīs.
So that I, following your example, may perfect my practice,
please approach and grant me your blessings."

When these verses were spoken, Guru Rinpoche and his retinue were seen approaching from the southwest surrounded by music, clouds of sweet-smelling incense, and a host of ḍākinīs dancing in the sky. In the midst of brilliant light, Guru Rinpoche himself appeared, seated in the middle of the mandala. And the king thought: "As I am the great Dharma King, I must prepare a throne for the Guru." But he was so overwhelmed by devotion and love that he was unable to prepare the throne.

Guru Rinpoche declared: "Before too long, quite soon, this king will have a grandson, a malevolent man, who will, for a short time, occupy the throne of his ancestors, the Great Dharma Kings. But the faith of this Dharma King here and now is so great that he need no longer occupy a body compelled by karma. He will manifest only for the benefit of beings. Simultaneously, he will achieve realization and liberation."

Prince Mu-rum prepared many cushions and asked the Guru to be seated. King Mu-khri then gave Guru Rinpoche one hundred mandalas of gold and turquoise, bowed to his teacher, and asked:

"E Ma Ho!
O manifestation of Jetsun Orgyan Padma!
One father of all beings in the land of Tibet!
Bad karma is a great burden pressing down upon me—
carrying it, I seem to flounder in a swamp of mud.
Without your compassion at this time, how can I ever escape?
Today through your great kindness you came here.
Please say you will stay with us always
and continue to turn the pure Wheel of the Dharma."

Thus he asked, and Padmasambhava answered:

"Listen carefully to my words, Dharma King, Lord of Gods!
How lucky you are—both great fortune and great faith are yours.
You were matured by the Guru's blessings;
you were liberated by the Lady's secret teachings;
you were realized by the mystic seal of your own mind;
you will reach your goal
in the centerless expanse of body, speech, and mind."

Then Padmasambhava placed his hand upon the head of the son of Khri-srong, and instantly, this great Dharma King simultaneously achieved realization and liberation.

Prince Mu-rum btsan-po then bowed low to Guru Rinpoche, circumambulated him, and offered him a veritable mountain of gifts: deerskins filled with gold and thirteen copper trays piled high with turquoise blue and clear as the sky. He asked the Guru:

"I, a king's son, am very proud. I am lazy and crave distraction and entertainment. I rejoice in wrongdoing, in war, in exerting power. Whatever I do is tainted by evil. I need a profound Dharma teaching, one that is easy to understand and joyful to practice, a great and powerful blessing, quick to give success, one that will destroy sin and fill me with virtue. This is the kind of teaching I seek."

Guru Rinpoche answered:

"Well said, well said, young prince!
Your prayer is pure and your karma is pure.
You have faith and nobility, Sad-na-legs, Discerning One.
Seven births from this one,
you will no longer need to take a karmic body,
but will manifest only to teach.
You will become one
with the Mind of the Buddhas of the three times.
And after one world age,
you will become the Buddha sKar-ma-'od."

Guru Rinpoche opened the Yang-dag Heruka mandala so that the prince would quickly achieve the deity siddhi. Specifically, he gave him the teachings called the Zab-chos-zhi-khro dgong-pa rang-grol and prepared him for realization and liberation, saying: "Hide this teaching at the foot of the mountain Dags-po-gdar. In the future, it will be of great benefit to many beings." Padmasambhava also gave him such lama sādhanas as the Bla-ma nor-bu padma'i phreng-ba, saying: "Hide these at the rock caves of Ra-mo-che."

Guru Rinpoche then went to the temple of sKar-chung where he stayed for seven days, giving blessings. The following morning, as he was again leaving for the land of Orgyan, Ye-shes mTsho-rgyal asked:

"Kye Ma!
Even sinful beings look, listen, remember, and feel . . .
your compassion quickly frees
those stuck in the mire of emotionality.
O Padmasambhava, Messenger of Buddhas,
continue to look upon the land of Tibet
with unbounded compassion!
I have completed all my acts of training—
now, Lord, I implore your mercy, I pray to you,
put an instant end to this meeting and parting!"

This she asked and received this answer:

"Kye Ma! Listen, daughter of mKhar-chen bza'!
The fire crystal of the sun is controlled by powerful forces;
thus day and night, and the four seasons come about.
But the openness of space knows nothing
of subject and object, grasping and grasped.
The nature of causation is such
that the final result must come forth—
like farmers who, once they plant,
cannot stop the plants from growing.

"Ye-shes mTsho-rgyal,
because your Pristine Awareness is far-reaching,
the seal which binds the aggregates of your existence
has been broken.
You are completely free from the stains of emotionality.

170

And though the limited samsaric mind
tries to hold on, it is powerless.

"Sentient beings who are drawn
to radiance, creativity, and perfection
will gain the Developing and Perfecting Stages,
and the Great Perfection.
Nothing can stop this process.
By destroying karma, destroying samsara's constituents,
destroying the need to be taught, and destroying the aggregates,
the five realms and the five elements are destroyed as well.
Beyond misery is a wondrous place!

"Fifty years from now, in the bird month, on the eighth day,
mTsho-rgyal will travel to the Lotus Light,
and a great host of ḍākas and ḍākinīs will welcome you.
Until then, strive to benefit beings."

Then Padmasambhava disappeared.

As mTsho-rgyal later explained: "Then, I, mTsho-rgyal, went back to the great meditation cave of lHo-brag in mKhar-chu. There I gave Nam-mkha'i snying-po instructions concerning patterning and energy to further his spiritual advancement, along with the siddhi practices of longevity. My students developed both the ordinary and the great siddhis.

"Then I meditated upon the actionless Great Perfection, and the Chos-nyid zad-pa, the highest of the Āti realizations, arose. I benefitted sentient beings by manifesting in various guises, and they saw me in various forms:

"To those sentient beings who were hungry,
I manifested as an abundance of food,
establishing them in bliss.
To those sentient beings who were cold,
I manifested as sun and fire,
establishing them in bliss.

To those sentient beings who were poor,
I manifested as myriads of jewels,
establishing them in bliss.
To those sentient beings who lacked clothes,
I manifested as apparel,
establishing them in bliss.
To those sentient beings without children,
I manifested as sons and daughters,
establishing them in bliss.
To those sentient beings desiring a woman,
I manifested as an irresistible maiden,
establishing them in bliss.
To those sentient beings desiring a husband,
I manifested as a handsome man,
establishing them in bliss.

"To those sentient beings wanting supernatural powers,
I gave the eight great siddhi practices,
establishing them in bliss.
To those sentient beings suffering from sickness,
I manifested as medicine,
establishing them in bliss.
To those sentient beings suffering from misery,
I manifested as satisfaction,
establishing them in bliss.

"Those sentient beings suffering under the laws,
I led to a land of harmony, friendship, and love,
establishing them in bliss.
To those sentient beings suffering from fear of wild animals,
I manifested as safety,
establishing them in bliss.
Those sentient beings who had fallen into abysses,
I brought forth from abysses,
establishing them in bliss.
To those sentient beings suffering by fire,

I manifested as water,
establishing them in bliss.

"To those sentient beings whose suffering was caused
by any of the five elements,
I manifested as the antidote,
establishing them in bliss.
To those sentient beings who were blind,
I manifested as eyes,
establishing them in bliss.
To those sentient beings who were crippled,
I manifested as limbs,
establishing them in bliss.
To those sentient beings who were dumb,
I manifested as tongues,
establishing them in bliss.

"From those sentient beings on the point of death,
I took away death,
establishing them in bliss.
Those sentient beings who had just died,
I led on the paths of transformation,
establishing them in bliss.
To those sentient beings wandering in the bardo,
I manifested as tutelary deities,
establishing them in bliss.

"Those sentient beings wandering in the hot hells, I cooled.
And those suffering from cold, I warmed.
Thus, to all beings suffering for any reason,
I manifested varied and appropriate aid,
establishing them in bliss.
To those sentient beings born as hungry ghosts,
I manifested as food and drink.
Those sentient beings wandering as animals,
I liberated from the suffering

of stupidity, dumbness, and servitude,
establishing them in bliss.

"Those sentient beings born as men
in barbarous or wrong-thinking lands,
I turned from the wrong paths,
establishing them in bliss.
Those sentient beings born as demigods,
I saved from quarrels, fights, and strife,
establishing them in bliss.
Those sentient beings born as gods,
I saved from the pain of falling to lower states,
establishing them in bliss.
Any beings who suffered from any kind of disharmony,
I saved from that disharmony,
establishing them in bliss.

"In short, wherever there is space,
the five elements are pervasive.
Wherever there are the five elements,
sentient beings are pervasive.
Wherever there are sentient beings, emotions are pervasive.
Wherever there are emotions, my compassion is pervasive.
That is how widespread my help has been.
For twenty years more,
I appeared and disappeared throughout the world."

At this time there came from India a lady who had been Guru
Rinpoche's body consort, a ḍākinī of the Pristine Awareness: a queen
of practice, a queen of healing, a knowledge-holder, another possessor
of auspicious marks, a sister of the gods, a flower—her name was
Mandāravā, and she came from the sky with seven students.

mTsho-rgyal met her, and for thirty-nine days they remained together sharing and discussing the higher Dharma teachings. In particular, Mandāravā asked mTsho-rgyal for twenty-seven of Guru
Rinpoche's technical Dharma teachings which had not been known

in India. mTsho-rgyal offered them to her. And then she asked Mandāravā, the ḍākinī of long life, the mistress of longevity, for seven technical instructions on longevity, as well as thirteen teachings including certain Hayagrīva practices. mTsho-rgyal then hid them as Dharma treasures.

Then mTsho-rgyal sang this song:

"OṀ ĀḤ HŪṀ!
Ḍākinī, you have the deathless Vajra Body;
you abide in space like the rainbow,
moving skillfully and at will, unhindered by objects.
Victor over the Demon Lord of Death,
subduer of the demons of the aggregates,
free from the bondage of emotionality, subduer of gods,
Mistress of Life, Ḍākinī, is this not you?

"From the highest heaven throughout the three realms,
mistress of all wondrous essences,
who achieved the Body of Great Bliss sealed by emptiness itself,
Mandāravā, Mother of beings, to you I bow.

"Beings are born and die,
the cycle is driven by karma—
the flow stirred up and impure
like the torrent from a water wheel.
I pray that I become realized, like you,
who have closed and barred the downward gate.
May even I obtain the mind of the Bodhisattva,
and end karma, end pleasure, end bewildered confusion,
end all the cycles of the three realms,
and end all conceptualization.
May I pass beyond bliss to the realm of Great Bliss,
never to be parted from Great Bliss, the All-good."

This was her prayer. Then mTsho-rgyal asked Mandāravā for many technical teachings that were unknown in the land of Tibet, and Mandāravā, queen of practice, sister of gods, answered her:

175

"Kye Ho!
You are the ḍākinī accomplished in the secret teachings;
you can manifest at will in both pure and impure realms;
you collected the quintessence of the Lotus precepts;
Great Mother, Prajñāpāramitā, is this not you?

"You entered the path and saw the truth of the Dharma;
in this very lifetime you totally renounced
the eight worldly dharmas;
you practiced the disciplines, gathered the nectar,
and controlled worldly appearances.
Pure and unspoiled, forever young, mTsho-rgyal, I bow to you.

"Though powerful karmic winds endlessly spin samsara,
you rescue sinful sentient beings with your skillful practice.
The ways of the wrong-minded, the demons, and Bon have declined,
and now the Dharma is established as custom.

"Powerful lady, you and I have become as one.
From here you will pass into a realm of infinite purity;
you will enter the land of the Lotus Light,
and within the brilliance of Padma Thod-phreng's compassion,
you and I will manifest charismatically to benefit beings.
May all beings in the three realms
rise out of the pit of samsara!"

Having made this prayer, Mandāravā disappeared into space.

After that, sBe Ye-shes snying-po, rMa Rin-chen-mchog, 'O-bran dPal-gyi gzhon-nu, Lang-lab rGyal-ba byang-chub rdo-rje, 'Dar-cha rDo-rje dpa'-bo, dBus-kyi Sūrya thad-pa, the Bhutanī girl bKra-shis spyi-'dren, the Nepalī Kālasiddhī, Li-bza' Byang-chub sgrol-ma, Shel-dkar rDo-rje mtsho-mo, mKhar-chen gZhon-nu sgrol-ma, and so forth, eleven disciples and seventy-nine other followers with faith accompanied mTsho-rgyal to the Zab-bu valley in Shangs where for ten years she concentrated on the completion of their training. Then she entered a meditation of complete transcendence.

Ye-shes snying-po together with six other students who had mastered their karma and other followers with faith went to mTsho-rgyal, asking her to continue to turn the Wheel of the Dharma and not to pass beyond the world of misery:

"Kye Ma Ho!
You are the Great Mother, the Perfection of Wisdom,
the Dharmakāya, endowed with all the auspicious signs!
If the wondrous sun and moon disappear into space,
whom can we turn to, we two-legged beings crawling the earth?
Stay a while longer and open the mandala of great wisdom.

"You are the Victorious One,
the moisture-granting cloud of the Sambhogakāya.
If the nectar of the teachings disappears into space,
whom can we turn to, we tender young sprouts living on the earth?
Stay a while longer and rain down the nectar of the Dharma.

"You are the place of refuge, mTsho-rgyal,
the Nirmāṇakāya teacher.
If your auspicious and revealing beauty disappears into space,
whom can we turn to,
ourselves and others like us, bereft of the Dharma?
Stay a while longer and teach, mature, and liberate us.
Pray hear us, wondrous mTsho-rgyal!"

Praying to her, they were choked with sadness, and mTsho-rgyal responded: "My children, please prepare a great mandala offering. A while longer I will open mandalas of many great and profound secret teachings and explain them to you. But on the eighth day, only my name will remain in the land of Tibet."

Though all her students were miserable and upset, they prepared a great mandala offering, and mTsho-rgyal took her place at its center. All her students, Dharma brothers and sisters, sat before her with downcast faces, and every time they looked at mTsho-rgyal, their eyes filled with tears. mTsho-rgyal told them:

"All of you gathered here, listen closely!
Direct the power of your minds to my voice.
You needn't despair, you should rejoice.

177

Because life is composite, it is impermanent.
Because objects are merely appearance,
they have no real foundation.
Because paths are confused, they are without truth.
Because the fundamental nature of things is emptiness,
objects have no real status.
Because the mind is merely dualistic concepts,
it has no ground or root.
I have never seen anything that is finally real.

"You faithful brothers and sisters gathered here,
you pray to me, the Mother, unceasingly,
but it is the expanse of the Great Bliss which gives blessings.
There is no such thing as meeting and parting.
My power is such that I am free from karma and can lead others—
I give refuge without distinguishing self and other,
and manifest compassion.
For me, the Mother, there is no suffering
from death or from change.
You need not despair, brothers and sisters,
that my deeds on this part of the earth are ending.
My Lord, the Orgyan Lord, predicted
that in this life I would help beings for two hundred years.
Now more years than that have passed.
No short time have I helped Tibet; a long time I have helped her.

"At thirteen, I became a queen;
at sixteen, the Guru in his compassion received me;
at twenty, I obtained empowerments and practiced the disciplines;
at thirty, I developed siddhis and worked to benefit beings;
at forty, I meditated upon the Enlightened Mind of the Guru;
at fifty, I conquered demons and guarded the teachings;
at sixty, I taught from texts and expanded the Sangha;
at seventy, I developed the Chos-nyid;
at eighty, Guru Rinpoche went to the Southwest;
at ninety, I saw the Chos-nyid mngon-sum;
at one hundred ten, I developed the Rig-pa-tshad;

at one hundred twenty, I was Dharma master to the Dharma King;
at one hundred thirty, I wandered throughout all Tibet;
at one hundred fifty, I hid gter and practiced to benefit others;
at one hundred sixty, Mu-khri passed away;
at one hundred seventy, I completed my students' training;
at one hundred eighty, I sent forth a manifestation to lHo-brag;
at one hundred ninety, I met my sister, supreme in practice;
I received excellent technical instructions
and longevity practices, and now I am freed
from the taint of birth and death.
Now two hundred eleven years have passed—
well, have I not helped Tibet long enough?
Aren't you grateful, all you gods and men?
Has anyone else experienced such pleasure and pain?
Now it seems the time is gone.

"Friends, do not be unhappy. Practice earnestly and deeply.
Meditate upon the actionless Great Perfection.
There is no other way to transcend misery.
This is the heart's blood of Orgyan Padma—
he gave it to me, now I give it to you.
Practice and you will achieve siddhi.
Give instruction to all beings who are ready,
but do not give it to those who are not.
Do not give it to those who have violated their vows.
And keep it from those with wrong views."

mTsho-rgyal explained further what she meant, and opened a mandala of the Āti Great Perfection for eleven of her root students. She
gave her final oral lineage teachings as well as one hundred technical
instructions which were like her heart. At that instant, all who heard
her voice were liberated.

Then mTsho-rgyal went to a meditation cave on the side of sPa-ma
snow mountain. In the two hundred and eleventh year of her life, on
the third day of the bird month, mTsho-rgyal said: "On the eighth day
of the month I will travel to the great spectacle of Zab-bu peak; soon
after I will reside again on the Copper-colored Mountain."

With eleven of her close disciples and fifty of her other followers, mTsho-rgyal set out for the peak of Zab-bu. On the seventh day, half way up Zab-bu mountain, they came to a cave shaped like two praying hands. There they stayed while she gave twenty-five different technical instructions and turned the great wheel of the lama's teaching. All her students gathered in front of her, and mTsho-rgyal told them: "It is the nature of sentient beings to be impermanent and to be taught."

Then bKra-shis spyi-'dren offered her a mandala of gold and asked:

"Mother, kind mistress,
one mother of sentient beings of the three realms,
if you do not stay to guard your children,
those knowing how to put hand to mouth will survive,
but many, not knowing, will die like hungry ghosts.

"You are like that great golden gem in the sky.
If you do not stay to clear away the darkness of beings,
those with the eye of wisdom may reach the path,
but those with ordinary eyes will fall into the abyss.

"You are the Teacher's regent, the one auspiciously marked.
If you do not stay to guard those who listen to the Dharma,
the Arhats and the self-sufficient may succeed,
but who will guard the Śrāvakas,
the listeners who find it difficult to understand?

"You are the ḍākinī, the lovely Sarasvatī.
If you do not stay to guard the people,
the lotsāwas and scholars may succeed,
but who will guide ordinary limited beings?

"Kye Ma! Alas, Lady of auspicious marks,
stay to look upon your followers with compassion!
This group of brothers and sisters gathered here
pleads for the nectar of your words."

bKra-shis spyi-'dren bowed many times, and mTsho-rgyal answered:

"Kye Ma! Listen, faithful Bhutanī girl,
I myself, the Lady mTsho-rgyal,

have not tired of benefitting beings.
But all Tibet is filled with the Dharma.
Many years, two hundred and eleven, have passed,
and now my work of teaching is surely complete.
There is no way I can stay, I cannot prolong it—
like all sentient beings, I must go beyond.
Now I will give you a few last words of counsel.

"Sisters and brothers gathered here, try to listen to me.
Though the black-headed beings are innumerable,
those who follow the teachings can be easily counted.
Those who have entered the Sangha are fewer still.
And those who have achieved siddhi
are like stars in the daytime—
it is scarcely possible to become a Buddha.
Thus the meaning of the Dharma is most important.
Some say there are eighty thousand Dharma doors,
some say four thousand or a countless number.
But they can be summarized in nine vehicles.

"The nine vehicles are arranged in three stages,
leading up to the Āti.
The meaning of the Āti is divided into
vision, meditation, action,
and fruit, which is the highest Dharma.
The vision is free from conceptualization as subject and object;
the meditation is the natural continuity of experience;
the action is unwavering centeredness, free from any delusion.
The fruit is the natural radiant creativity
and perfection of the Three Kāyas.

"The foundations of the Dharma are indicated:
Externally, follow the teachings of the Vinaya,
and you will naturally be respected by others—
there will be no contradiction between inside and outside.
Internally, follow the Dharma practices of the Sūtras,
and you will naturally accumulate the causes of virtue.

Rely upon the basic Abhidharma philosophy,
learn the tenets of the different schools,
and you will end all doubts, exaggeration, and prejudice.
These three are the foundation of the Dharma—
without these means, you cannot grasp the Teachings.

"Be heedful of Kriyā teachings on pure behavior,
and you will cleanse the stain of habitual proclivities.
Be heedful of the Upāya teachings on purity of mind,
and you will naturally become accustomed to Dharma meditation.
Be heedful of the Yoga teachings on vision and realization,
and blessings and compassion will naturally pervade your being.

"Enter the devotional practice of the Mahāyoga,
and vision, meditation, and action will naturally arise.
Enter the patterning and energy of the Anuyoga practice,
and you will naturally bring forth powerful realization.
The Āti itself purifies the snying-thig,
and instantly Buddhahood is achieved.
You need no other teaching.
Rely on the example of my life,
all you who follow after me, the Mother,
and you will find benefit for both yourselves and others,
and achieve the fruit."

Then the Bhutanī girl Kālasiddhī bowed low and circumambulated
mTsho-rgyal many times and asked:

"If you, the Mother, pass into the expanse of space,
how can we in Tibet enter the Mantrayāna?
How can we master the profound path?
Who will help us clear away obstacles
and bring forth the benefits of our own being?
Please stay and guard the land of Tibet with your compassion."

mTsho-rgyal answered her:

"Kye Ma!
Listen, lineaged girl, Mantra-born youthful siddhī-ma,

teacher of the virtuous Dharma to sentient beings.
You have an enlightened attitude and the conditions for growth.
In the future those on the Mantra path will gather here.
Whoever would practice the profound path—
first seek a teacher with the appropriate characteristics.
Ask the teacher with all the right signs
for empowerment and offer perfect commitment in return.
Practice continuously until you bring
patterning and energy under your control.
Ask for the three empowerments, and purify your passions.
Explore the meaning of the Four Joys for six months,
or until you perfect the auspicious bodily marks and signs.
Mingle male and female energies,
and mix upper and lower energies in the proper manner.

"Let male aid female, and female aid male—
let each penetrate the other as in weaving.
Develop your potential,
increase and purify your creativity and bliss.
If you do not merge emptiness with bliss,
it is senseless—not at all the Mantra path.
Practice the co-emergence of bliss and emptiness,
guard the yab and yum commitments as you would your eyes.

"Skillfully handle the five ritual implements;
avoid the demon obstacles.
Do not let the vitality diminish
and explore perfect creativity.
If your understanding begins to lessen,
strive to make it complete.

"Do not lose yourself in ordinary physical agitation—
that is for ordinary men and women.
Meditate upon me with the intensity of a deity.
Visualize me in your four root cakras
as a central figure within a host of deities.
Strive for mantric energy in your speech—
without that energy, your practice is merely ordinary passion.

"Spread the world of illusion before you
and pierce it to the marrow.
Search every part of it, drive into it with your mind.
Let vitality itself pervade your mind.
If you let the signs of vitality lessen,
it is like killing a Buddha.

"Bring whatever happens under your own power.
Hold on to ecstasy and find its essence—
otherwise the secret teachings are meaningless.
Perfect the fruit of your passion, the Great Bliss.

"Carefully guard the naturalness of experience.
Protect your commitment as if it were your life and body—
if you let it go, there is no expiation.
Take all this to heart; this is the teaching.

"Those who enter the door of the secret teaching
may develop great desire—control this.
Cast deceit and pride into the sea!
Burn desire, burn it with the fire of your mind's intensity.
Throw profit, gain, and transgression to the winds.
Let doubts and confusion disappear.

"Keep your secret behavior from others—
vow not to reveal the secret doors.
If you succeed, if marks and signs of heat appear,
do not show them.
Do not let go of the three roots,
the lama, the yidam, the ḍākinī, and rely upon your yidam.
Do not stop the continuous cycle of practice.
Keep a compassionate enlightened mind and help others.

"Dedicate merit, and remain detached from its object.
All this is appropriate general behavior.
Act thus for the heart of siddhi.
You and I are the same, one in essence—
we will manifest together in the future to benefit beings."

Then sBe Ye-shes snying-po asked:

"E Ma! Ye-shes mTsho-rgyal-ma!
For my benefit, and that of others like me,
I ask for your oral instructions.
Stay and bless us with your compassion –
please never part from us."

mTsho-rgyal answered him:

"Kye Ho! Listen, Ye-shes snying-po!
Ask the Lord Lama for blessings,
ask the four ḍākinīs how to act effectively.
Portents and signs will come when they are needed.
Here is a simple explanation of how to act:
Listen once again, Ye-shes snying.

"Behave in a respectable manner,
following the basic Vinaya teachings;
this way you will easily guide the common people.
But practice the Mantrayāna energetically,
and you will quickly achieve realization.

"In your practice of the Dharma, earnestly follow the Sūtras,
so that the source teachings take root.
Do the practices of the yidam,
and you will attain siddhi and whatever you desire.

"Questions will clear up with study of the Abhidharma,
and you will be freed from all doubts.
Integrate the practices of patterning, energy, and vitality,
and as you perfect them, signs of warmth will quickly come.

"Practice the purifications of the Kriyā teachings,
and soon all stains will be cleared away.
Strengthen the essences of vision, meditation, and action,
and you will certainly reap future benefits.

"Meditating upon the fruit, the actionless Great Perfection,
the Chos-zad transcends the subjective mind –

this is the Great Perfection.
Your prayers for sentient beings will be boundless,
without distinctions,
and you will do immeasurable good for all beings."

Then rMa Rin-chen-mchog asked:

"Lama, Lady mTsho-rgyal-ma!
If you go to the land of Orgyan,
what will the brothers and sisters gathered here do?
Who will give us blessings?
Is there no way for us to stay together—
must we be separated from you?"

As he finished, tears streamed down his face, and Ye-shes mTsho-rgyal
answered him:

"Kye Ho! Listen, yogi!
You have achieved the mantric siddhis;
you have an excellent mind and can benefit beings.
I, the Lady Ye-shes mTsho-rgyal,
by the compassionate blessings of the Guru,
now have achieved the fruit, complete creativity and perfection.
Tomorrow I go to the land of Orgyan.
Brothers and sisters gathered here, ask and blessings will come.
Hold fast to the supreme Dharma for your own good,
and help others without arrogance or pride.
Through vision, meditation, and action you will be freed.

"Rely on my words which you have asked for;
draw reverence and humility from your very bones.
Meditate only on the brilliance
of the Lama's pure awareness; visualize the Lama;
let the visualization penetrate you,
so that you and the lama become one.
Whatever experiences arise, just let them be.

"I am the master of all samsara and nirvana.
If you know Ye-shes mTsho-rgyal—

you know she resides in the hearts of all beings,
and manifests in all realms and all sense fields,
and incarnates again and again
in all the twelve links of dependent origination.
You know that we are inseparable;
we always have been and always will be together.
But if you do not know me, you are tied to outside appearances.

"If you cut away the root, the one mind-itself will arise from within
and pervade all the 'outside' with great Pristine Awareness.
Innate bliss will whirl like the ocean,
and insight will penetrate like the golden eye of the great fish.

"Use and guard this deep experience and bliss;
leap beyond and through to perfect creativity;
run and roll through the fields of appearance;
disappear and fly up into space.
In the broad expanse of great Pristine Awareness
merge into the ocean of the nectar of Great Bliss.
Amid vivid symbols and dancing forms,
amid letters of flashing light,
the Chos-nyid mngon-gsum
and the Nyams-snang-gong will expand.
The Rig-pa-tshad will mightily take hold
until it dissolves into the primordial expanse
of the Chos-nyid zad-tshad.
Use this means, and we will never be parted."

Thus she spoke. Then 'O-bran gZhon-nu-dpal asked:

"Kye Ma! Ye-shes mTsho-rgyal-ma!
If you go to the land of Orgyan,
how can ordinary apathetic uninspired people like me
produce vision, meditation, and action?
Would you give me a few more words of instruction?"

Thus he asked, and she answered him:

"E Ma Ho! Listen, faithful gZhon-nu-dpal!
Until you perfect the skills of the six vehicles,

I will not see you flying with joy and ease,
like birds that nest upon the cliffs.
But by the powerful beating of the wings
of creativity and perfection,
you can cut through the razor-like winds
and go or stay wherever you desire.

"I myself as well, the Lady mTsho-rgyal,
when first I practiced, had not perfected my creativity and skill,
and though I wished for enlightenment,
my body was slow to respond.

"But when I had perfected that creativity
through the Developing and Perfecting Stages,
through the Great Perfection,
my heavy corporeal body was transformed into light.

"Soon I will stand before the Orgyan Guru,
so I give you a few last words.
Vision is the general defining characteristic of the Dharma.
What does this mean?
Your practice is not just emptiness—
clear-seeing radiance and pure awareness are present.
But as nothing is established as eternal,
this presentation is naturally empty.
The essential nature of experience is called vision.
With regards to vision, how does it work?
When you do the visualizations of the Developing Stage,
this is the transformation of yourself into deity.
When the visualization reaches out to all sentient beings
and returns, this is responsive compassion.
When Perfection is attained, this is Mahāmudrā.
The essential nature of vision is free
from either the eternal or the transitory.
This vision is self-realized, seeing itself.
It is not a looking upon the realization, the seeing,
but that very seeing awareness.
This is what is designated vision.

"Meditation is the ground of the Dharma.
What does this mean? In the flow of your practice,
through continually and steadily inspecting
the essential nature of vision,
you create a meditation completely unbounded.
This is called evenness and composure.
How does this meditation work?
Whether you are practicing the Developing or Perfecting Stages,
the experience is significant and yet unconceptualized.
Whatever happens, happens within continuing concentration.
A meditation of either the Developing or Perfecting Stages
must be free from three conditions:
instability, cloudiness, and dullness.
Hold the experience without distraction and without concepts—
such evenness and composure is meditation.

"Action is the activity of the Dharma.
What does this mean? In the flow of your practice,
when you reach the meditation endowed with the depth of vision,
you will see all the various kinds of action,
all characterized by continuity and nondistraction.
How does this action work?
The exact manifesting of action is not specific;
whatever happens, you remain continuously
and incontrovertibly with the experience,
using the experience for spiritual advancement.

"In truth, whether walking, moving, sleeping, eating, or sitting,
on all the paths of action, remain in contact with your practice,
be it the Developing or Perfecting practice,
the Great Perfection practice, or some other.
Never allow yourself to be separated from your practice.
By such action you are endowed with the very epitome of action.

"This is my final spoken instruction,
and now I am going to rNga-yab Island.
Fill all Tibet with these teachings,
and all who are filled with devotion will be blessed."

Thus she spoke. Then Shel-dkar-bza' rDo-rje-mtsho asked:

"Kye Ma! Mother of all Tibet!
Most special Guide of all gathered here, there is no other like you.
Please don't take your compassion from me!
Please take me with you to Padma-'od.
But if my evil karma is so heavy that I cannot follow you,
please give many more teachings and instructions."

Choked with tears, she was barely able to speak and collapsed on the ground. When she had come to herself, mTsho-rgyal answered her:

"E Ma Ho! Listen, faithful daughter of Shel-dkar-bza'!
Wisdom Ḍākinī, Vajra Ocean!
This body, formed of flesh and blood, is a fetter,
and being inferior, oppresses you.
But if you meditate using the patterning and energy practices,
you will have the means to wander through space.

"If you bring energy and mind under your own power,
you will truly achieve what is called siddhi.
Though your mind is deceitful and fraught with the five poisons,
though your life stream is naturally unsettled
and your communication bound by ordinary conceptualization,
they can be purified.

"If you want to achieve Buddhahood,
meditate upon the Mahāmudrā.
Liberation—the unity of openness and Pristine Awareness—
is not different from Buddhahood.

"The transitory aggregates are deeply deceitful,
the ground of all good and evil.
Cut them off. If you want to obtain the Rainbow Body,
meditate upon the Great Perfection Āti.

"If you employ the Chos-nyid zad-sa,
you will be truly spontaneous and free from karmic action.
Then you have the means to move freely through space.
For a little while only, until enlightenment, your body is coarse.

"If you want to know the way to Padma-'od
listen to this teaching.
Do not for an instant lose contact with your own root lama.
Visualize him, honor him, respect and have faith in him;
pray and ask for the four empowerments and blessings.
Meditate upon him as a burning light always within your heart,
and visualize merging with his three gates
until you become one and inseparable.

"Meditate thus upon the Mahāmudrā.
Follow the path, gain understanding, and guard your insight,
draw forth your wisdom, and carefully cultivate
creativity, openness, and bliss.
Bring dualistic and obsessing objects into the path.
Purify them profoundly in the Great Perfection,
and enter the ground of the final Āti.
You will have eleven more births,
aiding beings of Tibet with your skillful means.
Then come to Padma-'od.

"Your manifestation will be known as
rDo-rje bde-chen Padma-mtsho.
You and the disciple Nam-mkha'i snying-po
will merge skillful means and discriminating wisdom.
Together you will scatter tens of millions of teachings
in the barbarous border countries of cannibals,
and benefit beings with meaning, not just words.
You will be the body consort of the one named Nam-mkha'i snying-po.
You will remain for thirty thousand years, as men count them,
and then you will come to Padma-'od,
never again parting from the Lord Guru."

Thus mTsho-rgyal prophesied and gave many instructions.

Then La-gsum rGyal-ba byang-chub bowed before mTsho-rgyal and circumambulated her many times. He presented mTsho-rgyal with a mandala of seven turquoises, the principal one radiating a thousand shining blue lights, and asked:

191

"E Ma Ho! Wonderful Lady who never forgets!
Master of the secret teachings of Padmasambhava,
Sarasvatī, Mistress of Great Bliss and the most profound wisdom,
mTsho-rgyal-ma, sole sun in the dark land of Tibet!

"Now, before you go to the southwest once and for all,
please give me, as a great blessing,
a few more words of instruction.
Let them be complete, essential, profound,
sharp and quick to succeed.

"I ask for the teaching that brings Buddhahood in one lifetime.
And I ask also, please, how many times will I be reborn,
and when will I meet with you again, ḍākinī?
Please, do not part from us yet—
protect us with your compassion."

When he asked for these teachings, Ye-shes mTsho-rgyal gave to him:
the mKha'-spyod sprul-sku'i snying-thig, the Phyi-mdo dang bstun-pa
mkha'-'gro sku-gsum rkang-sgrub, and the sPyod-yul 'dul-ba dkar-po,
the Thog-'beb drag-spyod rnam-gsum, the Bla-ma sku-gsum rkyang-
sgrub, the Byin-rlabs dbang-gi sgo-mo, and the gZer-'joms lta-ba cig
chod, the rTags-tshad so-ba dgu 'dres, the gNad-kyi me-btsa' rnam-
gsum, the rDzas sngags dmigs-yul brgya-rtsa, the rJes-gcod lcam-bu
gzer-them sogs spyi tshan-bcu, the Nang gsang-sngags dang bstun-pa
bla-ma mkha'-'gro zung-'jug-tu bsgrub-thabs, the bsGom-pa sgyu-ma
'phrul-'gros, the rTsa-rlung 'gag don bcu-pa, and the Man-ngag gcig
chog zab-mo, the bsGyur-sbyang sbel-ba rnam-gsum, the mKa'-'gro'i
bang mdzod mig gcig, the mKha'-'gro'i dmar-pa snying-gcig, the
mKha'-'gro gnyen-po srog gcig, the Man-ngag sngags-kha sum-sbrel,
the 'Od-zer zhabs-pa rnam-gsum, the dPa'-bo gyad stobs rnam-gsum
spyi tshan bcu-gcig, the gSang-ba man-ngag ltar bla-ma mkha'-'gro
rang lus dbyer-med-du bsgrub-thabs, the lTa-ba phyag-rgya chen-po,
the 'Bras-bu rdzogs-chen chig-chod, the Man-ngag gtum-mo sum-
sbrel, the gDams-ngag thos chog rnam-gsum, the Nyams-len bsgom-
pa rnam-gsum, the gCig chog mun chos rnam-gsum, the Las-phran
dgos-pa rnam-gsum, the rTen-'brel me-long rnam-gsum, the rGyab
chos dgos-pa rnam-gsum, the bKa'-srung myur mgyogs rnam-gsum,

and the Drag sngags gnad-kha rnam-gsum, and so on, and twelve various final teachings.

rGyal-ba byang-chub and seven other disciples, having received these teachings, reached the liberation of the highest radiant light and were freed.

Then Ye-shes mTsho-rgyal made these prophecies:

"E Ma Ho! Listen attentively, rGyal-ba byang-chub-pa.
Listen well, Lord Dharma Protector.
You were Ārya Sa-le, my heroic consort of skillful means.
In a former time, the time of Sa-le, when you were that Ācārya,
you and I merged skillful means and wisdom.
Together we practiced profound and secret teachings,
and because of those blessings,
I achieved liberation in this life.
And yet, though you and I were intimate friends then,
still sometimes you had doubts, you wavered, you scoffed.

"Thus, you will continue to undergo future rebirths,
and though you will be a great siddha,
you will meet with obstacles.
You will be troubled by gossip,
exaggerated praise and blame, abuse and evil counsel.
Your benefit to beings will be counteracted by hindrances.
But whatever happens, remember, this is due to previous actions.
Finally, you will become one with Padmasambhava and mTsho-rgyal.

"For thirteen future births, you will aid beings:
In the future, toward the end of that time,
you will manifest to the west of this Mount Meru
as a most wrathful being.
You will have the name of Nam-mkha'
and the form of a fierce Vajra Ḍāka.
Three births more and you will be called sTag-shams,
and you will stop the winds of karma and come to Padma-'od.
Then you and I will part no more.

193

With means and wisdom we will manifest
to break the transmigratory cycle for beings.

"That will be a time to meditate,
developing the profound power of altruistic prayer;
a time to expand, with the essences of many profound secret teachings;
a time to mature, as the result of profound meditation;
a time to develop, stirring up the creativity
of the profound Developing and Perfecting Stages;
a time to be born,
as the good result of profound transformative karma;
a time to move, like the great clouds of profound blessing;
a time to make fall the rain
from the expanse of profound compassion.
You will achieve your goal, Ārya Sa-le-ba.
The power of truth will come, rGyal-ba byang-chub-pa.
For now, take this carefully to heart and practice."

Then night fell on the evening of the eighth day.

Then, it is said, there came flying from the Dākinī Island of Orgyan,
the twelve types of nyul-le spirits and one hundred twenty million
different dākinīs. At midnight the life-lords arrived with the breath-
takers, the flesh-eaters and blood-drinkers, the bone-chewers, and the
like, the twelve types of dākinīs who devour parts of a human being.
They numbered fifty million and five thousand and five hundred, so it
is said. Then came beasts of prey from the regions of the land and sky.
When half had passed by, one hundred twenty million and one hundred twenty thousand dākinīs of the world and of the twelve times of
day rose up and mounted upon the backs of the animals.

Some rode upon the various carnivorous beasts, like the lions; others
rode upon the various kinds of winged creatures, like the garudas.
Some rode upon the various powerful animals, like the elephants;
others rode the various game animals, like the antelopes. The whole
region was filled with all sorts of creatures of varied forms, fearful apparitions, as well as men of all sorts, and other kinds of beings.

At dawn, ḍākinīs came from the four regions of Orgyan and the twelve islands. Some were pure white, others were varied colors—red, green, blue, and so forth. Some were light yellow or reddish, light green or blue or brown, as well as white; others were red and white, or yellow and white, or green and white, or deep blue and white. Some were half white and half red, blue, yellow, or green.

In their hands the ḍākinīs held various signs of their lineages: various types of ritual implements, daggers, and such. They wore silk robes, bone garlands and diadems, scarves and swirling skirts and veils. They carried musical instruments—thighbone trumpets, skull drums, and such like, too many to enumerate . . . but it is said there were fifty million and two hundred thousand of them.

From the break of dawn until sunrise, the ḍākinīs danced in sixty-eight mandalas around strikingly beautiful female figures of great power and skill who, themselves, danced upon lotuses. Rainbows crisscrossed the sky, all the earth was filled with the smell of incense, and all of space was filled with ḍākinīs.

During the time between midday and dusk, it is said the ḍākinīs came from thirty-two holy places, ten dwellings of the Herukas, the eight great cemeteries, and two hot springs, each demonstrating her special skills.

They did various dances and showed various gestures, made various different kinds of music, sang many different songs, and performed many dances. They demonstrated their great dexterity, and then made various offerings accompanied by various different kinds of glances, praising mTsho-rgyal and honoring her. Then all together, they stopped and seated themselves upon the ground.

mTsho-rgyal circled the great assembly and magically distributed the offering sweets to all the men and women who were gathered there; to the ḍākinīs, she gave even more wondrous things. Then each drank a skull cup of beer and, totally satisfied, sat down to listen to mTsho-rgyal.

mTsho-rgyal spoke the symbolic initiations of the secret ḍākinīs to all the beings gathered there. Ḍakinis and ordinary people mingled together, and all were established on the level of Non-turning-back, soon to reach liberation.

At dusk of the ninth day, they went from the heart cave on the side of the mountain of Zab-bu, to the mountain peak of the Copper-colored Mountain. At first light, mTsho-rgyal opened the mandala of one letter, the blessing of the Lama's heart. At the same time, there came spirits and demons of all kinds beyond measure, uncountable, innumerable, incomparable beings. Some had three heads, some one head, some no head, some five heads, some nine heads, some one hundred heads, and so on. Some had one leg, some up to one hundred thousand, and some even more.

In the midst of a radiant blue light, the queen of demonesses appeared, sent by the Lotus Guru with an invitation for mTsho-rgyal. Lights rushed about in the sky as she passed among the crowds of beings. Then, at daybreak, the entire assembly circumambulated mTsho-rgyal. Her eleven faithful close disciples and others—humans, ḍākas, ḍākinīs, demons, gods, and spirits—all bowed with great faith before the Lady. With tears streaming down their faces, they asked her:

"Kye Ma! Kye Hud! Ye-shes Ḍākinī!
Guru of mankind, Ye-shes mTsho-rgyal-ma!
You, the sole mother of all Tibet, are leaving for the sky.
What can we preta-like hungry orphans do now?
Please, stay a while longer to protect Tibet.

"But if you cannot stay, if you must go, what will happen?
Will the teachings in Tibet flourish or decline?
What will happen to the followers of the doctrine?
What will happen when demons manifest in the world?
And what can we do to counteract such occurrences?
We ask you to tell us.

"In particular, how will you manifest,
with what teaching, in what place, and with what name?
Please, do not hide anything, do not keep it a secret,
do not speak symbolically or in fragments.
All-wise and powerful one, we ask you to answer.

"Specifically, what will become
of the three parts of your life story?
What will become of your oral lineage,
higher and lower, mother and son, one and many?
Especially what of the heart-drops of your body,
your ḍākinī incarnations?
What of your spoken treasures?
What worthy people should prepare them?
Where should they be hidden, and who should hide them?
What gter masters will come, and when will they find them?
We ask you to explain completely and precisely what will occur.

"We brothers and sisters gathered here, what will we do?
Where will we go, where look for hope?
Who will clear up our obstacles
and help us when the time comes to die?
Alas! Alas! Look quickly upon us with compassion!"

Having said all this, they looked to mTsho-rgyal for extensive predictions, which are presented in summary here:

"E Ma Ho! Listen attentively, gods and men of Tibet!
Listen well, faithful, blessed ones.
I myself, the great Mother, Ye-shes mTsho-rgyal-ma,
have been protecting Tibet now for 111 years.
The Dharma Protector King Ral-pa-can, Khri Ral-phyag-rdor,
incarnation of Vajrapāṇi,
will continue to support the Sūtra and Mantra teachings
as did his ancestors.

"But his younger brother, the demon manifestation Glang,
will conspire with the ministers.
The elder brother will be killed, and Glang will seize power.
Not so much as the names of the early Sūtra and Mantra
will be left in Tibet.

"This king will encourage the ten unwholesome acts
and the five inexpiable sins;

he will instigate improper laws harmful to the Buddhadharma.
The greatest Dharma practitioners will be killed,
the lesser ones banished,
and the ordinary ones made servants.

"But yogi priests in the villages will keep the teachings alive.
Although lHa-sa and bSam-yas will be left in ruin,
dPal-gyi rdo-rje will remember the prophecy.

"He will kill the demon king and then go to lower Khams.
sMar and gYo both will preserve the Vinaya texts
like the last precious flame in a lamp.
Then ten monks will assemble at Glang-thang sGrol-ma.
The teachings will enter dBus and gTsang again
like a shining light,
and again the Dharma will grow and spread throughout Tibet.

"The wisdom, power, and nobility of the Mantrayāna
will fill the earth,
though some will still perform
improper and hypocritical practices.
The incarnation of the speech of Orgyan,
the Master of Peace, Śāntarakṣita,
will be called Atīśa. He will do much to spread
both the Sūtra and Mantra teachings.

"I, mTsho-rgyal, will be reborn as Jayākarā,
appearing in the family of the 'Brom.
I will be close to the great lotsāwa and will spread the teachings.
When the lifespan is seventy years,
I will fill the world with brilliance
by explaining the Sūtra and Mantra Dharmas.

"After that, a time will come when the lifespan is sixty years.
The Dharma King will manifest as one named Sa
and uphold the teachings.
Later his lineage will decline in power
and the patron-leader relationship
with Mongolia will be disconnected.

"At this time Padmasambhava will produce a body manifestation
called 'Brog-mi who will spread the teaching
of path and result, increasing and establishing
a strong tradition of both Sūtra and Mantra.

"For a while it will seem
like the time of Śākyamuni Buddha,
but then a time will come when the land will become fragmented.
The secret teachings will prosper again
when the lifespan is fifty years,
and the Dharma tradition will spread as it did in former times.

"A heart manifestation of Padmasambhava
will come from the southern valleys.
He will be called Mar-pa and will spread the Mantrayāna teachings.
Again, I, mTsho-rgyal, will be his body consort,
and one known as Mi-la will develop siddhi
after practicing austerities.

"Padmasambhava's quality incarnation will arise at Dvags-po,
and the 'Bri, sTag, Kar, and 'Brug schools
will flow forth like rivers from Mount Ti-se,
forming an ocean of Dharma
and leading beings to the place of ultimate bliss.

"When men are old by age forty,
the teachings will become divided;
men will come to rely on the Mongols,
and the teachings will lose their subtlety.
The land of Tibet will again be fragmented,
and a time will come when the vision of the world is diseased.

"Then Padmasambhava's activity incarnation will be known as Karma.
The teachings will spread in the country of Tibet
and be prolonged for thirty years.
The whole realm will be filled with the sounds of MAṆI.

"Then, when men age in thirty years,
the teachings of dGe-ldan will arise;

Padmasambhava's heart incarnation will come from dBus,
and Tibet will be joyful and happy like a land of the gods.

"A powerful man from Zahor
will spread the Buddha's teachings
throughout dBus, gTsang, and Khams.
After that རྗ྄ེན་ཀཁ་བ྄ས྄ན྄ལ་ཕ྄ན྄ ཆ྄ཐ྄ན྄ཕ྄ཆ྄ལ྄ཕ྄ན྄
the land of Tibet will fall upon unhappy times,
and again be divided into many parts;
the Mongols will become very influential
and be looked to for support.

"When men are old at twenty years,
a speech incarnation of Padmasambhava
will come from lHo-brag
and establish all beings in bliss.
A Dharma ruler with a birthmark on his shoulder
will appear from the land of Li-yul.

"When aging occurs at ten years,
the teaching will be found only in the border regions.
Then, after manifesting a kalpa and an era,
the essence of earth will deteriorate,
and there will come the dark age
of bDud-'joms Nag-po gya-chu.

"After that, Maitreya will come and lift up the world.
For an era, things will look up,
and for two ages they will go downhill.
Then will come three more eras and four periods,
long and short, so it is said.
These are only the very general characteristics
of things to come.

"Throughout these times of change and trouble,
look to the teachings of Padmasambhava
for ways to counteract these trends—
these words of truth will never fail you.

"I myself, Ye-shes mTsho-rgyal,
will also never take my compassion from Tibet;
I will continue to manifest in the future for all beings.
I will lead all beings to bliss
by emanating the light rays of skillful means.

"In particular, I will produce
five body, five speech, and five heart incarnations,
five quality, and five activity incarnations.
These twenty-five will continually protect Tibet.
They will produce again ten millions of manifestations,
remanifesting, and manifesting again beyond that,
until the world of beings is completely exhausted.
All of these will be Great Mothers, possessing bliss,
representations of the All-good,
uniting space and being, openness and Pristine Awareness
in the centerless expanse of bliss.

"I will simply summarize the next five hundred years:
Tibet will come to be like a great military camp,
bristling with spears.
For a time it will be filled with fortresses,
on the plains and in the mountains,
at the ends and mouths of canyons.
Heretic demonesses will lead beings on wrong and twisted paths.
For a time a reversed gcod teaching will spread across the land.

"The speech incarnation of my body aspect
will appear with the characteristics of Tārā.
The body incarnation of my body aspect
will come as Kun-dga' bzang-mo.
The heart incarnation of my body aspect
will come as dPal-mo of dBus.
The quality incarnation of my body aspect
will be called gYas-ru-bu.
The activity incarnation of my body aspect
will be from Tam-yul in Khams.

And they will establish
the profound and secret Mantrayāna teachings,
and will bring forth the teachings of the gCod
and the profound Perfections.

"Bu will train beings by the four lion edicts,
but after some time, Tibet will become
cemetery food for the Mongols.
dBus and gTsang will be separated like the eyes on dice,
but the pure Buddhadharma will be like a burning butter lamp.

"In a time when a whirlwind of terrible obstacles
clouds the air, Padmasambhava has prophesied
the coming of one hundred gter masters.
The hidden treasure teachings of the Mantrayāna
will fill the world with bliss.

"But a hundred heretical and false gter masters
will also come fabricating their own treasures—
the use of black magic and witchcraft
based upon the false gter will spread.

"At that time, the body incarnation of my speech aspect
will manifest at mNga'-ri:
She will be named sNyan-grags
and will distinguish the true and false gter.

"The speech incarnation of my speech aspect
will come as a lady from dBus:
She will manifest the signs of Orgyan
and will reinstate the ways of practice,
showing the marks and powers of Mantrayāna achievement.

"The heart incarnation of my speech aspect
will come from rTa-shod;
She will manifest the signs of the Lotus
and will perform profound gter activities,
giving siddhis to those who are ready.

"The quality incarnation of my speech aspect
will come from Kong-po:
Named Bu, she will comfort those in low conditions,
and will completely remove the obstacles
working against the gter Masters.

"The activity incarnation of my speech aspect
will come from gTsang:
She will be named Jo-mo
and will perform the Vajravārāhī practices,
filling the world with the blessings of Vārāhī's countenance.

"After that, there will come a time of great border wars,
violent as a stormy sea.
The Sa and the 'Bri will fight incessantly,
each holding tightly to his own sectarian bias.
The old and new traditions will split apart,
and divisiveness will reign.
It will be a time of impurity
for both Dharma and non-Dharma.

"The body incarnation of my heart aspect
will come from Nyag-sa:
Named Orgyan, she will be a great Siddhā
and increase meditative experience and realization.

"The speech incarnation of my heart aspect
will be called bSod-nams dpal-'dren:
She will be a commoner from the North,
and will teach those who are ready
how to realize siddhi at the time of death.
She will aid many worthy ones and give them siddhi.

"The heart incarnation of my heart aspect
will be called E:
She will come from dBus
to lead those with proper connection to the lands of the ḍākinīs.
She will show the path of freedom
to many practitioners of patterning and energy.

"The quality incarnation of my heart aspect
will come from lHo-brag:
But it is uncertain what form this incarnation will take
in leading beings to bliss.

"The activity incarnation of my heart aspect
will come from the land of Nepal:
She will establish many beings in the Dharma
by using skillful means.

"Some time after, the Dharma King will manifest five emanations.
The ruler in gTsang will be like a firefly;
the palaces will be like mirages;
good news will be like the distant song of gandharvas;
the bad advice of the clever will spread like poison;
and the Dharma teachings will be like a light about to go out.
Tibet will patronize the Mongols, and give them gifts of brocade.

"The body incarnation of my quality aspect
will be a ḍākinī from dBus.
The speech incarnation of my quality aspect
will be sGrol-ma from Khams.
The heart incarnation of my quality aspect
will be sNye-mor sprul-sku.
The quality incarnation of my quality aspect
will be a teacher from the North.
The activity incarnation of my quality aspect
will be from gTsang-rong.
It is uncertain exactly how they will manifest,
but by their magical abilities and extraordinary perception,
they will lead those who are ready to Great Bliss.

"After that, the highlands and lowlands will go their own ways;
the mountains, valleys, and roads will be divided up.
The populace will rise up, and everyone will want to be a ruler;
the deceitful will take the part of the Mongols.

"Even the Dharma practitioners will fight—
the monks will become militant,

while the paṇḍitas carry on the burden of plowing.
Businessmen, ladies, and ordinary people
will pronounce upon the Dharma.
People will act like children and create much bad karma.
lHa-sa will be destroyed by water, bSam-yas by wind,
Khra-'brug will not last; its four corners will fall to ruin.

"The body incarnation of my activity aspect
will come to mChims-phu.
The speech incarnation of my activity aspect
will manifest at mNga'-ri.
The heart incarnation of my activity aspect
will appear at sPu-bo.
The quality incarnation of my activity aspect
will come from mDo-khams.
The activity incarnation of my activity aspect
will be dPon-mo from dBus.
There is some uncertainty as to their various forms.
They will lead bounded beings to unbounded places;
all those who are ready they will lead to Great Bliss.

"The dispersal of the succeeding manifestations
and their reincarnations is uncertain,
but they will continue to clear away obstacles
and benefit all beings.
From now until this cyclical world is emptied,
they will manifest and reincarnate
innumerable times without cessation.

"In the future, whoever meditates upon patterning and energy
will experience a loosening of hard materiality
until the world assumes the form of a dream.
Again and again I will manifest as the Great Seal, the Mahāmudrā.
The obstacles of the worthy will be removed,
and their spiritual development procured.
Quickly they will develop bliss and warmth,
and make friends with realization.

"Concerning the three sections of my life story,
the story of the mother,
the expanded version should be concealed here
at the peak of Zab-bu Mountain.
The summary version should be hidden at lHo-brag,
at the stairs to heaven.
The medium version should be hidden in Khams,
in a southern valley.
The higher and lower versions
of my special transmission teachings
and the mKha'-'gro'i snying-thig,
each of these I have given as oral instructions.
In the future, those three fortunate ones,
sBe, Byang-chub, and rMa, will bring them forth.

"In particular, there are nine auspicious circumstances
connected with this history:
First, if one named Chos-dbang finds a gter treasure,
his benefit to beings will be famous throughout the realm,
and his reputation as a teacher will reach even to China.

"But even if this auspicious omen
does not come about in the proper order,
a certain bKra-shis, who comes from upper Tibet, will appear;
or if one Ral-pa lcang-lo-can draws a gter forth,
he will benefit beings throughout dBus and gTsang,
and finally spread his teachings to Nepal.

"But even if this auspicious event
does not occur in the proper order,
one called rDo-rje, said to be a great Hero, a dPa'-bo,
will appear in the southern valleys and snow mountains.
If he draws forth a gter,
the teachings will extend throughout mDo-khams,
and finally even Hor will receive his aid.

"But should this not occur in the proper order,
one called Ra-dza from the lowlands will find gter,

after having accumulated great power through ascetic practices.
Another rDo-rje from sPu-bo in the east,
who is also called Kun-dga', will draw them out.
Beings will be benefitted, but less and less.

"But should none of these happen, still there is one final chance.
The gter will be found by three ladies,
or just spontaneously appear.
If that happens, only the immediate region will reap the benefit.

"Such are the nine auspicious omens which may occur in the future.
Should only one be successful,
the teachings will still grow and spread,
continuing for five times five hundred years.

"There will be a place called Ka-thog in the east,
a center for the teachings of Guru Seng-ge sgra-sgrog;
Padmasambhava buried thirty treasures there,
on the shoulder of a mountain like a haughty lion.
The discovery of these profound treasures
will be a great and good omen in the future,
and Padmasambhava and his consort
will again help the beings of that region.

"I, mTsho-rgyal, will manifest as Dam-pa rgyal-mtshan.
The secret mantric Āti teachings will last until the end;
though from time to time, they may decline,
yet again their power will gradually rise.
This has been the final disclosure of mTsho-rgyal's teachings.
I have given you many kind words of counsel and instruction.

"Now mTsho-rgyal cannot stay much longer.
Meditate and pray—speed up your practice!
All of you gathered here and all who will study in the future,
keep my teachings and predictions within your hearts."

After disclosing all this, mTsho-rgyal placed her right hand upon the
Bhutanī bKra-shis spyi-'dren, and an eight-petalled blue lotus appeared
which changed into the syllables HŪM PHAṬ and dissolved into the

right side of the Lady's heart. Her left hand she placed upon the Nepali Kālasiddhī, and a sixteen-petalled red lotus appeared, which became sixteen vowels and the symbol for HRĪ which dissolved into the left side of the Lady's heart.

At dusk of the ninth day, the Lord of the four Great Guardians, and those beings bound by inner, outer, and secret oaths, twelve representatives of the eight classes of spirits, came and welcomed mTsho-rgyal, saying: "Now, this is the final invitation to rNga-yab Ḍākinī Island. Come, Knowledge-holder, Great Radiant Blue Light."

All the gods and men of Tibet tried their hardest to postpone her departure one last time. They pleaded with her and circumambulated her nine times. All the great mountain spirits and land gods of Tibet appeared to entreat her: rDo-rje legs-pa of gTsang, rMa-chen spom-ra of the east, Rong-btsan me-'bar of the south, mTsho-sman rgyal-mo of the north, Gang-bzang-ha'o of the west, and Li-byin har-legs of dBus, and more. Many great and fierce lords from all the land of Tibet and its neighbors assembled.

In particular, there came the twelve earth goddesses who asked for and received many teachings relevant to gods and men. Much more occurred, but it all cannot be included here for fear of making this account too long.

The next morning, at the dawn of the tenth day, there appeared a radiant eight-petalled lotus of shining light, drawn by four ḍākinīs who beckoned to mTsho-rgyal and invited her to enter.

Again, the Lady raised up her body. In her right hand she held a skull drum, and in her left hand a skull cup. Surrounded by a sphere of light, mTsho-rgyal entered into the radiance of the lotus. At the same time, all of those gathered there cried out: "What will become of Tibet now? What will we do?"

And she answered:

"Kye Ma! Listen, faithful Tibetans!
I am merging with the fundamental, the ground of all that is—
physical pain and suffering are disappearing.

"The conditioned mTsho-rgyal is expanding
into the unconditioned,
and all of the pain and agony of the body's constituents
are disappearing.

"Even the illusion of a body is dissolving,
and all needs for medicines, for cures and bleeding,
are disappearing.

"This is the time for the essentials of training,
and concern with permanence and material things
is disappearing.

"The holy Dharma has transformed my body into light;
this bag of skin and pus and dark flesh
is disappearing.

"The Mother mTsho-rgyal is disappearing into the A;
she need no longer cry out 'Ah!' in pain.

"The son, the inner elements of my body,
is reuniting with the mother, the outer elements.
Her physical remains will disappear into earth and stone.

"The compassion of the Guru has never left me;
his manifestations fill all the world and call out to welcome me.

"This wild lady has done everything;
many times have I come and gone, but now, no longer.
I am a Tibetan wife sent back to her family.
I shall now appear as the Queen, the All-good, the Dharmakāya.

"This self-sufficient black lady
has shaken things up far and wide;
now the shaking will carry me away into the southwest.

"I have finished with intrigues,
with all the fervent cascades of schemes and deceptions;
I will take my winding way into the expanse of the Dharma.

"I have mourned many men of Tibet who have left me behind—
but now I am the one who will go to the land of the Buddhas.

"Do not suffer needlessly. Depend on prayer—
mTsho-rgyal will never depart from those who have devotion.
Just call upon me and I will appear—
dear friends, just summon me and I will return—
I wish the greatest happiness for you all."

Thus she spoke, and at the same time a beautiful five-colored rainbow appeared. Within it was an exquisite deep blue light in the shape of a sesame seed, and mTsho-rgyal disappeared within it. Four ḍākinīs grasped the lotus by its petals and drew it up into the sky, higher and higher, until it disappeared.

All prayed and cried out in one voice:
"Kye Ma! Kye Hud! Ye-shes mTsho-rgyal-ma!
What a terrible thing you are doing!
What little compassion you show us!
If you will no longer protect the Tibetans,
who will help those sentient beings stricken with evil karma?

"When you, Mother, go to the Pure Land,
who will protect the impure and wicked Tibetans?
Mother, when you have gone to the Pure Expanse,
who will lead those beings
caught in the ripening of their bad karma?

"When you, Mother, go to the land of Great Bliss,
who will lead the anguished ones wandering in samsara?
When you, Mother, go to the Lotus Light,
who will lead the beings of Tibet
caught in dark and wild canyons?

"When you, Mother, go to join Padmasambhava,
who will save those of us lost in the desert without refuge?
Kye Ma! Kye Hud! Look upon us still with compassion!
Please, we ask for a few words
of blessing for the land of Tibet.

We also ask for a few words
of farewell for your countrymen.
Have you any way to soothe the sorrow
of those of us gathered here together?
Mother, Lady, enfold us in your compassion.
Ḍākinī, we ask you to lead us to the Lotus Light."

For a long time they lamented, calling out such pleas, bowing to the ground, and crying. Then a brilliant luminous radiance appeared before them, and they heard these words, though no one appeared:

"Kye Ma! Listen, faithful Tibetans!
I am the great Ye-shes mTsho-rgyal-ma!
My destructible parts have united
with the indestructible expanse;
they have become one with the Buddhas
in the realm of Padma-'od, the expanse of the Dharma.
Do not suffer needlessly. Be happy!

"The sentient beings of Tibet suffer endlessly,
harmed by many and varied karmic actions.
But your suffering is self-produced—can't you see that?
The Three Jewels are the refuge place of sufferers—
pray to them one-pointedly with your whole being.
I, the great Ye-shes mTsho-rgyal-ma,
have gone from the impure, the defiled, into space,
but I can still magically manifest to help beings.
Do not suffer needlessly. Rejoice!

"This world is so heavy, weighted down
by the ripening of impure karmic actions.
Don't you see how relying on emotionality leads to misfortune?
The holy Dharma is the way to gain maturity.
Take to heart its teachings on the ten virtues,
such as effort and the others.
I, the great Ye-shes mTsho-rgyal-ma,
because of spiritual maturation,
have gone to the realm of total purity.

My deeds were all for the teaching's benefit,
which will continue without end when I am gone.
Do not suffer needlessly. Be joyful!

"These many and varied unwholesome actions—
don't you see their fruit will ripen in hell?
Exert yourself in the wholesome use of body and speech,
and the lower realms will be purified.
Focus all three doors on striving for the wholesome Dharma.
I, the great Ye-shes mTsho-rgyal-ma,
have gone to the expanse of Great Bliss, free of defilement.
Those connected with me know the means to never fall back.
Do not suffer needlessly. Sing and dance!

"The ocean of samsaric suffering is endless.
To see it is to fear it—if you understand
the suffering pent up in your karmic actions,
you have the means to escape: the holy Lama.
Should you meet an appropriate teacher,
whatever he says, you must do.
I, the great Ye-shes mTsho-rgyal-ma,
have gone to the expanse of space, the Lotus Light.
I will be born into the perfectly pure lotus.
Do not suffer needlessly. Have faith!

"The land of Tibet is dark and savage;
can't you see the stupidity
of fighting painful battles and vying for narrow valleys?
Rely on your meditation retreat, without needs, without actions.
Practice patterning, energy, and vitality,
the Mahāmudrā, the Great Perfection.
I am the great Ye-shes mTsho-rgyal-ma.
If you practice with devotion, my compassion will enfold you.
I go to stand before the Teacher, Padmasambhava—
do not suffer needlessly. Pray!

"Like helpless bubbles are bodies and deeds.
When you see impermanence, that the time of death is uncertain,

when you stop grasping for permanence,
you achieve the siddhi of long life.
Practice until you reach the final stage of Āti.
Kye Ho! Listen, dear ones, and don't cry!

"My compassion will never change or fade—
to see me as gone is an eternalistic viewpoint.
I have not died, I have not gone anywhere.
Pray to me—even if I do not appear in person,
I will give the desired siddhis
to those with one-pointed devotion.

"From now until the final generations,
Tibetans who are disciples of the Lotus Guru
will mature in the land of the great compassion.
Mañjuśrī's incarnation made this a land of the teachings;
the Secret Lord, Vajrapāṇi, provided glory and power.
The teachings will ever remain as a great undisturbed ocean;
the wrong-minded heretics cannot hurt them;
all the demons and demonic powers have been made calm.
The Wheel of the Sūtra Dharma will continue to be turned,
and the secret teachings will gain power and success.

"May all the land of Tibet be filled with those who practice!
May all those living in this land of Tibet
in the future rely upon the Triple Gem,
gain power over both pleasure and pain,
pursue the ten virtues, and avoid the ten non-virtues.
May the noble teachings be your guide
for both inner and outer pursuits.
Padmasambhava's words reveal what is right and what is not;
Khri-srong's rules tell what is lawful and unlawful.
In Tibet, the laws were made according to the Dharma.
Though enemies arise in all four corners,
they will be subjugated by the power of Dharma.
The compassion of the gods and the Three Jewels
will turn back all harm.

"Practice harmoniously, the spiritual way,
acting according to the Dharma.
Respect the Dharma as father, mother, and saint.
Treat the high ones with unmeasured respect,
and offer what you have to the poor and lowly.
Pray with steadfast mind to the Lord Padmasambhava,
always repeating, for your own sake and others',
the six-syllable prayer.

"Dear students of my lineage,
respectfully and humbly take up the four initiations.
Repeat the name of mTsho-rgyal as much as you can,
ask for the four empowerments, and let them permeate your mind.
But do not fixate on anything whatsoever.

"For all the future,
Tibetans will retain Padmasambhava's inheritance.
Those who strive to practice the Lama sādhana
will themselves be transformed into the Lotus One,
and great waves of compassion will flow forth.
Practice both the long and short versions of the sādhanas,
and I promise you will attain Buddhahood in one lifetime.

"Recite the Vajra Guru mantra,
the essence of the essence of mantra.
Remember the tenth, eighth, and fifteenth days of the month
are especially auspicious.
On those days, make many offerings and prayers.
If you do the Gaṇacakra perfectly even one time,
all evil births will be gone forever,
and you will never revert to samsara.
You must understand this: It is absolutely certain.
This is the heart of the Teacher, the Guru Siddhi.

"The lives of all the Buddhas of the three times
is the syllable HŪṀ,

the siddhis of all victorious yidams
is the syllable DHI,

the charismatic activity of all holy ḍākinīs
is the syllable SID,

cutting through the delusion of all sentient beings
is the syllable MA,

the supreme Buddha realms of all the three times
is the syllable PAD,

stopping the karmic winds which afflict the three gates
is the syllable RU,

the heart initiation of Pristine Awareness
is the syllable GU,

the great Mahāmudrā, indestructible emptiness,
is the syllable JRA,

the symbol of the primordial Dharmadhātu
is the syllable VA,

the Nirmāṇakāya which takes form to train beings
is the syllable HŪṀ,

the assembly of perfect enjoyment emanating from the Sambhogakāya
is the syllable A,

the pure Dharmakāya, the All-good, Samantabhadrā
is the syllable OṀ.

"These twelve syllables are the very essence of Padmasambhava.
Recite them, and you reverse samsaric proclivities—
one hundred thousand times
and you will clean away the sins of the three doors;
two and you cut the evil karma of the three times;
three and you will not return to this world;
seven hundred thousand and
you will meet Padmasambhava in this lifetime;
one million and you will realize the four charismatic acts;
six million and you shake off samsara;
ten million and you are one with Amitābha—
you will certainly attain the siddhi of whatever you desire.
The benefits of surpassing this number are truly wonderful.

"This mantra is the antidote,
the means to pass from and reverse all misery:

OM is the bringing together
of the five body aspects of all the Tathāgatas,

AH is the gathering together
of the essence of the five aspects of their speech,

HŪM is the five aspects of their mind,
the unification of the four kāyas as the Svabhāvakāya,

VA is the sign of the unchangeable Mahāmudrā,

JRA is the compassionate enlightened activity
of the diamond scepter,

GU is the Lama Herukas of the three times,

RU is the seed of the essence of maturation and liberation,

PAD is the opening of the blissful realm of Sukhāvati,

MA is the entrance into the womb of the Great Bliss,

SID is the forceful radiant activity
and responsive compassion of the enlightened mind,

DHI is the power to satisfy all desires,

HŪM is absolute being eternally realized.

"This mantra is the wish-fulfilling gem.
It can also be interpreted
according to the twelve links of dependent origination,
or in terms of the great Mother,
the very essence of the ten pāramitās.
It can be performed in various ways.
You beings here now, and you who are yet to come,
please practice and rely upon this essential mantra.
Now, until the dualistic identity mind melts and dissolves,
it may seem that we are parting.
Please be happy.
When you understand the dualistic mind,

there will be no separation from me.
May my good wishes fill all the sky."

After she had spoken, colorful dazzling lights burst forth which slowly dissolved into darkness as mTsho-rgyal disappeared in a vivid radiant halo into the southwest, in the direction of rNga-yab.

All those left behind bowed down countless times and prayed fervently. They were so upset that tears ran down their faces, their breath came in gasping sobs, and they stumbled about, barely able to stand. Slowly they drew themselves together and went west to the cave of Zab-bu to practice.

sBe Ye-shes snying-po and La-gsum rGyal-ba byang-chub and rMa Rin-chen opened the mandala of the Lama and ḍākinī and practiced for seven months. They realized the inseparableness of the Lama and the ḍākinī and received many blessings and predictions. Then the great Dharma Protector King of Tibet, Khri Ral-pa-can, invited the lotsāwas to come help him set down rules for translating.

When mTsho-rgyal realized the Chos-nyid zad-pa, the Fourth Stage of the rDzogs-chen teaching, some people saw her dissolve into a basket of pearls. The glittering remains of her nasal bones and teeth and nails and hair were all that was left where her body had been, and these were kept as relics, inspiring beings to have faith. It is said her body disappeared as did the Buddha's.

Some say that she gave teachings in the bird year, the eighth day of the bird month. At dusk of the tenth day, she subjugated all demons. At midnight she turned the Wheel of the Dharma. During the middle of the night, she meditated. At dawn she obtained enlightenment. At break of day, while her body was erect and straight, she passed beyond all misery. All that remained of her body were small white ring-bsrel relics, which the Dharma Protector King gathered up to place into an urn.

All this has been recorded faithfully. I, rGyal-ba byang-chub, along with sBe Ye-shes snying-po, rMa Rin-chen-mchog, 'O-bran dPal-gyi gzhon-nu, 'Da' Cha-ru-pa rDo-rje dpa'-bo, dBus-kyi nyi-ma, Li-bza' Byang-chub, Shel-dkar-bza' rDo-rje mtsho, and at least a hundred others, labored long and hard to write this down, and agreed completely on its contents.

MANTRAS OF SEALING

This has been the life story of the Lady Ye-shes mTsho-rgyal of Tibet, as it was hidden and later brought forth. This was the eighth chapter which shows the manner in which mTsho-rgyal achieved her final prayer, how her body entered into the expanse of the Dharmadhātu and she achieved Buddhahood.

MANTRAS OF SEALING

"I, rGyal-ba byang-chub, blessed by the Lady Ye-shes mTsho-rgyal who achieved realization in one lifetime, and Nam-mkha'i snying-po of lHo-brag, inseparable from the great Teacher Padmasambhava who was free of the marks of birth and death, added nothing to the words of the Lady, nor did we delete anything. We have exaggerated nothing. The text was written on flat yellow paper and placed in the hands of the Dharmapāla sTong-rgyug, the Black Water Lord. In the future, as prophesied by the Lady, it will be delivered into the hands of a boy. May these words, now sealed, be found in the future and spread."

MANTRAS: PROFOUND SEAL

SEALED TO BE FOUND BY THE DESIGNATED

"Such a one was I, a southerner from a southern lineage,
in a land of narrow canyons,
believing myself bereft of the mercy of Padmasambhava,
hampered by sin and bad karma, my attainments a pittance,
even my retreat only conventional display of spiritual practice.
In a sinful and unwholesome land, a land of hunters,
a land where dark men wear dark garments,
a place where black food is eaten, and black beer drunk,

a land where the black karma of the world increases,
in a village of dark beings in dark houses,
with black friends and bad parents,
the black birth of a man born of black karma,
given a black name, dPa'-bo sTag-sham, that is I.
From the hand of the Black Water Lord I took this,
and copied it upon a flat paper with black ink.

"In a dark retreat in the dark forest I practiced;
at a dark time, the twenty-ninth, I finished.
May all dark sentient beings without exception
be rid of their dark karma and become Buddhas.
May all black beings be freed!
Having purified all defilements and black materialism,
I truly pray that I become inseparable from you:
the Radiant Blue Light of the dark blue ḍākinī,
who dwells in the highest blue-black place of 'Og-min.
By these words of truth, this highest aspiration,
pray come here today!
These words I spontaneously write from memory,
with a sense of wonder.

dPa'-bo sTag-sham rDo-rje, gTer-ma Master

MANTRAS OF SEALING

Glossary

Abhidharma   systematic teachings which analyze elements of experience and investigate the nature of existence, thus dispelling wrong views and establishing analytic insight.

Ādibuddha   the all-pervasive primordial Buddha from whom radiates the five Dhyānibuddhas; the representation of dynamic energy that brings form into existence.

Akaniṣṭha (Tib. 'Og-min)   the highest of the heavens of the form realm.

Akṣobhya (Tib. Mi-bskyod)   one of the five Dhyānibuddhas; his Sambhogakāya form is Vajrasattva.

Amitābha (Tib. sNang-ba mtha'-yas)   lit. 'Buddha of Boundless Light'; one of the five Dhyānibuddhas.

Amitāyus (Tib. Tshe-dpag-med)   lit. 'Buddha of Infinite Life'; Buddha associated with the 'Long life initiation'; the Sambhogakāya aspect of Amitābha, spiritual source from which Avalokiteśvara emanates.

Amoghasiddhi (Tib. Don-grub)   one of the five Dhyānibuddhas.

Ancient Kings of Tibet   The ancient kings of Tibet, descended from the Licchavis of India, ruled Tibet for hundreds of years. There were five dynasties which reigned before the great Dharma Kings: the Seven Khri beginning with gNya'-khri; the Two lTengs; the Six Legs; the Eight lDe; and the Five bTsan, the last of whom was lHa-tho-tho-ri gNyan-btsan. During his reign, the Dharma entered Tibet in the form of Buddhist relics, dhāraṇīs, texts, and mantras. Although the king did not understand the full significance of these things, he recognized the holiness of these objects, and so kept and preserved them carefully.

221

After lHa-tho-tho-ri, four kings ruled before the first of the Dharma Kings: Khri-gnyan gzungs-btsan, 'Bro-gnang-lde, sTag-ri gnang-gzigs, and gNam-ri srong-btsan.

Anuyoga   see Tantra.

Ārya (Tib. 'Phags-pa)   lit. 'exalted'.

Ārya Sadāprarudita (Tib. rTag-tu ngu)   lit. 'Ever-weeping'; a great Bodhisattva in the Prajñāpāramitā literature who manifested great fortitude in attempting to obtain the Prajñāpāramitā teachings during the time of the Buddha Dharmodgata.

Ātiyoga   see Tantra.

Avalokiteśvara (Tib. sPyan-ras-gzigs)   known as the Bodhisattva of Compassion, he is an emanation of the Dhyānibuddha Amitābha. Avalokiteśvara manifested in Tibet as King Srong-btsan sgam-po in order to help the Tibetan people and to lay the foundation for the spread of the Dharma.

Bardo   the state of consciousness between death and rebirth; the 'space' between waking and sleeping; the 'space' between thoughts, etc.

Bodh Gayā   place in Northern India, west of Rājagṛha, where the Buddha, seated under the Bodhi tree, gained enlightenment.

Bodhisattva (Tib. Byang-chub sems-dpa')   a being in whom the thought of enlightenment has arisen, one who has formed the intention to strive for complete enlightenment for the benefit of all sentient beings. After practicing the Dharma for countless lifetimes, a perfected Bodhisattva is reborn in the world to demonstrate the way to enlightenment by becoming a Buddha.

The Bodhisattvayāna is the vehicle of the Bodhisattva. Beginning with the generation of the mind dedicated to enlightenment, the Bodhisattva develops compassion and wisdom, the perfect knowledge of śūnyatā, the emptiness of all existence. He practices the six pāramitās which begin as ordinary virtues (giving, morality, patience, effort, meditation, and wisdom) and culminate in perfect transcendent action. From within the six, four further pāramitās arise: skillful means, vows, power, and primordial wisdom. The Bodhisattvayāna has ten stages, the first beginning with entry into the Path of Seeing: the Joyous, the Immaculate, the Light-giving, the Radiant, the Invincible, the Realizing, the Far-reaching, the Immovable, the Beneficial, and the Cloud of Dharma.

Bon   a native religion of Tibet, whose founder is said to be gShen-rab who came from either Ta-zig (which may be Persia) or Zhang-zhung, an area of western Tibet.

Brahmā   chief of the gods residing in the realm of form; often described as the creator of world-systems.

Buddha (Tib. Sangs-rgyas) lit. 'awakened'; the Enlightened One; a perfected Bodhisattva, after attaining complete, perfect enlightenment in a human form, is known as a Buddha. The Buddha generally referred to is Śākyamuni Buddha, the Buddha of this era, who lived in India around the 6th century B.C. But there have also been perfected Bodhisattvas in ages past who have manifested the way to enlightenment. In the current fortunate era, there will be one thousand Buddhas, Śākyamuni Buddha being the fourth. In some eras, no Buddhas appear at all.

Cakras there are four main cakras, which are located at the head, throat, heart, and navel. Three channels (nāḍī) pass through these cakras, acting as the conductors of energy and vital forces. Patterning (Tib. rtsa), energy (Tib. rlung), and vitality (Tib. thig-le) refer to the interrelationship of these elements.

mChod-rten (Skt. stūpa) lit. 'foundation of offering'; monuments often containing relics of Buddhist saints. Stūpas are built according to universal principles of harmony and order. Often quite large, they focus and radiate healing energy throughout the six realms of existence.

gCod a tantric system based on Prajñāpāramitā and introduced to Tibet by Dam-pa sangs-rgyas in which all attachment to one's self is relinquished. Ma-gcig Slab-sgron, an incarnation of Ye-shes mTsho-rgyal, was a central figure in the propagation of this teaching.

Ḍākas (Tib. mkha'-spyod) a class of sky-going beings; masculine counterpart of ḍākinīs; tantric deities who protect and serve the Dharma.

Ḍākinīs (Tib. mkha'-'gro-ma) a class of sky-going beings; ḍākinīs represent the inspirational impulses of consciousness leading to understanding and wisdom; goddesses or female tantric deities who protect and serve the tantric doctrine.

Ḍāmaru small ritual drum used in tantric ceremonies.

Dependent Origination see Twelve Links of Dependent Origination.

Desire Realm lowest of the three realms that make up a world-system; inhabited by hell-beings, pretas, animals, humans, and the lower gods.

Developing Stage (Skt. utpannakrama, Tib. bskyed-rim) stage of tantric practice focussing on the processes of visualizations—oneself as deity, the outer world as a mandala, and the beings within as gods and goddesses. See also Tantra.

Dharma (Tib. chos) the Teaching of the Buddha; the truth, the true law; individual things, elements, or phenomena are all referred to as dharmas.

Dharma Kings three great Tibetan kings who encouraged the transmission of Buddhism to Tibet and became known as the three great Dharma Kings: Srong-btsan sgam-po, Khri-srong lde'u-btsan, and Ral-pa-can.

Srong-btsan sgam-po (7th century)   first great Dharma King, who united the Tibetan kingdom. He married two Buddhist princesses, Bhṛkūṭī of Nepal and Wen-ch'eng of China. He built the first Buddhist temples, established a code of laws based on Dharma principles, developed the Tibetan script with the help of his minister Thon-mi Sambhoṭa, and also began the translation of Buddhist texts into Tibetan. Srong-btsan sgam-po was succeeded by: Gung-srong, Mang-srong, 'Dus-srong, and Khri-lde gTsug-btsan (Mes-ag-tshoms).

Khri-srong lde'u-btsan (8th century)   second great Dharma King, who invited to Tibet Padmasambhava, Śāntarakṣita, Vimalamitra, and many other Buddhist teachers including Jinamitra and Dānaśīla. With the aid of Śāntarakṣita and Padmasambhava, he built bSam-yas, the great monastery and teaching center modelled after Odantapurī. He proclaimed Buddhism the religion of Tibet, and during his reign the first monks were ordained. Paṇḍitas and lotsāwas translated many texts, and large numbers of practice centers were established. He was succeeded by: Mu-ne and Khri-lde srong-btsan (Sad-na-legs).

Ral-pa-can (9th century)   third great Dharma King, who supported the standardization of new grammar and vocabulary for translation and the revision of old translations. He renewed old centers and invited many Buddhist scholars to Tibet. He was renowned for his devotion to the Dharma.

Dharmadhātu (Tib. Chos-kyi dbyings)   lit. expanse of the Dharma; ultimate reality, synonym of voidness or openness.

Dharmakāya   see Three Kāyas.

Dhyāna   meditation.

Disciplines   see Eight Great Disciplines.

Eight Great Disciplines   ascetic practices concerned with food, dress, speech, body, mind, teaching, benefitting others, and compassion.

Eight Heruka Sādhanas   the eight Heruka Sādhanas are part of the meditative realization transmission which preserves essential instructions for practice. Each of these sādhanas is connected with a particular root text and with various specific practices containing everything necessary for enlightenment. They were transmitted from Padmasambhava to eight of his disciples who were known as the Eight Great Ācāryas. The Eight Heruka Sādhanas are: 'Jam-dpal-sku (gshin-rje); Padma-gsung; Yang-dag-thugs; rDo-rje phur-ba 'phrin-las; bDud-rtsi yon-tan; Ma-mo rbod-stong; 'Jig-rten mchos-bstod; and dMod-pa drag-sngags.

Enlightenment (Skt. bodhi, Tib. byang-chub)   the state of Buddhahood characterized by perfection of the accumulations of merit and wisdom, and by the removal of the two obscurations.

Five Branches of Learning   the five sciences: language; dialectics; science of medicine; science of mechanical arts; religious philosophy.

Five Buddha Families   Buddha, Karma, Padma, Ratna, and Vajra; see also Five Dhyānibuddhas.

Five Dhyānibuddhas   Vairocana, Ratnasambhava, Amitābha, Amoghasiddhi, and Akṣobhya. These five Buddhas are associated with various aspects of existence, for example the five skandhas: Vairocana (consciousness), Ratnasambhava (sensation), Amitābha (perception), Amoghasiddhi (volition), and Akṣobhya (form).

Five Elements   earth (the solid), air (the gaseous), fire (the incandescent), water (the liquid), and space. The five elements can also be associated with the five Dhyānibuddhas and with the cakras.

Five Eyes   the physical eye through which we perceive our physical surroundings; the eye of the gods which can see what ordinary mortals cannot; the eye of wisdom which penetrates all appearances; the eye of the Dharma which sees reality without obscurations; and the eye of the Buddha, the omniscient and most perfect seeing of all aspects of the cosmos.

Five Kāyas   see Three Kāyas.

Five Paths   five aspects of the complete path to enlightenment, following one another in succession: preparation or accumulation; application; vision or seeing; cultivation; no more learning.

Five Types of Pristine Awareness   each of the five types of Pristine Awareness is associated with one of the Dhyānibuddhas: Mirror-like Awareness (Skt. Ādarśajñāna, Tib. Me-long ye-shes) is associated with Akṣobhya; Awareness of Fundamental Sameness (Skt. Samatājñāna, Tib. mNyam-nyid ye-shes) is associated with Ratnasambhava; All-encompassing Investigating Awareness (Skt. Pratyavekṣaṇajñāna, Tib. So-sor rtogs-pa'i ye-shes) is associated with Amitābha; All-accomplishing Awareness (Skt. Kṛtyānuṣṭānajñāna, Tib. Bya-grub ye-shes) is associated with Amoghasiddhi; The Awareness of the Expanse of Dharma (Skt. Dharmadhātujñāna, Tib. Chos-dbyings ye-shes) is associated with Vairocana.

Form Realm   realm between the desire realm and the formless realm inhabited by the higher gods.

Formless Realm   highest of the three realms that make up a world-system; inhabited by the highest gods.

Four Empowerments   Vase Empowerment, Secret Empowerment, Wisdom Empowerment, Creativity Empowerment.

Four Immeasurables   love, compassion, joy, equanimity.

Four Joys   each of the four joys is associated with one of the four cakras: Awakened Joy (forehead cakra); Joy of Limitless Good Qualities (throat cakra); Supreme Joy of the Mahāmudrā (heart cakra); and Spontaneous Transcendent Awakened Joy (navel cakra).

Four Kāyas   see Three Kāyas.

Four Means of Conversion   giving, kind words, assisting the development of others, consistency between words and actions.

Four Noble Truths   suffering, cause of suffering, ending of suffering, and the eightfold path to liberation from suffering.

Fulfillment Stage   see Perfecting Stage.

Gandharvas   beings living in the desire realm in cloud-like castles; they are known for their beautiful music.

The Great Perfection (Tib. rDzogs-chen)   lit. 'All-perfect'; the highest realization of the Ātiyoga; a practice in which one can obtain enlightenment in one lifetime.

Hayagrīva (Tib. rTa-mgrin)   tantric deity always shown with a horse's head within his flaming hair; wrathful aspect of Amitābha, Lord of Speech.

Heart Bone   a small white round bone-like substance which appears in the hearts of the great practitioners, and is often discovered in the ashes of the great tantric lamas after they have been cremated.

Heruka   manifestation of tantric energy; activation of the positive qualities of the mind.

Indra   also known as Śakra or Kauśika; chief of the Thirty-three Gods who reside in the heaven of the desire realm known by that name.

Jina   lit. 'Conqueror'; one of the titles of the Buddha.

bKa'-ma   a vast collection of rNying-ma Tantras that have had a continuous transmission. Three sections, mDo, sGyu, and Sems, form the theoretical and philosophical basis of the inner Tantras. The bKa'-ma was transmitted especially through Padmasambhava, Śrī Siṁha, Vimalamitra, and Vairotsana. gNyags Jñānakumāra, gNubs-chen Sangs-rgyas ye-shes, and the Three Zur continued the line of transmission. In the fourteenth century, Klong-chen-pa greatly contributed to the bKa'-ma tradition, systematizing and transmitting the Ātiyoga teachings; gTer-bdag gling-pa, the great gter-ston, also held the entire bKa'-ma tradition, and together with his brother Lo-chen Dharmaśrī, revived and promulgated these teachings during the seventeenth century.

Karma (Tib. las)   lit. 'action'; its wider meaning encompasses the causal connections between actions and their consequences.

Kha-byang   see gTer-ma.

Kīla   lit. 'dagger'; used as a symbol in certain tantric ceremonies.

Lotsāwa   Tibetan translators of the canonical texts who usually worked with Indian paṇḍitas.

Lung-byang   see gTer-ma.

Mahākāla   great wrathful tantric deity; wrathful aspect of Avalokiteśvara.

Mahāmudrā (Tib. Phyag-rgya chen-po)   lit. 'Great Gesture' or 'Great Seal'; all-encompassing, and unchanging; the indivisible unity of the Developing and Perfecting Stage; attainment of Pristine Awareness.

Mahāyāna (Tib. Theg-pa chen-po)   lit. 'Great Vehicle'; the way of those who follow the Bodhisattva ideal, intent on achieving liberation for the purpose of freeing all beings from the misery of samsara. Two paths lead to the realization of the Bodhisattva: the Sūtrayāna, the way of those who follow the teachings of the Sūtras, and the Mantrayāna, the way of those who follow the teachings of the Sūtras and Tantras.

Mahāyoga   see Tantra.

Mandala (Tib. dkyil-'khor)   lit. 'concentric circle'; a mandala is a symbolic, graphic representation of a tantric deity's realm of existence, as well as the arrangement of offerings in tantric ritual.

Mañjuśrī (Tib. 'Jam-dbyangs)   Bodhisattva of Wisdom. Mañjuśrī manifested in Tibet as King Khri-srong lde'u-btsan in order to help the Tibetans firmly establish the Dharma.

Mantra   syllables and words whose sound can communicate the nature of tantric deities, grant supernormal powers, or lead to purification and realization.

Mantrayāna   see Vajrayāna.

Māra   lord of the desire realm, master of illusion who attempted to prevent the Buddha from attaining enlightenment at Bodh Gayā.

Mount Meru   world axis; the mountain at the center of a world-system, ringed by chains of lesser mountains and lakes, continents, and oceans.

Mudrā (Tib. phyag-rgya)   gestures symbolizing particular spiritual attributes or steps toward perfection. There are technically four types of mudrā: the symbolic seal (Skt. Upāyamudrā, Tib. Dam-tshig phyag-rgya); the female partner in tantric practices or the visualized partner who represents Pristine Awareness (Skt. Karmamudrā or Jñānamudrā, Tib. Las-kyi phyag-rgya or Ye-shes-kyi phyag-rgya); the seal of the Absolute (Skt. Dharmamudrā, Tib. Chos-kyi phyag-rgya); and the Great Seal (Skt. Mahāmudrā, Tib. Phyag-rgya chen-po).

Nāgas   powerful long-lived serpent-like beings who inhabit bodies of water and often guard great treasure. Nanda was one of their great kings. He helped protect the Buddha from the elements when the Buddha was seated at Bodh Gayā, and gave Nāgārjuna various treatises from the nāga treasure.

Nirmāṇakāya   see Three Kāyas.

Nirvana (Tib. mya-ngan-med-pa)   lit. 'blowing out'; extinguishing of the emotional fetters; the unconditioned state, free from birth and death.

sNying-byang   see gTer-ma.

rNying-ma   see Tibetan Schools of Buddhism.

Orgyan   also known as Uḍḍiyāna or Odiyan; home of many ḍākinīs, and birthplace of Padmasambhava; thought to be located in the Swat valley northwest of India, which borders on modern Afghanistan.

Padma Thod-Phreng-rtsal   lit. 'the Lotus-one ornamented by a rosary of skulls'; an emanation of Padmasambhava.

Padmasambhava   the 'Lotus-born' Guru of Odiyan; his eight major manifestations are: Padma 'byung-gnas, Padma rgyal-po, rDo-rje gro-lod, Nyi-ma 'od-zer, Śākya seng-ge, Seng-ge sgra-sgrog, Blo-ldan mchog-sred, and rDo-rje 'chang.

Paṇḍita   great Buddhist scholar; usually refers to the Buddhist scholars from Kashmir or India.

Path of Accumulation   see Five Paths.

Path of Application   see Five Paths.

Perfecting Stage (Skt. Sampannakrama, Tib. rDzogs-rim)   a non-conceptual stage in tantric practice; in the Perfecting Stage, the visualizations of the Development Stage dissolve into an experience of openness.

Prajñāpāramitā (Tib. Pha-rol-tu phyin-pa)   lit. 'Perfection of Wisdom'; six pāramitās are generally referred to: giving, morality, patience, effort, meditation, and wisdom.

Pristine Awareness (Skt. jñāna, Tib. ye-shes)   discriminating awareness born from wisdom; knowing in itself (not specific knowledge *of* anything); intrinsic knowledge inherent in all manifestations of existence.

Rainbow Body (Tib. 'ja'-lus)   the transformation of the bodily substance into multi-hued light.

Ransom Ceremony   the Bon practice of offering the skin of another living being to disease-causing demons to effect a cure; the skin is the substitute or ransom for the man.

Ratnasambhava (Tib. Rin-chen 'byung-gnas)   one of the five Dhyānibuddhas.

Ril-bu   medicinal capsule, which often contains holy substances and has been blessed by a lama.

Ring-bSrel   small, very hard glittering objects found in the burnt ashes of certain very great lamas.

Sādhanas (Tib. sgrub-thabs)   lit. 'means of attainment'; special tantric practices for gaining certain spiritual attainments.

Śākya   the clan into which the Buddha was born; their lands in northern India bordered on Nepal. The Śākyas were destroyed by neighboring peoples during the Buddha's lifetime.

Śākyamuni   lit. 'the Sage of the Sakyas'; name of the Buddha.

Samādhi (Tib. ting-nge-'dzin)   meditation or concentrative absorption.

Samantabhadra (Tib. Kun-tu bzang-po)   lit. 'the All-good'; the Ādibuddha who through ceaseless meditation gives rise to the Dhyānibuddhas; representation of the ultimate nature of reality.

Samantabhadrā (Tib. Kun-tu bzang-mo)   lit. 'the All-good'; the Mother of all the Buddhas of the three times; the female or prajñā (wisdom) counterpart of the Ādibuddha Samantabhadra.

Sambhogakāya   see Three Kāyas.

Samsara   the cycle of birth, death, and rebirth within the six realms of existence, characterized by suffering, impermanence, and ignorance.

Sangha   the community of those practicing the teachings of the Buddha, united by their vision and their commitment to the path. In order to lay the foundation for Dharma practice, various forms of discipline are undertaken. Eight traditional kinds of Sangha exist: bhikṣu and bhikṣunī: fully ordained monks and nuns; śramaṇara and sramaṇī: novices who have taken preliminary vows; śikṣamaṇa: aspirants too young to join the community but who follow special rules; upavasta: laymen or laywomen who take monk's vows for a certain limited time; upāsaka and upāsikā: laymen and laywomen who practice Buddhist teachings and follow five precepts: not to kill, not to steal, not to lie, not to take intoxicating substances, not to engage in sexual misconduct.

Sarasvatī   goddess of Euphony and patron of the arts and sciences; early known as goddess of a sacred river in northern India and as the goddess of speech and learning; traditionally regarded in India as the source of the Sanskrit language and Devanāgarī letters.

gShen-rab   according to the Bon tradition, the founder of the Bon religion.

Siddha   one who has accomplished the siddhis.

Siddhi (Tib. bsgrub)   lit. 'success, complete attainment'; there are eight 'common' siddhis developed by the practice of yoga. Among these are clairvoyance, clairaudience, the ability to fly through the air, the ability to read thoughts, and control of the body and external world, enabling one to transform both at will. The supreme siddhi is enlightenment.

Śrāvaka (Tib. Nyan-thos)   lit. 'Hearer'; one who listens to the teachings of the Buddha, realizes the suffering inherent in samsara, and focuses on understanding that there is no independent self. By conquering emotionality, he liberates himself, attaining first the stage of Stream Enterer at the Path of Seeing, followed by the stage of Once-Returner who will be reborn only one more time, and the stage of Non-returner who will no longer be reborn into samsara. The final goal is to become an Arhat. The vehicle of the Śrāvaka is known as the Śrāvakayāna.

Stūpa   see mChod-rten.

Sumeru   see Meru.

Sūtra   discourses given by the Buddha on the Dharma.

Tantra (Tib. rgyud)   advanced teachings which offer many skillful means for obtaining liberation rapidly. Although in some systems the Tantras are considered to fall into only four categories, the Kriyā, Caryā, Yoga, and Anuttarayoga, the rNying-mas accept three outer and three inner Tantras.

The three outer Tantras are the Kriyā, Caryā, and the Yoga Tantras. The Kriyā Tantras emphasize purification of body and speech through ritual and cleansing activities, establishing a relationship between the deity and the practitioner similar to the relationship of master and servant. Realization can be gained within sixteen human lifetimes.

The Caryā Tantras place emphasis on purification of body and speech through ritual and meditation, establishing a relationship between the deity and the practitioner similar to that between brothers or friends. Realization can be gained within seven human lifetimes.

The Yoga Tantras have two divisions: outer Yoga Tantra (Upayoga) which emphasizes meditation on nonduality and the practice of the four seals (Mahāmudrā, Dharmamudrā, Samāyamudrā, and Karmamudrā); and inner Yoga Tantra (Anuttarayoga).

The Anuttarayoga Tantras are themselves divided into three sections: Father, Mother, and Non-dual. The Father Tantras are concerned with the Developing Stage, and the Mother Tantras are concerned with the Perfecting Stage. Father Tantra may be related to Mahāyoga, Mother Tantra to Anuyoga, and Nondual Tantra to Atiyoga. Realization can be gained within three human lives.

The inner Tantras include the Mahāyoga, Anuyoga, and Ātiyoga Tantras. The Mahāyoga Tantras are based on the sGyu section of the bKa'-ma; important texts are the root text (Guhyamūlagarbhatantra) and eighteen Mahāyogatantras. Emphasis is on visionary meditative experience.

The Anuyoga Tantras are based on the mDo section of the bKa'-ma. The root text is the Gongs-pa 'dus-pa; important texts include the five Anuyogasūtras. Emphasis is on the unity of appearances and openness.

The Ātiyoga Tantras are based on the Sems section of the bKa'-ma; these are the Absolute Perfection teachings. They are divided into three parts: the Sems-sde, or Mind section; the Klongs-sde, or Unending Experience of Being section; and the Man-ngag-gi-sde, or Guidance section which contains the sNying-thig, the 'Quintessential Instructions'. The first of the Āti realizations: Chos-nyid mngon-gsum; second realization: Nyams-snang-gong; third: Rig-pa-tshad; fourth and highest: Chos-nyid-zad-pa. The Āti is also divided into vision, meditation, action, and fruit.

Tantrayāna   see Vajrayāna.

Tārā (Tib. sGrol-ma)   the redemptress venerated as a great Bodhisattva of Compassion. King Srong-btsan sgam-po's two Buddhist queens were considered to be emanations of Tārā.

Tathāgata (Tib. De-bzhin-gshegs-pa)   lit. 'Thus-gone' or 'Thus-come'; one of the titles of the Buddha.

Ten Spiritual Levels   see Bodhisattva.

Ten Virtues   to abstain from killing, stealing, sexual misconduct, lying, slander, abusive speech, senseless speech, coveting, ill-will, and wrong views.

gTer-byang   see gTer-ma.

gTer-ma   Concealed treasures of many different kinds, including texts, ritual objects, relics, and natural objects. gTer-ma convey essential teachings suited for the time and place in which they are discovered. Through the blessings of Padmasambhava, the discoverer, or gter-ston, can locate and decipher the gter.

The gter-ston receives various aides to help in his discovery. These include the kha-byang, the gter-byang, the yang-byang, the snying-byang and the lung-byang. These are lists of books to be found in certain locations, precise descriptions of places where the gter will be found, lists of gter which have been hidden twice, and various other predictions concerning the hidden treasures. Padmasambhava predicted three grand gter-stons, eight great gter-stons, twenty-one powerful gter-stons, one hundred and eight intermediate gter-stons, and one thousand lesser gter-stons. The gter-ma lineage preserves very pure and undistorted teachings especially necessary in the present era, the Kāli Yuga.

The three great gter-stons are Nyi-ma 'od-zer, Chos-kyi dbang-phyug, and Rig-'dzin rgod-ldem 'phru-can. Nyang-ra Nyi-ma 'od-zer (12th century) and Guru Chos-kyi dbang-phyug (13th century) are known as the Sun and Moon. gTer-ma they discovered are called Upper and Lower Treasures, or gter-kha gong-'og. Rig-'dzin rgod-ldem 'phru-can (14th century) was editor and compiler of gter known as the Northern Treasures.

The eight great gter-stons are Ratna gling-pa, Padma gling-pa, Orgyan gling-pa, Sangs-rgyas gling-pa, rDo-rje gling-pa, Karma gling-pa, Orgyan rDo-rje gling-pa, and Orgyan Padma gling-pa. These gter-stons all lived during the 14th and 15th centuries.

Three Great Temples lHa-sa, Khra-'brug, and Ra-mo-che built by Srong-btsan sgam-po.

Three Kāyas The Mahāyāna recognizes the three aspects (Trikāya) of the Buddha: Dharmakāya (Tib. Chos-kyi sku), lit. 'Dharma body'; Sambhogakāya (Tib. Longs-spyod-kyi sku), lit. 'Enjoyment body'; and Nirmāṇakāya (Tib. sPrul-sku), lit. 'Representation body'.

The Dharmakāya is voidness and its realization, beyond time and space, and is pure transcending awareness. The Sambhogakāya, the pure enjoyment aspect of the Dhyānibuddhas, also represents the aspect of communication. The Nirmāṇakāya forms are embodiments taken by Buddhas among earthly beings in order to clarify the way to enlightenment.

The Sambhogakāya and the Nirmāṇakāya are sometimes known together as the Rūpakāya (Tib. gZugs-sku), lit. 'Form body'; all three kāyas are sometimes considered aspects of a fourth body, called the Svābhāvikakāya (Tib. Ngo-bo-nyid-sku).

Three Protectors (Tib. Rigs gsum mgon-po) Avalokiteśvara, Vajrapāṇi, and Mañjuśrī.

Three Roots lama, yidam, ḍākinī. The guru is the root of all blessing, the yidam is the root of all siddhi, and the ḍākinī is the root of Buddha-activity.

Tibetan Schools of Buddhism these come under the two general headings of rNying-ma (the ancient ones) and gSar-ma (the new ones).

The rNying-ma maintain the lineages that were carried to Tibet during the early transmission of the Dharma from the 7th through the 9th centuries. These lineages were established in Tibet by the great masters Padmasambhava, Vimalamitra, Śāntarakṣita, and Vairotsana, and were supported by texts translated at that time by outstanding paṇḍitas and lotsāwas. This early transmission was furthered by the patronage of the great Dharma Kings Srong-btsan sgam-po, Khri-srong lde'u-btsan, and Ral-pa-can.

232

rNying-ma-pas maintain a complete Sūtra and Mantra tradition, and recognize nine different vehicles for realization. Principal types of transmission are bka'-ma and gter-ma. Practices are based on both outer and inner Tantras, with practice of the inner Tantras being a distinguishing characteristic of the rNying-ma school. There is an emphasis on the balance of study and practice as a foundation for the higher practices which lead to complete realization.

The gSar-ma is the general heading of all the Tibetan schools of Buddhism which developed after the 10th century.

The bKa'-gdams was the first of the gsar-ma, or new, schools, and was based on the teachings of Atīśa (10th–11th century), the great Buddhist teacher from Vikramaśīla who spent thirteen years in Tibet. Three lineages branched from Atīśa's teaching, carried by three of Atīśa's disciples; Khu-ston Shes-rab brtson-'grus, rNgog, and 'Brom-ston, who established the structure of the bKa'-gdams school. The bKa'-gdams-pa teachings were continued by Po-to-pa Rin-chen gsal (11th century) and Blo-gros grags-pa. The bKa'-gdams-pa were noted for the rigor of their Vinaya practice and for the study of Prajñāpāramitā and Mādhyamika śāstras. Their teachings were later assimilated by other schools, especially by the bKa'-rgyud and dGe-lugs schools.

The bKa'-rgyud school was founded by Marpa (10th–11th century), the great yogi and translator who was the disciple of the Mahāsiddhas Maitri-pa and Nāropa. His own disciple, Mi-la-ras-pa, was the teacher of Ras-chung-pa and sGam-po-pa. From these two disciples came a number of flourishing subschools such as the 'Brug-pa and Karma bKa'-rgyud. The bKa'-rgyud traditions emphasize devotional and yogic practices and have produced numerous siddhas.

The Shangs-pa teachings were based on the lineage brought to Tibet by the siddha Khyung-po rnal-'byor (11th century?), a great tantric master who has studied with many teachers, including ḍākinīs. Khyung-po lived in Shangs in gTsang, central Tibet, where six disciples became his spiritual sons. Thus, this school is sometimes known as the Seven Treasures lineage (the Master and his six sons) or as the Ḍākinī lineage. The teachings of this school, which are powerful and practice-oriented, have been assimilated into the other schools, particularly the bKa'-rgyud and dGe-lugs schools.

The Zhi-byed teachings were brought to Tibet by Dam-pa sangs-rgyas, a siddha who visited Tibet several times around the 12th century and introduced the gCod teachings. His disciple, sKyo-ston bSod-nams bla-ma, founded the Father lineage of gCod which followed the Sūtrayāna teachings according to Āryadeva; Ma-gcig Slab-sgron, a great female siddhā, founded the Mother lineage, based on Prajñāpāramitā. Zhi-byed emphasizes teachings suited to the individual's consciousness rather than adhering to specific texts. gCod teachings continue within other schools, especially rNying-ma and bKa'-rgyud.

233

The Sa-skya school traces its lineage to 'Brog-mi Śākya ye-shes (b. 1147), who studied with the Mahāsiddha Virūpa. Five great masters continued the lineage: Kun-dga' snying-po, bSod-rnams rtse-mo, Grags-pa rgyal-mtshan, Kun-dga' rgyal-mtshan (Sa-skya Paṇḍita), and 'Gro-mgon chos-rgyal ('Phags-pa). The Sa-skya tradition emphasizes both study and practice, especially favoring the Hevajra Tantra.

The Jo-nang-pa teachings emphasize the practices and doctrines of the Kālacakra Tantra and developed a controversial interpretation of śūnyatā. The Jo-nangs traced their Kālacakra lineage to Yu-mo Mi-bskyod rdo-rje (12th century), a Kālacakra master and siddha. His spiritual son Dharmeśvara continued the lineage which later included the siddha Dol-bu-pa (Dol-po) and Tāranatha (Kun-dga' snying-po), one of the last Jo-nang-pa scholars. Officially closed in the 17th century, its teachings have endured within other schools.

The dGe-lugs school was founded by Tsong-kha-pa (15th century), a master of the Vinaya lineage who was revered as an incarnation of Mañjuśrī. His Lam-rim chen-mo, based on Atīśa's lam-rim texts, became the central focus of the practice and study of this school, which thus assimilated much of the bKa'-gdams-pa tradition. Tsong-kha-pa's two main disciples, rGyal-tshab-rje and mKhas-grub-rje, continued the lineage.

Transmission Lineages   After the Great Dharma King Ral-pa-can was killed by anti-Buddhist factions of the government, his brother, Glang-dar-ma, took the throne. During his reign, traditional studies were halted, monks forced to return to lay life, and monasteries closed. Esoteric practitioners continued secretly, and all lineages were preserved.

The Vinaya transmission was maintained in the East through gYo, Rab, and dMar, Bla-chen, and Klu-mes, who returned to Central Tibet; the Abhidharma transmission was maintained in the East through lHa-lung dPal-gyi rdo-rje and his disciples; the Prajñāpāramitā transmission was maintained through sKa-ba dPal-brtsegs, Cog-ro Klu'i-rgyal-mtshan, and Ye-shes sde; the Tantra transmission was maintained through gNyags Jñānakumāra, gNubs-chen Sangs-rgyas ye-shes, and the Three Zur.

Triple Gem   the Buddha, the Dharma, and the Sangha.

gTum-mo   practice to develop the mystic inner heat in one type of tantric yoga.

Twelve Links of Dependent Origination (Skt. pratītyasamutpāda, Tib. rten-cing 'brel-bar-'byung-ba)   the twelve-fold cycle of causal connections which binds beings to samsaric existence and thus perpetuates suffering: ignorance (Tib. ma-rig-pa) which gives rise to karmic dispositions (Tib. 'du-byed) which gives rise to consciousness (Tib. rnam-par-shes-pa) which gives rise to name and form (Tib. ming-dang gzugs) which give rise to the six senses (Tib. skye-mched drug) which give rise to contact (Tib. reg-pa) which gives rise to feeling (Tib. 'tshor-ba) which gives rise to craving (Tib. sred-pa) which gives rise to grasping (Tib. nye-bar-len-pa) which gives rise to existence (Tib. srid-pa) which gives rise to birth (Tib. skye-ba) which gives rise to old age and death (Tib. rga-shi).

Twenty-five Main Disciples of Padmasambhava   in various lists these include Vairotsana; Mandāravā; Ye-shes mTsho-rgyal; rGyal-ba mchog-dbyangs; Nam-mkha'i snying-po; dPal-gyi ye-shes; dPal-gyi seng-ge; Ye-shes dbyangs; Ye-shes sde; dPal-gyi rdo-rje; Khri-srong lde'u-btsan; mKhar-chen dPal-gyi dbang-phyug; gYu-sgra snying-po; dPal-gyi seng-ge; rMa Rin-chen-mchog; Sangs-rgyas ye-shes; rDo-rje bdud-'joms; rGyal-ba blo-gros; lDan-ma rtse-mang; sKa-ba dPal-brtsegs; 'O-bran dbang-phyug; Jñānakumāravajra; Sog-po lHa-dpal gzhon-nu; Lang-gro dKon-mchog 'byung-gnas; rGyal-ba byang-chub; Dran-pa nam-mkha' dbang-phyug; Khye'u-chung mKha'-lding; Cog-ru Klu'i rgyal-mtshan; Ting-nge-'dzin bzang-po.

Vairocana (Tib. rNam-par snang-mdzad)   one of the five Dhyānibuddhas.

Vajra (Tib. rdo-rje)   'diamond scepter'; the active symbol of the means for attaining wisdom.

Vajradhara (Tib. rDo-rje 'chang)   lit. 'the Bearer of the Vajra'; all-embracing Buddha nature.

Vajrakīla (Tib. rDo-rje phur-bu)   one of the major Herukas; wrathful aspect of Amoghasiddhi.

Vajrasattva (Tib. rDo-rje sems-dpa')   the Sambhogakāya aspect of Akṣobhya.

Vajravārāhī (Tib. rDo-rje phag-mo)   a female tantric initiation deity.

Vajrayāna (Tib. rDo-rje theg-pa)   lit. 'the diamond vehicle'; also known as the Mantrayāna, Tantrayāna, and Phalayāna, the vehicle of the result. This way offers innumerable skillful means to enlightenment, based on the Sūtras and Tantras. When followed under the guidance of an accomplished teacher, this rapid path can result in liberation within one lifetime. Transmitted by the Vidyādhara lineage of Knowledge-holders, this vehicle produces the deepest and most far-reaching realization particularly in the Kāli Yuga when powerful techniques are necessary to liberate human consciousness.

Vajrayoginī   the highest ḍākinī who embodies all of Buddha wisdom; she is the driving force of all wisdom; she is identical to the indestructible and immutable nature of the vajra, and her activity represents the dynamic power of vajra wisdom.

Vidyādhara (Tib. rig-'dzin)   lit. 'wisdom holder'; holder of the Enlightened Lineage; those who have attained great spiritual and magical abilities. Having received and manifested the teachings of the enlightened lineage, they are able to transmit these teachings to others.

Vinaya (Tib. 'dul-ba) teachings which establish the discipline and moral conduct (śīla) that support all Dharma practice.

Wheel of the Dharma the cycle of teachings given by the Buddha; three such cycles, known as the Three Turnings of the Wheel of the Dharma, were taught by Śākyamuni Buddha during his lifetime.

Wisdom Eye see Five Eyes.

Wish-fulfilling Gem a gem which grants the fulfillment of all one could desire; thus the Buddha is often called a wish-fulfilling gem.

Wrathful Deities deities in fierce forms representing wisdom that overcomes emotionality.

Yab-Yum tantric symbol of male and female energies in mystic union.

Yamāntaka (Tib. gShin-rje gshed) wrathful form of Mañjuśrī, representing wisdom that subdues death.

Yang-byang see gTer-ma.

Yidam tutelary deity; a personal protector of one's practice and guide to enlightenment.

Yogatantra see Tantra.

Yoginī a female practitioner of yoga, the path of mystic union.

Zhi-byed see Tantra.

Index

A-shad 66
Abhidharma 33, 90, 182, 185
Akaniṣṭha 7, 60, 145
All-accomplishing Pristine
    Awareness 58
All-investigating Pristine
    Awareness 57
Amitābha 1, 12, 29, 53, 57, 215
Amitāyus 90, 101, 103, 104, 112
Amoghasiddhi 58
animals 96, 157, 172, 173, 194
    sacrifice of 119, 125ff
Anuyoga 182
Ārya Sadāprarudita 11
ascetic practices 82ff
Asura 64
Atīśa 198
Ātiyoga 55, 98, 113, 146, 147, 150,
    157, 167, 171, 179, 181, 182, 190,
    207, 213
    realizations of 147, 157
attachment 69, 96
    purification of 52
Avalokiteśvara 5, 90, 118

bandits 56–59, 105, 139
bar-do 66, 173
Bar-lam 136
sBe Ye-shes snying-po 156, 176, 185,
    206, 217
Bhutan 12, 16, 99, 100, 107, 145,
    163, 180
Blo-gros-skyid 141
Bodh Gayā 128
Bon 15, 43–45, 109, 117, 188ff, 137,
    138, 144, 159, 176
    ministers-of-state 43–45
Brag 73, 163
    -dmar 163
    Yang-rdzong 73
Brahmā 132
'Bre 44, 73
'Brog 28
'Brog-mi 199
'Brom 198
Bu-chu 136
dBu-ru 74
Buddhakāya 55
Buddhas of the 3 times 6, 11

dBus 28, 161, 167, 198, 200, 201, 202
Bya Rog-rgyung 41
Bya-rung kha-shor 58
Bya-tshang 136
Byams-gling yan 109
Byang-gi gnam-mtsho-do 74
Byang-kha 161
Byar 28, 161
Bye-me'i brag 74

cakras 47, 49, 66, 183
    eight 47, 51–54
Caryātantra 90
cemeteries 7, 80
central channel 66
mChim-phu 24, 25, 31, 33, 73, 74,
    133, 134, 136, 143, 145, 160,
    161, 167
China 7, 16, 19, 28, 98, 107, 118, 135,
    137, 161, 206
Chos-nyid mngon-sum 147, 178, 187
Chos-nyid zad-pa 171, 185, 187,
    190, 217
circumambulations 82, 94
Clear light 66
gCod 102, 202
Cog-ro-bza' 106, 132, 138
Cog-ro Klu'i rgyal-mtshan 44, 74,
    133, 144
commitments 35–40, 68, 69, 75, 99,
    146, 179, 183, 184
compassion 48, 56, 67, 83, 84, 151,
    157–159, 174, 178, 185, 213, 216
    misplaced 107
Copper-colored Mountain 179, 196
craving 54

'Da' Cha-ru-pa rdo-rje 157, 217
ḍākinī 5, 17, 29, 49, 59, 61, 67, 75, 85,
    101, 141, 151, 152, 154, 155, 168,
    171, 175, 184, 185, 194–197, 203,

108, 210, 215
    of four lineages 12
    Orgyan 79–81, 194–197
    Wisdom 30
Dam-pa 103
lDan-ma rtse-mang 73, 132, 144
'Dar-cha rDo-rje dpa'-bo 176
dates 17, 151
bDe-ba-mo 89, 106, 156
bDe-chen-mo 141
death 54, 63–64, 66, 86, 91, 148, 149,
    173, 175, 178, 212
    revive from 63, 64, 68, 69, 133, 134
debate 127ff
demons 6, 80, 83, 99, 100, 105, 112,
    123, 128, 132, 175, 183, 196, 213
dependent origination 53, 54,
    114, 187
desire 139
Developing Stage 39, 65, 82, 139, 149,
    171, 188, 189, 194
Dhānakoṣa 145
Dharma Protectors 13
Dharma vehicles 25, 30, 33, 34
Dharmakāya 5, 17, 18, 54, 59, 72, 97,
    98, 113, 124, 150, 177, 209, 215
Dharmamudrā 38
Dharmapāla sTong-rgyug 218
Dharmodgata 11
mDo-khams 161, 163
rDo-rje bde-chen Padma-mtsho 191
rDo-rje bdud-'joms 73, 106, 132
rDo-rje dbang-phyug of
    Zur-mkhar 21
rDo-rje gro-lod 107, 130, 145
rDo-rje gzhon-nu 105, 108, 156
rDo-rje khro-bo 47
mDong-chu 136
Dran-pa nam-mkha' 74, 122, 133
dreams 16, 17, 66
Dvags-lung 136
Dvags-po 136, 199

E in lower Nepal 97
E-khram mandala 106
E-rong valley 56
E-yi gTsug-lag-khang 64
Ekajātī 107
emotions 51–53, 66, 101, 156, 170,
    174, 175, 211
Empowerments 29, 34, 48–51, 55, 75,
    108, 178, 183
    four 49–55, 111, 139, 140, 214
Emptiness 178, 183, 188
energy 49, 55, 66, 79, 86, 91, 112, 140,
    171, 183, 185, 190, 203
Enlightenment 22, 52–54, 102, 108,
    183, 217

faith 92
fast-runners 70
Five Buddha Families 48, 90
Five Kāyas 40
Four Joys 51–53, 66, 69, 85, 139,
    140, 183
Four Kāyas 69
Four Noble Truths 33

gandharvas 5, 7, 93
Ganges River, goddess of the 11, 93
Glang 108, 197
Glang-thang 136
Gling 163
Glu-gong 134
Glu Gung-btsan-po 41
Golden Isle 56
Gong-thang-pa 15
mGos-rgan 42, 45, 127
sGrags-gi se'u valley 13
sGrags-pa 15
grasping 52, 54
Great Bliss 12, 29, 48, 50, 51, 57, 65,
    83, 88, 101, 112, 139, 140, 150,
    175, 178, 184, 187, 192, 212, 216
Great Perfection 55, 60, 66, 113, 140,

151, 167, 171, 179, 185, 188,
    189, 212
Great Vehicle 35
Gru-gu U-be 44
Grva-pa mNgon-shes 102
Gung-btsan-po 41, 71
Gung-thang la-thog 146
Guru Drag-po 25
rGya 161
rGya-tsha lHa-nang 70
rGyal-ba blo-gros 73, 132
rGyal-ba byang-chub 74, 133, 157,
    176, 191, 193, 194, 217, 218
rGyal-ba mchog-dbyangs 73, 132
rGyal-tham 136
rGyu-bon 118ff
rGyud rGyud-ring-mo 41

lHa-dpal 106
lHa-lung dPal-gyi seng-ge 106
lHa-nang 70
lHa-sa 118, 120, 122, 136, 161, 164,
    198, 205
lHa-tho-tho-ri 117
Has-po-ri 134, 138
hatred 57
Hayagrīva 49, 56, 101, 125, 132, 175
healing 93, 101
heart-bone 76, 87
hell 29, 30, 37, 53
Heruka 13, 38, 49–52, 85, 100, 101,
    102, 103, 106, 156, 169
    sādhanas 38, 103, 106, 195
lHo-brag 45, 69, 73, 106, 148, 171,
    179, 200, 204, 206
lHo-rong 162
Hor 28, 161
Hva-shang 160, 161

ignorance 53, 58
illusion 184
immortality 138, 159

impermanence 88, 148, 150, 178, 180, 212
India 7, 107, 135, 137, 160

'Ja' 97
'Jang 28, 107, 136, 161
jealousy 58
Jñānakumāravajra 74, 133
Jñānamudrā 38
Jo-mo-nang 136, 138, 141, 162

sKa-ba dPal-brtsegs 44, 74, 133, 144
Kālasiddhi 7, 141, 144, 176, 182, 208
Kamalaśīla 160
sKar-chung temple 167, 170
karma 28, 29, 33, 34, 35, 50, 56, 58, 61, 63, 66, 69, 92, 108, 114, 124, 148, 149, 150, 152, 169, 170, 171, 175, 176, 178, 190, 193, 194, 205, 210, 211, 212, 215
Karmamudrā 37
Kashmir 135, 136
Kathog 207
mKha'-'gro snying-thig 47
Kha-rag 138, 139, 141
Kha-rag rdzongs 163
Khams 16, 28, 107, 118, 136, 145, 198, 200, 201, 206
mKhar-chen rDo-rje-mgon 15
mKhar-chen dPal-gyi dbang-phyug 15, 16–21, 26, 27
mKhar-chen gZhon-nu-pa 15
mKhar-chen gZhon-nu sgrol-ma 176
mKhar-chen-pa 15
mKhar-chu 148, 171
mKhar-chu-pa 15, 21–24, 26, 27
Khe'u-chung mKha'-lding 74
Kho-khom-han 59
Khra-'brug 120, 136, 161, 164, 205
Khra-mgo 41
Khri-sgo 135
Khri-srong lde'u-btsan 11, 25, 27–31,

41–45, 59, 69–77, 119, 120ff, 137, 179
laws of 135, 213
Khung-lung 73
Khye-'dren 93, 100. See also Khyi-'dren and bKra-shis sphyi-'dren.
Khye'u-chung 133
Khyi-'dren 105, 107. See also Khye-'dren and bKra-shis spyi-'dren.
Kīla sādhanas 105, 106, 108, 112
Klo-yul 163
Klu-btsan (sTag-ra) 41
Klu-gong 43, 135. See also Glu-gong.
dKon-mchog 'byung-gnas 74
dKon-mchog 'byung-ldan 133
Kong 28
Kong-po 118, 136, 162, 163, 203
bKra-shis spyi-'dren 7, 100, 102, 106, 176, 180, 207. See also Khye-'dren and Khyi-'dren.
Kriyātantra 90, 182, 185
Kucha 7

La-phyi 136
La-stod 103
lama 5, 56, 75, 79, 86, 98, 184, 185, 186, 191, 196, 212
Lang-gro 44, 133
Lang-lab Byang-chub rdo-rje 157, 176
Li-bza' Byang-chub sgrol-ma 176, 217
Li-yul 200
lo-ro 161
lotsāwas 76, 122ff, 146, 180

Ma Ma-zhang 41
rMa Rin-chen 70, 74, 106, 133, 176, 186, 206, 217
Ma-zangs-gling 60
Ma-zhang 41

magical manifestations 95, 96, 98, 130ff

Mahākāla 124

Mahāmudrā 38, 49, 50, 52, 65, 74, 140, 145, 188, 190, 205, 212, 215, 216

Mahāyāna 55, 83, 93

Mahāyoga 90, 182

Maitreya 200

Manasarowar Lake 107

mandala 13, 25, 28, 38, 40, 41, 47, 48, 49, 50, 51, 52, 56, 67, 73, 75, 76, 84, 90, 91, 101, 105, 112, 139, 141, 144, 156, 168, 169, 177, 191, 195, 196

Mandāravā 7, 174ff

Mang-yul 156, 161

Mañjuśrī 11, 90, 120, 137, 213

mantra 6, 13, 16, 17, 25, 39, 40, 43, 47, 49, 50, 60, 63, 82, 90, 103, 112, 133, 134, 143, 175, 183, 207

  black 131, 133, 139

  six-syllable 118, 145, 146, 214

  three-syllable 145, 146

  twelve-syllable 214ff

Mantrayāna 6, 7, 12, 25, 29, 30, 31, 35, 39, 46, 47, 59, 69, 70, 73, 98, 104, 108, 117, 122, 139, 182, 185, 198, 202

sMar 198

Mar-pa 199

Māra 46

Me-nyag 136, 161

medicine 93

meditation 56, 57, 84–87, 89, 95, 97, 109, 113, 181, 189

Mi-la 199

mind 64–66, 70, 98, 112, 113, 130, 169, 178, 184, 187

miracles 33

Mirror-like Pristine Awareness 57

Mon 28, 161

Mon-bu Sa-le 101, 102, 106

Mongolia 7, 16, 19, 107, 135, 198, 199, 200, 202, 204

Mount Meru 28, 48, 91, 121, 193

Mu-khri btsan-po 137, 141, 144, 160, 167, 168, 179

Mu-ne btsan-po 137

Mu-rum btsan-po 167, 168, 169

mudra 37–38, 40, 50, 133

  four types of 37, 38

  finger-pointing 63, 134

Muni 92, 93

music 153

nāgas 7, 92, 100, 157

Nam-mkha'i snying-po 44, 73, 106, 132, 136, 144, 171, 191, 218

gNam-ri srong-btsan 15

Ne-ring 94, 112, 163

Nepal 16, 19, 56–64, 98, 107, 137, 140, 146, 162, 204, 206

New Year 41, 129

mNga'-ri 161

mNga'-ris man 136

mNga'-ris-skor gsum 28

Ngang-chung dPal-gyi ryal-mo 167

Nirmāṇakāya 5, 11, 12, 17, 18, 124, 177, 215

nirvana 48, 53, 72, 87, 186

gNub-bza' dGe-mtsho 15–21

sNubs 44

gNubs-yul 73

gNya'-khri btsan-po 15, 117

Nyams-snang-gong 147, 187

sNye-mo 74, 162

'O-bran dbang-phyug 74

'O-bran gzhon-nu 133, 157, 176, 187, 217

'Om-bu 122, 134

'Om-bu'i tshal 120

'On-phu 157

'On-phu Tiger Cave 25, 34, 75, 101,
    112, 122, 145
Orgyan 12, 18, 34, 140, 167, 187, 194,
    198, 202

dPa'-bo sTag-sham rDo-rje 219
sPa-gro Tiger Cave 104, 107, 112, 145
sPa-ma gang 157, 179
Padma Thod-phreng-rtsal 6, 55, 100,
    159, 163, 176
Padma-bkod 163
Padmasambhava 5, 6, 12
dPal Chu-bo-ri 74
dPal-dbyangs 101, 102, 106, 138,
    144, 156
dPal-gyi dbang-phyug 15–21, 26, 27
dPal-gyi gzhon-nu 21, 157, 176
dPal-gyi rdo-rje 108, 109, 133, 198
dPal-gyi seng-ge (lHa-lung) 106
dPal-gyi seng-ge (shud-bu) 44, 74
paṇḍitas 122ff
Path of Vision 53
patterning 49, 55, 79, 86, 91, 112, 140,
    171, 185, 190, 203
Perfecting Stage 39, 65, 82, 149, 171,
    188, 189, 194
sPo-bo 136
Prabhādharā 7
Prajñāpāramitā 176, 177
predictions 71, 101, 102, 103, 113,
    121, 122, 151, 152, 170, 191ff,
    194, 197ff
Pristine Awareness 18, 40, 49, 51, 52,
    65, 66, 81, 93, 94, 101, 105, 140,
    148, 170, 174, 187, 190, 201, 215
    five types of 57, 58
Pristine Awareness of the Expanse of
    All-that-is 58
Pristine Awareness of Sameness 57
procrastination 81
prostrations 82, 94
Pu-rang 161

Ra-mo-che 118, 120, 170
Rab-gang 136
rainbow 17, 151, 152
Rainbow Body 5, 46, 88, 112, 138,
    175, 190
Ral-pa-can 197, 217
ransom ceremony 119, 159
Ratnasambhava 57
reality 66
Rig-pa-tshad 147, 157, 161, 178, 187
ril-bu 113
Rin-chen bzang-po 74
Rlang lHa-dpal 106
Rong-lam 136
Rong-pa 15

Sa-le 56, 59–72, 75, 89, 101, 105,
    193, 194
sādhanas 48, 73, 75, 82, 90, 175, 214
Śakra 157
Śākya clan 117
Śākya De-ma 7, 64–67
Śākyamuni 6, 11, 122, 130, 199
gSal-bkra 141
bSam-yas 12, 24, 25, 28, 34, 70, 71,
    120ff, 129ff, 141, 160, 161, 164,
    198, 205
samādhi 38, 49, 91, 97, 103, 104
Samantabhadra 5, 17, 60, 63, 91, 98,
    145, 175
Samantabhadrā 35, 72, 113, 201,
    209, 215
Samāyamudrā 37
Sambhogakāya 5, 11, 12, 17, 18, 54,
    103, 124, 177, 215
samsara 21, 24, 53, 58, 59, 67, 68, 72,
    83, 87, 89, 117, 143, 171, 176,
    186, 212, 215
Sangha 33, 122, 135, 137, 161, 178, 181
Sangs-rgyas ye-shes 73, 132
Sanskrit 118, 144
Śāntarakṣita 59, 120, 121, 122, 130,

135, 136, 137, 141–143, 198
Sarasvatī 11, 12, 13, 17, 33, 55, 93, 180
secret teachings 30, 71, 84, 184, 194
Seng-ge rdzong 112
Seng-ge sgra-sgrog 207
Sham-po gangs 139
Shan Khra-mgo 41
Shang 74, 157, 163, 176
Shel-brag 133
Shel-dkar rDo-rje mtsho-mo 176,
    190, 218
Shud-bu dPal-seng 44, 70
siddha 6, 18, 93
siddhi 6, 7, 103, 113, 152, 171, 178,
    179, 181, 185, 186, 199, 213
bSod-nams dpal-'dren 203
Sog 28
Sog-po lHa-dpal 74, 133
Spiritual levels 53–54
Śrāvaka 92, 180
Srong-btsan sgam-po 15, 118, 120,
    121, 129
stūpa 16, 58, 71, 124, 141, 143, 145
subjective and objective poles of
    experience 58, 101
suffering 35, 171ff, 178, 211–213
    antidote of 215
Sūrya thad-pa 176
Sūtra 90, 103, 181, 185
Sūtra and Mantra path 33, 43, 108,
    117, 136, 137, 142, 143, 145,
    197, 198
Svābhāvikakāya 53, 216
symbolic experiences 82

sTag-ra Klu-btsan 41, 43, 71, 134, 135
sTag-shams 193
Tārā 18, 102, 118, 201
Tārā Bhṛkuṭī 12
Tathāgata 37, 113, 124, 130, 150
gter-ma 46, 109, 112, 144–146, 148,
    161ff, 175, 197ff, 218

proofs of validity 144–147
testaments 153–156
Thang-nag 132
mThar-byed Dril-bu 46
Thon-mi Sambhoṭa 118
Three Kāyas 5, 72, 112, 146, 149, 181
Ti-se-man 109
Ti-sgro 46, 60, 67, 70, 75, 76, 79, 84,
    111, 147, 157, 160, 161
Tiger cave 107, 145
Ting-nge-'dzin bzang-po 74, 133
Ting-nge-'dzin rtog-sa-pa 133
sTon-pa gShen-rab 117
sTong-dbon 41
sTong-rgyus 132
Triple Gem 5, 213
rTsang 28, 67, 118, 136, 138, 156, 161,
    198, 200, 202, 203
rTse-pa 15
Tsha-shod rong 146
Tshe-spong-bza' 44
gTum-mo 66, 82, 84, 85, 111
Turkestan 7, 12, 16, 19, 24

uḍumbara 47
'Ug-pa-lung 139, 141

Vairocana 58, 123, 124
Vairotsana 73, 76, 131, 132, 136, 144
Vajra Body 6, 42, 46, 88, 101, 138,
    150, 175
Vajra Guru Mantra 151
Vajraḍākinī 17
Vajradhara 44, 48, 55, 70, 103, 104
Vajrakīla 38, 105–108, 134
    Byi-to-to-ma Tantra 106
Vajrapāṇi 74, 90, 197, 213
Vajrāsana 83
Vajrasattva 31, 57, 74, 85, 108
Vajravārāhī 7, 49, 55, 101, 112, 203
Vajrayāna 85
Vajrayoginī 5, 12, 17, 81

Vase Empowerment 53, 139, 155
Vasudhara 64
Vidyādhara 101, 112
Vimalamitra 123, 130, 135, 136, 137
Vinaya 33, 90, 181, 185, 198
visualization 151, 183, 186, 190
vitality 49, 55, 79, 91, 101, 112,
    184, 185
vows 35–40

war 27, 203, 204
Wheel of the Dharma 59, 69, 87, 93,
    142, 146, 150, 151, 159, 168,
    177, 213
wish-fulfilling gem 57, 61, 68, 142
women in the Dharma 102

gYa'-ma-lung 33, 41, 42, 46, 74
gYa-ru Shang-gi-brag 74
yab-yum 13, 49, 51, 80, 183
Yang rdzong 73, 133, 136
Yang-le-shod 64
Yar-lung 122, 161
Yer-pa 74, 133, 136, 161

yidam 39, 56, 75, 79, 86, 91, 112, 138,
    184, 185, 214
gYo 198
Yoga of longevity 75, 104, 105, 106,
    145, 175, 179, 213
Yogatantra 90, 182
yogi 102, 105
yoginī 18, 63, 102
gYu-sgra snying-po 133, 144
gYung 44

Zab-bu 147, 157, 163, 176, 179, 180,
    196, 206, 217
Zahor 120, 135, 136, 200
Zhang ministers 120, 127
Zhang sTong-dbon 41
Zhang-zhung 118, 122, 135
zhi-byed 103
gZho 70, 157
mZho-mdar 71
gZho-stong 45
Zhong-mdar 120
Zur 156
Zur-mkhar 122
Zur-mkhar-pa 15, 25

Ekajātī